W9-BZT-810

PRIMA OFFICIAL GAME GUIDE

Prima Games
An Imprint of Random House, Inc.
3000 Lava Ridge Court, Suite 100
Roseville, CA 95661

www.primagames.com

SCRIBBLENAUTS

Written by Catherine Browne

Product Manager: Todd Manning

Associate Product Manager: Sean Scheuble

Copyeditor: Cathleen Small

Editorial Assistant: Jenkey Hu

Guide Design: Jamie Knight & In Color Design

Layout: In Color Design

Manufacturing: Stephanie Sanchez

eProduction: Cody Zimmer

Important:

Catherine Browne

Catherine grew up in a small town, loving the proverbial "great outdoors." While she still enjoys hiking, camping, and just getting out under the big sky, Catherine also appreciates the fine art of blasting the Covenant in *Halo* as well as arranging a perfect little village in *Animal Crossing*. (Seriously, you cannot just plant apple trees all willy-nilly. Neat rows, people!)

We want to hear from you! E-mail comments and feedback to cbrowne@primagames.com

ISBN: 978-0-3074-6550-4
Library of Congress Catalog Card Number: 2009907695
Printed in the United States of America

09 10 11 12 LL 10 9 8 7 6 5 4 3 2 1

TABLE OF CONTENTS

INTRODUCTION

You are about to experience one of the most inventive videogames ever released—and do you know why? Because you made it. Sure, the box says it was developed by 5TH Cell. And technically, they did do all of that coding and stuff that makes the game actually boot up when you turn on your Nintendo DS. But once you join the game's little hero, Maxwell, the spotlight is entirely on you. You are a movie director, inventor, chef, professor, zoologist, surgeon, soldier, author, and artist all at the same time. That is the magic of *Scribblenauts*. It is a game that celebrates the creative spirit and the zillion different ways humans express it.

WHAT DO I DO?

While the ultimate goal of the game is to collect 220 Starites—shiny little tokens—the way you go about doing so is a little more nebulous. That's by design, though. With your trusty stylus, you conjure up objects that help Maxwell solve a series of levels. Some of them are pretty simple, such as helping a lumberjack cut down a tree. Conjure up a chainsaw, right? But soon you are trying to rescue a Starite dangling over boiling lava by a mere thread—and if Maxwell crosses the tripwire near the Starite, the thread breaks and drops the prize right into the molten earth.

So, again, what do you do?

You simply *create*. Maxwell has a magical Notepad that allows him to jot down any object he can think of (there are thousands of objects in the game) and then make it real. Once the object has been pulled into the game, you manipulate or position it so it helps Maxwell circumvent obstacles and collect the Starite.

Call upon a Pegasus for a ride through the skies. Attack enemies with a charnosaurus. Lure a cow to safety by holding clover in front of it. Summon Mrs. Claus to make a certain someone at the North Pole happy. Write down "black hole" to devour hazards with the greatest power of the known universe. Or just hand a puppy to an enemy soldier to make him set down his weapon.

The beauty of it all, though, is that there is no single correct way to solve a level. There are many, many ways to get from A to B, and most of them require making detours to C, D, and E along the way. After all, what's more fun? Saving a Starite with just a hammer and a set of wings? Or writing in a fighter jet, a tire iron, and an emperor penguin to get the job done?

This guide will help you solve all 220 levels in *Scribblenauts*. Now, you could follow our object suggestions to the letter and get every single Starite. But we hope that while certainly using many of the objects we offer for each level, you also use our suggestions as inspiration to experiment and come up with some of your own crazy contraptions or concepts. We know you'll dream up things we never even thought of. But that's okay. That's the whole point of *Scribblenauts*. No two people will play this game the same. And 5TH Cell wouldn't want it any other way.

Octopus

Jellyfish

Wolf

Chameleon

Hot Air Balloon

Windsurfer

Scissors

Chariot

This guide explains exactly how *Scribblenauts* works, offers full solutions to all of the levels, and gets you started with the game's robust level editor. Here is how each section breaks down, so you know exactly where to look for the tips and tricks you need:

"Introduction." A quick overview of the game, peeling back the curtain on the wonderful world just waiting at the tip of your stylus.

"How to Play." A complete explanation of how everything in this game functions, from moving Maxwell to creating objects via the Notepad. We explain how different groups of objects work and the in-game currency, called Ollars, which helps Maxwell buy new levels and outfits.

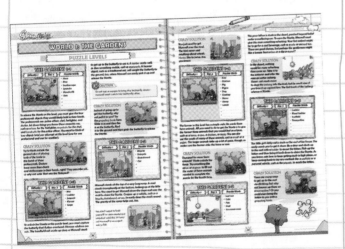

"Walkthrough." Detailed strategies for solving all 220 levels in the game, complete with lists of potential words and objects. We even include Crazy Solutions to show you how you can really think outside the box when collecting a Starite.

"Level Editor." Scribblenauts comes complete with a Level Editor that lets you create your very own levels to share with your friends via Nintendo Wi-Fi Connection. We show you exactly what's possible and offer plenty of our own examples to get those creative sparks...er, sparking!

"Word List." While we definitely do not have the room to show you all of the tens of thousands of words in the game, our Word List calls out some of the most intriguing objects just waiting to be made real by your stylus.

"Bonus Content." Learn more about the inspiration behind Scribblenauts in our interview with Jeremiah Slaczka, Co-Founder and Creative Director of 5TH Cell.

HOW TO PLAY

When you first start *Scribblenauts*, you spot Maxwell standing in a field. The little hero is enjoying a summer's afternoon and a light breeze. With his magical Notepad, he's ready to take on the world. All he's missing is you. But before joining Maxwell on his incredible adventures to collect the Starites, you better make sure you can keep up with him. If you pursue the Starites with full knowledge of how the entire game universe works, from how to create objects for Maxwell to how to glue two objects together, your time with Maxwell will be all the more fun.

THE BASICS

Your view into Maxwell's universe is nice and simple. There is no complicated heads-up display with a bunch of meters and gauges. You just have a Notepad for creating objects and a magnifying glass for identifying objects in a level. The top screen of the Nintendo DS shows all of the needed details for each level.

Here is how the basic game screen breaks down:

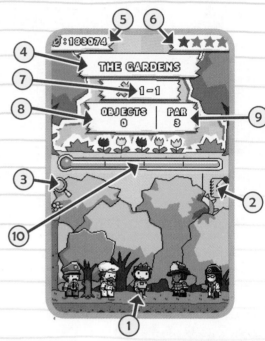

1. **Maxwell**

2. **Notepad**: This is where you write down objects you want to place into the current level to help Maxwell achieve his goal. Just tap the Notepad with the stylus to open it. When manipulating an object, the Notepad turns into a trash can. To remove an object, drag it into the trash can.

3. **Magnifying Glass**: Tap the magnifying glass to go into an object identification mode. Now you can tap on any object in the level and see what it is called. To exit this mode, just tap the magnifying glass again.

4. **World Name**: This is the world you are currently exploring. There are 10 worlds.

5. **Ollars**: Ollars are the currency in *Scribblenauts*. Maxwell earns Ollars when he successfully completes a level.

6. **Difficulty**: These stars measure how tough the current level is. The more stars, the harder the level.

7. **Current Level**: Each world has 22 levels. This tracks your current level.

8. **Objects**: This is the number of objects you have placed in the level since the start of the level.

9. **Par**: Each level has a set number of objects you should stay at or under when solving it to help maximize the amount of Ollars earned for that level.

10. **Object Meter**: You only have so much ink for writing in objects. The larger an object, the more this meter fills. When the meter is full, you can no longer add another object to the level without first deleting one.

When you first look into Maxwell's world, he is just hanging out at the Playground. This is a great place just to get acquainted with the basics of the game, such as how to make Maxwell walk

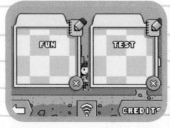

around and how to create objects. There is an Object Meter that prevents you from writing in an unlimited number of objects, but there are no threats either. You can just try stuff out here, from placing Maxwell on the back of a pterodactyl to handing the little guy a sword. Or giving him a sword and then mounting him on the back of a pterodactyl, turning Maxwell into a hero straight out of some strange sci-fi novel...

Once you tap Start on the Playground, you move into the Profile Menu. Here, you select which of two possible profiles you want to use when playing the game. Each profile tracks the player's supply of Ollars, how many Starites have been collected, which levels have been completed, and which merits have been earned when completing levels.

You can select the background of the Playground by tapping the ticket. Try opening new backgrounds by writing different objects!

After selecting a new profile and typing your name, you are directed to the game's Main Menu. From this screen, you can choose to enter Challenge Mode, which is where you go to select different worlds

and complete levels, try out the Level Editor to create your very own worlds, or enter the Ollar Store. The Ollar Store is a cool spot to spend your collected cash on new avatars (you don't always have to hang with Maxwell—you can play with an alien, a pirate, and more) or purchase different music to listen to while you play the game.

NOTE

For more on the Level Editor, please see the "Level Editor" chapter of the guide. The Ollar Store is explained in greater detail later in this chapter.

Once you select Challenge Mode for the first time, you are directed to a tutorial at the game's University. Under a professor's watchful eye, Maxwell gets a crash course in writing. The professor goes through the basics, such as how to create an object and what a Starite is.

NOTE

You can replay the tutorial at any time by tapping the University from the world select screen.

Picking Levels

As soon as you complete the tutorial, you can then dive right into the first world: The Gardens. This world select screen shows 10 levels, though! How do you open

up new worlds? After earning enough Ollars, you buy your way into new worlds.

Each world has a price to enter:

World	Ollars
The Gardens	0
Metro	2,000
The Peaks	4,000
Ancient	8,000
Shoreline	10,000
Outer Wild	12,000
Stunt Park	16,000
Frontier	18,000
Dark Hollow	20,000
Mish Mash	25,000

To enter a world, just tap on it from the world select screen. You are taken right into the world's menu, where you can see which levels are ready to play and which are still locked.

Each world has 22 levels: 11 puzzle levels and 11 action levels. To switch back and forth between the two, tap the lower-right corner of the screen. Tap the jigsaw piece to switch to puzzle levels. Tap the explosion to switch over to the action levels. There are distinct differences between the two types of levels.

Puzzle levels do not show the Starite at the beginning of the level. You must figure out how to solve the problem proposed at the start of the level. Usually, you receive some help in the form of a little hint.

Once you jot down the correct objects to solve the puzzle, the Starite appears, and you must move Maxwell over to it in order to finish the level.

NOTE

Puzzle levels are usually a little slower paced, although they can be frantic from time to time.

Action levels reveal the Starite right at the beginning of the level. You must write in objects in order to reach the Starite, whether it is being held behind bars or in the clutches of an enemy creature. These levels often have people or monsters that must be neutralized or hazardous obstacles (such as lava or an abyss) to overcome in order to seize the Starite.

To start a level, just tap on it. Within seconds, you're helping Maxwell in that level.

Maxwell's Controls

Maxwell is controlled entirely with the stylus on the touch screen of the Nintendo DS. To make Maxwell walk or run, tap along the floor where there are no objects to interact with. Maxwell automatically jumps across small gaps, so tapping the opposite side of a hole in the ground makes him leap across it.

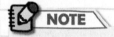 **NOTE**

To look around a level, use the D-pad to move the camera. If the camera is left alone for a few moments, it snaps back to Maxwell.

To interact with an object, tap on it. If the object has a single function or is small enough for Maxwell to pick up, he automatically does so without any further input from you. However, if an object has multiple functions, a small menu pops up and asks what you would like to do, such as Interact or Shoot.

When Maxwell is holding an object or equipment he can interact with, just tap Maxwell. If you have given Maxwell a weapon, such as a pistol or a grappling hook, tap on a target and then select Shoot. If Maxwell is holding something he can throw, tap on a target and choose Throw.

To place Maxwell inside a vehicle, just drag the object on top of him. When the object turns yellow, that means Maxwell will hop inside of it as soon as you lift the stylus from the screen. Once Maxwell is in the vehicle, move it around just as if you were making Maxwell walk or run.

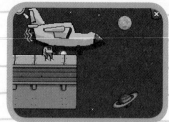

NOTEPAD

The Notepad is where the magic happens. When you are in a level (or on the Playground), tap on the Notepad to bring up a keyboard or a small tablet, depending on your personal preference. Spell out an object you want to place in the level and tap the green check mark. Voila!

Creating an Object

The Notepad is very easy to use. You have two ways in which to write in an object. You can use the traditional QWERTY-style keyboard you see on a computer, or you can tap the small ABC button below the keyboard

and bring up what looks like a blank sheet of paper. Now, one at a time, write each letter of the object you want to create. After lifting the stylus, the game will translate your writing into a letter along the top of the screen.

Use large capital letters for best results when spelling out objects in the Notepad.

There are a few basic rules to follow when coming up with objects to create:

- No proper names. "Steve" will not bring up your friend Steve.
- No trademarked objects.
- No general shapes.
- No alcohol or illegal substances.
- No races or cultures.
- No vulgarity, so don't bother trying.

If you misspell a word, the game offers a few suggestions. Select one from the list or tap Go Back to try another word.

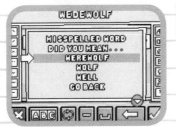

There are tens of thousands of words in the game, from gypsum to magic carpet to mech. Chances are good that if you have an idea for an object you want to use in a level, you can jot it right down and get to work. If the word is accepted, you are taken back to the level, and the object is ready to use.

Using an Object

When you have written in an object and moved back to the level, the object is still not part of the level yet. It hovers just above the action. You "pick up" the object with the stylus and can then move it around by sliding the stylus across the touch screen.

While holding the object, you may rotate it by using the shoulder buttons on the Nintendo DS. Not all objects can be rotated. Some can only be flipped horizontally; others cannot be repositioned at all. When you remove the stylus from the screen, the object is then dropped into play. Depending on where you place the object, several things can happen. If you have created a monster and placed it next to an enemy or a creature that will hurt Maxwell, the monster follows its instinct and attacks. If you create an inanimate object, such as a rock, it just drops to the ground.

You cannot just place an object anywhere in a level and have it work. There are some limitations on object placement. You can place an object on top of a character in the level, such as Maxwell or a creature, and have those automatically interact. For example, if you create a ball, dragging it on top of Maxwell and letting go hands the ball directly to Maxwell.

There is a color system that helps you determine exactly how an object will work within the level when you release it. There are four colors: blue, yellow, red, and green. Here's how the colors break down:

- **Blue**: When an object turns blue, that means it will be picked up by the character you are holding it over once you release it. In this example, pulling the stylus from

the screen hands the missile launcher to the cowboy. If an object does not turn blue when you're holding it over a character, that means it is either too big for the character to hold or the character would not naturally interact with that object. While you can hand Maxwell a baseball, you cannot hand him a girder. It's too big.

- **Yellow**: When you drag a vehicle-like object over Maxwell and there is enough space in the immediate area for you to release the object, it turns yellow. This means Maxwell will automat-

ically enter the object when you pull the stylus away. The example shown here is a helicopter. Maxwell will automatically hop into the pilot's seat when the stylus is removed. However, in a larger vehicle that has multiple seats, such as an airplane, Maxwell's location matters. If you let the object go while Maxwell is not under the pilot's seat, he just sits in the plane as a passenger, and you cannot fly it. Maxwell must be in the pilot's seat for you to be able to control the vehicle.

- **Red**: When an object appears red, that means it cannot be dropped into the level in its current position. The area is not large enough to fit the object, or the object is being held over a surface

such as a wall or floor. You must move the object until it is not over that feature.

If you release the object while it is red, it appears with a giant X over it. The object remains in the level but not in play. Characters can walk behind it and will not interact with it at all. For example, a dragon normally would slash at everything around it. But if it is red, it will do nothing.

There is actually a good use for dropping objects into a level while they are still red. If you know you are going to use something later in the level, you can place it close to where you will need it. When it is time to use it, just grab the object and then move it into the level. This is also a good way to reuse the same object. Let's stick with the dragon example. Let's say you cleared out a menacing bear with the dragon, but there are still creatures in the level that will attack Maxwell. Just pick up the dragon and move it over a wall or the ground. Release it, and the dragon is no threat to Maxwell. Do what you need to do with Maxwell and then, when the dragon is needed again, move it back into play.

• **Green**: When you attempt to connect two objects, such as attaching a rope to a crate, the objects appear green. When you release the object you are moving, it will attach to the other object and remain connected unless removed by force—or by you tapping the object you connected and pulling it away.

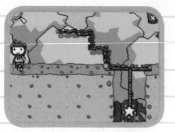

Connecting Objects

As mentioned, some objects can be connected. There are multiple ways to connect two objects. But to start, you have to imagine that almost every object—including the Starite—has particular points on it where it will "accept" a connection. When you try to link the objects, these connection points appear as small dots. These are the only places where the connection can occur. If you try to connect the object at another spot, it will either just fall away or appear red.

Now, in the case of connecting a rope or a chain to an object, you do not need anything else but the rope or the chain. These objects (and other rope-like objects, such as bungee cords or extension cords) automatically tie themselves to objects when you release them over a connection point.

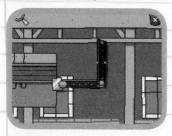

To connect other objects, though, you need to use an adhesive, such as glue or tape. It is likely that you will use glue the most. To glue one object to another, write "glue" in your Notepad. A small gray wad of glue then appears. Drag it over an object and attach it at a connection point. Once the glue is in place, you can then attach another object, as long as it will fit in that area with the two connection points—the glue's and the object's—touching. If the object you are trying to connect is red, it will not work.

 TIP

Not all adhesives are created equal. Tape is much flimsier than glue. It will hold two objects together, but there is quite a bit of wiggling going on between the two objects.

So, why should you connect objects? Connecting objects is a great way to build contraptions that help solve levels. If you know the Starite is going to fall from a great height when you trigger a tripwire, you can

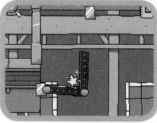

build a bucket out of glue and girders to catch it. You can also glue weapons to vehicles, such as cementing a mortar to the top of a UFO.

CAUTION

You cannot glue objects to Maxwell, to other people, or to animals. However, you can attach ropes and whatnot to them, just as if they were inanimate objects. They may not exactly go willingly, though, when you try to drag them.

Object Categories

With so many objects in the game, it helps to have an idea of what's in the game's lexicon and what objects are capable of doing. This is by no means a complete list, because there are so many objects, but these are the kinds of things to look for and what their general functions are. There is a large word list of objects later in this guide that will also help you figure out what kinds of objects you can type up and use.

• **General Purpose**: These are everyday objects that you are familiar with, such as ladders, balloons, or rocks. You know exactly what these objects do and what to expect from them. Of course, you can

always find interesting things to do with them, especially if they are connected to another object.

- **Vehicle**: There are many types of vehicles, from cars to bicycles to skateboards. These are good for getting places quickly or pulling objects. If a cart is too heavy to pull uphill with just Maxwell, for example, hook it up to the back of a stock car.

- **Weapon**: These come in two categories—melee and projectile. Melee weapons include things such as swords and clubs. You must walk up to an enemy and hit them with it. Projectile weapons includes guns and launchers. These let you attack from a distance.

- **Rope**: This category includes ropes, chains, and cords. These are useful for tethering two objects together or for pulling something. Attaching one end of a rope to a person and the other to a helicopter will let you pick the person up and cart him or her somewhere else in the level.

- **Swim Gear**: Scuba, wetsuits, and flippers are examples of swim gear that lets Maxwell travel underwater.

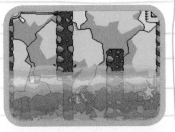

- **Flight**: Maxwell needs to fly around many levels to collect the Starites, so you must give him objects such as wings or a jetpack so he can take to the air. There are flying vehicles, such as helicopters and jets, too.

- **Food**: Some levels are solved by giving animals or people food. Certain creatures are partial to specific foods. A dog, for example, would prefer a steak over a pistachio. Sometimes you can lead animals around by holding their favorite foods in front of them.

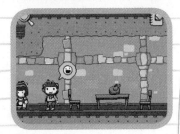

- **Clothes**: Maxwell and other people can wear clothes that change their appearance. Some levels are solved by putting on specific costumes.

- **Attack Creature**: There are a lot of hostile creatures in the levels. While Maxwell can try to avoid them or attack them himself, he can also jot down a monster or a creature to attack on his behalf. A bear or a dragon will attack if dropped next to a hostile creature or an enemy. One catch, though—these creatures do not stop after finishing off the enemy. If Maxwell wanders too close, the attack creature will take a swipe at him. Call it instinct.

- **Peaceful Creature**: Some creatures are completely docile, such as a cow or a cat. That said, these creatures can be coaxed into attacking their natural prey. The same cat that stands next to Maxwell and looks cute turns ravenous if you drop a mouse near it. Perhaps you can use this to your advantage in a level. Maybe tie something to an animal and then place its natural prey in front of it to make it pull another object?

 **NOTE**

If you feed a person or a creature three times, it falls asleep for a few moments.

Typical Object Interactions

Though there are thousands of objects in the game, there are some specific types of objects and interactions you will return to time and time again to solve puzzle or action levels.

- **Digging**: In some levels, Maxwell comes across softer soil that he can burrow through—but he needs a digging utensil to do so. When you spot loose dirt (typically sandy or light brown in color),

jot down a shovel or a spade in the Notepad and give it to Maxwell. When you tap on the soil while Maxwell is holding the shovel, he digs into it. It takes multiple taps to burrow through a wall.

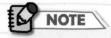 **NOTE**

While holding a shovel or another object, Maxwell cannot hold anything else.

- **Breaking**: Sometimes, Maxwell must break things to get through an area, such as bashing a wall or a stalagmite. Give Maxwell an object, such as a hammer or a tire iron, to smash through the object.

Just tap on the object you want Maxwell to break while he holds the hammer, and Maxwell goes to work.

- **Shooting/Throwing**: Maxwell can fire weapons and throw objects. To shoot or throw, give Maxwell an appropriate object. Type in a laser pistol and give it Maxwell. Now he can shoot it. Tap

on an object or a character and select the Shoot option from the menu. Maxwell then opens fire. The exact same principle works with throwing balls or other handheld objects, such as a rock or a lime.

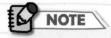 **NOTE**

Many guns have limited ammunition. After the ammo is spent, the object falls from Maxwell's hands and disappears.

- **Swimming**: Maxwell can swim on the surface of water without any assistance. However, if you need to sink beneath the waves, you must give Maxwell something like flippers, a snorkel, or scuba

gear. Any diving equipment will work. When Maxwell has the object on, tap underwater, and Maxwell swims in that direction.

 **NOTE**

While swimming with gear such as scuba, Maxwell can hold another object.

 **CAUTION**

Electronic items short out in water. If you accidentally drop into water while wearing a jetpack, it breaks, and you cannot use it again. However...what if you dropped a TV in the water next to something bad, such as a shark?

- **Flying**: Many situations call for Maxwell to fly. Perhaps he needs to reach a high ledge or cross a wide gap in the ground. There are three ways Maxwell can fly. You can jot down a flying object,

such as wings, a jetpack, or a magic carpet, and drag it onto Maxwell. Now, when you tap in the air, Maxwell takes flight. These objects do not work forever, though. They can be reused over and over, but their flight paths do not last long. If you try to fly for too long, the object sputters and Maxwell falls.

Maxwell can also fly in a vehicle, such as a plane or a helicopter. These do not have limited flight times like wings or jetpacks do. Some flying vehicles, such as a fighter jet, even have onboard weapons.

Alternatively, Maxwell can fly on the back of certain creatures, such as a pegasus, a pterodactyl, or a sphinx. These are inherently friendly creatures that will not attack Maxwell. Just drag the creature onto Maxwell and release it when it turns yellow. You can also place the creature in the level and then tap it. Choose Ride from the menu, and Maxwell hops on. Flying creatures can soar much, much longer than an object.

 **CAUTION**

If the creature you are flying on is attacked, it drops Maxwell and refuses to let him back on again. You must write in another creature if you want to fly again, or you can try a vehicle.

HOW TO SOLVE A LEVEL

Now that you know how to create an object and interact with it, it's time to look at how to actually solve a level in *Scribblenauts*. It was mentioned earlier that there are two types of levels: puzzle and action. Although the general setup of each type of level is different, the goal is the same—capture the Starite. Once Maxwell holds the Starite is his hands, the level ends in success.

Sample Level

Let's look at an early puzzle level in the game and break down exactly what happens to solve the level. For this example, we'll use Puzzle Level 1-4. The goal here is to give a farmer three animals. Already,

you have an idea of what is required. Write down a cow, a chicken, and a pig and then place them near the farmer. When you draw up each animal and place it in the level, you see two balloons appear. The farmer, protective of the flock, shows a shield over his head. The animal shows a flag over its head. That flag indicates that the animal is indeed an appropriate solution and counts toward the goal.

However, let's say you create an animal that the farmer doesn't want. You jot down kangaroo in the Notepad, and when the animal bounds across the level, nothing happens. No balloon. Then you have to scrap the kangaroo by dragging it into the trash and try another animal. You just used up one object. This level only has par 4, so you are going to come in right at par. That means no bonus Ollars for you for finishing the level with fewer objects than allowed.

> **NOTE**
>
> Use the balloons that appear over character and creature heads as indicators of behaviors.

Well, that's definitely better than the alternative. If you had conjured up a bear, you'd see a much different reaction. For one thing, the farmer is afraid of the bear, so you'd see a purple face over his head. The bear is violent, so it attacks the farmer. (Attacking creatures have a red sets of boxing gloves in their balloons.)

The bear and the farmer then attack each other. Each injures the other, which is noted by the orange upset faces in their balloons.

But when you do give the farmer the three farm animals requested, the Starite finally appears overhead. It falls to the ground. Tap the Starite, and Maxwell picks it up. Great—you're all finished with the level, right? You can move on to 1-5?

Not so fast...

Multiple Solutions

To truly finish a level, you must come up with four solutions. Only after completing the level a fourth time does a gold Starite appear over the level in the level select screen. Now you have finished the level. You can replay it as many times as you like after that, though.

Sticking with 1-4 as an example, you then need to go back into the level and come up with three different farm animals. You cannot use the same object twice in a level while you are going for the four needed solutions. If you used a pig, a cow, and a chicken in the first solution, you must pick three different animals in your second attempt. Maybe the next time, you try a dog, a sheep, and a horse. Those work. But then it's on to the third attempt.

After you successfully solve a level the third time, something different happens. You are not sent back to the level select screen. The level automatically restarts. You must solve the level a fourth time without backing out to the level select screen. This is designed to challenge you to think hard about different objects or solutions. If you do quit the level without solving it for the fourth time, you must then start back on your second solution and work your way up to the fourth solution again. You can use the same objects as before, if you'd like, in this situation.

Not to confuse you, but although you cannot use the same object in different solutions to the same level, you can use multiples of the same object during a single solution. For example, you can write in four rocks in a single solution, but then you cannot use a rock in the next solution attempt.

Rewards

After you solve a level, you are rewarded for your efforts. Depending on your performance, those rewards vary. You always earn at least a few Ollars when you solve a level, but coming in under par adds bonus Ollars. For each object you are under par, you earn 120 Ollars. You earn style Ollars for having creative solutions. And the quicker you solve a level, the more Ollars you earn.

PAR:	-1	120
STYLE:		30
TIME:	01:16	348
OLLARS WON:		498

These Ollars are then multiplied by the merits you earn. On the bottom screen of the reward dispensation, you are told what merits you earned for the solution you used. There are many merits, each awarded for doing different activities or using specific types of objects. These merits are logged in a merit journal in your profile. The more merits you earn for a single solution, the more bonus Ollars you receive for completing a level. If you are particularly creative, you can bank thousands of Ollars with just a single solution.

MERIT GET!
- ★ NEW OBJECT
- ☺ SAVIOR

OK

Here is a full list of all of the merits and what is needed to earn them:

5TH Cell: Spawn a 5TH Cell developer.

All New: Complete a level with an object you've never used before.

Architect: Write in two buildings.

Arrrrrr: Attach the Jolly Roger to a flagpole.

Audiophile: Write two or more instruments or audio objects.

Bioterrorist: Introduce the plague and infect two or more people.

Botanist: Write two or more plants.

Chauffeur: Drive a vehicle with more than one passenger.

Chef: Write two or more foods.

Closet: Write two or more clothes.

Combo: Combine any two objects.

Cupid: Shoot a humanoid with Cupid's arrow.

Decorator: Write two furniture objects.

Electrolysis: Shock someone with electricity.

Elemental: Write more than one element.

Entertainer: Write two or more entertainment objects.

Entomologist: Write two or more insects.

Environmentalist: Write two or more environmental objects.

Explosive: Write two or more explosive devices.

Exterminator: Two or more humanoids or animals start in a level and are destroyed.

Fantasy Novel: Write two fantasy objects.

Fashion Designer: Clothe Maxwell's head, body, legs, and feet and give him an accessory.

Genius: Complete a level twice in a row.

Glutton: Feed someone or something three times in a row.

Gold Digger: Write three or more precious stones.

Grab and Go: Write two or more grabbing tool objects.

HaxxOr: Write five or more developers.

Healer: Write two or more medical objects.

Herpetologist: Write two or more reptiles.

Humanitarian: Write two or more humans.

Infected: Write a zombie and have it infect two humanoids.

Janitor: Write two or more cleaning objects.

Jockey: Use an animal as a vehicle.

Joust: Defeat a knight while Maxwell is mounted.

Knight School: Slay a dragon with a melee weapon.

Luddite: Short out three or more objects.

Lumberjack: Cut down three or more trees in a level.

Mad Hatter: Place a hat on four or more humanoids or animals.

Magician: Use the magic wand to turn something into a toad.

Marine Biologist: Write two or more fish.

Mechanic: Jump start a vehicle.

Messiah: Turn a humanoid into a deity.

Militant: Use two or more weapons or one weaponized vehicle.

Miner 49er: Dig a massive hole.

Miser: Reach 300,000 Ollars total.

New Object: Write a completely new item.

Novice Angler: Catch a fish with a fishing pole.

No Weapon: Don't write a weapon to complete the level.

Old School: Write two or more classic video game objects.

Organ Donor: Write two or more organs.

Ornithologist: Write two or more birds.

Paleontologist: Write two or more dinosaurs.

Pariah: Make three humanoids or animals flee.

Pi: Earn 314 Ollars in a single level.

Picasso: Write two or more drawing tool objects.

Pilot: Write two or more air vehicles.

Prodigy: Complete a level three times in a row.

Pyromaniac: Set at least four objects on fire in a level.

Reanimator: Bring a corpse back to life.

Roped In: Write two or more rope objects.

Russian Doll: Place an object inside an object and then inside another object.

Savior: Two or more humanoids or animals start and finish a level alive.

Sea Two: Write two or more sea vehicles.

Shoveler: Write two or more digging tool objects.

Series of Tubes: Go here—scribblenauts.com/nauts

Smasher: Write two or more melee weapons.

Smuggler: Hide a weapon in a container.

Split Personality: Write two or more cutting or splitting tools.

Stealth: Destroy a security camera.

Sweet Tooth: Write two or more junk foods.

Tooling Around: Write two or more tool objects.

Washington: Chop down a cherry tree.

Water Jockey: Use a sea animal as a vehicle.

Whisperer: Ride a hostile animal.

Zookeeper: Write two or more animals.

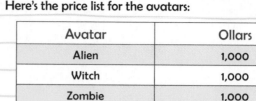

Ollar Store

Now that you've pocketed all of those Ollars, what do you do with them? You use them to both unlock new worlds and purchase music tracks and new avatars. Avatars are replacements you can use instead of Maxwell when playing levels.

Here's the price list for the avatars:

Avatar	Ollars
Alien	1,000
Witch	1,000
Zombie	1,000
DJ	2,500
Pirate	2,500
Bride	2,500
Ninja	5,000
Robot	5,000
Shaman	5,000

GENERAL TIPS AND STRATEGIES

So, you're about to step into the world of *Scribblenauts*. As you jot down objects in the Notepad and discover solutions for the levels, keep in mind these general tips and strategies. They are sure to save you not only time, but also spare you the sight of a Starite dropping into lava or Maxwell falling into the void.

1. Flying objects like wings and jetpacks only work for a few seconds at a time. Then, the object needs to recharge for a second or two before Maxwell can use it again. If you are in a level with tall ledges or wide chasms, you risk coming up short. While crossing a gap in the floor or a wide lava pit, running out of juice with the jetpack is a real disaster.

2. Friendly flying creatures like a pegasus or a pterodactyl do not require rest periods like the jetpack or helibackpack. However, they are rendered unusable once they are attacked by another creature or struck by a level hazard. The creature just refuses to let Maxwell ride it again. You must either come up with a new route through the level or create another flying creature. Just make sure not to use a different one in a level or else you eliminate two potential objects in a single solution and must figure out something completely different by the time you reach the fourth solution.

3. Water always shorts out electronic objects. Flying through rain in a jetpack or helibackpack is a recipe for trouble. If a level has rain clouds, stick to wings, a magic carpet, or a flying creature.

4. Once an electronic object has been shorted out by water, it cannot be reused.

5. Sources of fire, like a match or a campfire, can be used and reused multiple times in a level. If you want to burn several ropes or melt through ice, just keep moving the fire around with your stylus. Watch out for accidentally turning a fire source upside-down and dropping it. If the flame hits the ground, it is extinguished.

6. The match is one the smallest objects in the game. If you need a tiny object to fit into a tight spot and set off a button, use a match and turn it sideways.

7. Many, if not most, creatures are afraid of fire. You can contain creatures and animals in smaller areas of a level by placing fire around them and then herding them into a corner by picking the fire up and moving it even closer to them. This is a great trick for keeping even the biggest monsters, like a minotaur, in check.

8. Most explosives require a fire source to set off. If you are fast with your stylus, you can ignite an explosive and then move the fire source before it is destroyed in the resulting blast.

9. Explosives are a good way to get rid of both monsters and obstacles. If you have a giant creature blocking your path or a huge ice block (or a huge monster inside of an ice block), set dynamite or a bomb next to it and drop a torch. The explosion is big enough to destroy a monster to the size of a dragon, which is one of the biggest creatures you encounter.

10. Don't be afraid of using monsters to do your dirty work. If you have some tough-looking creatures ahead, deploy a behemoth or dragon to take them on. If the monsters are in the water, consider using a kraken or sea serpent to take them on. (Alternately, you can also remove monsters or attacking creatures in the water by just dropping a TV right next to them.) Just make sure you delete the monster before getting close to it. Most monsters will not care that Maxwell created them—they will attack him all the same.

11. Give Maxwell a magic wand and then launch an attack on a creature or attacking humanoid. The spell turns the creature into a harmless frog.

12. Many creatures in *Scribblenauts* share the behaviors of their real-life counterparts. Dogs chase cats. Horses eat apples. Mice like cheese. Use these behaviors in the game to solve puzzles, such as tying the Starite to a dog and then taunting it with a cat or bone to make it drag the Starite straight to Maxwell.

13. Reuse an object as many times as possible in a solution. For example, after you've thrown a ball, you can also use it to hold down a button.

14. The black hole is one of the most powerful objects in the game, but it is also quite dangerous. A black hole placed next to a dragon or a spiked steel ball will destroy it. But like an explosion, the black hole does not discriminate with its targets. The black hole will also pull in innocent civilians, Maxwell, or even the Starite if it is placed too close.

15. One more thing about the black hole: it disappears after just two seconds. However, those two seconds are only measured while the object is actually in the level. While you hold it with the stylus, it is not considered active and that "timer" stops. If you practice and get quick with the stylus, you can move a black hole around a level and destroy multiple targets with a single deployment.

16. You can create projectiles like a fireball or tranquilizer dart and then use them directly on an enemy without needing a weapon. Drop a fireball or electric shock on a monster to do damage. Use a tranquilizer dart to put a monster to sleep.

17. Feeding a creature three times puts it to sleep for a few moments. However, this uses up a lot of objects and can push you close to or over par.

18. If you need to reach a high ledge and do not necessarily want to use a flying object for a particular solution, look into a fixed ladder. This ladder is over twice as tall as a regular ladder.

19. There are a handful of special weapons—like a freeze ray or shrink ray—that do not injure a target, but make them a lot more manageable. The freeze ray in particular is useful for levels where you must protect something from attack. Encasing a friend in ice, for example, does not hurt them. While they're in the ice, you have a few seconds to deal with the attackers.

20. Ropes and other tethers do not need glue to be attached to another object. You can also tie multiple tethers to each other to create extra-long ropes and chains.

21. Maxwell can survive in lava for only a few seconds. If you fall in from a low ledge, immediately tap the ledge to jump back out before Maxwell perishes.

WORLD 1: THE GARDENS

PUZZLE LEVELS

THE GARDENS 1-1

Difficulty: 1	Par: 3	Possible Words:

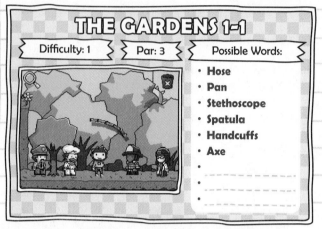

Possible Words:
- Hose
- Pan
- Stethoscope
- Spatula
- Handcuffs
- Axe

To release the Starite in this level, you must give the four professionals objects they would likely hold in their hands. The professionals are: police officer, chef, firefighter, and doctor. Jot down things you know these careerists use, such as a hose for the firefighter, a spatula for the chef, and handcuffs for the police officer. You need to think of two objects total per attempt at this level (one for one professional and one for another).

CRAZY SOLUTION

Try to think outside the general idea of placing tools of the trade in the hands of these professionals. Doctors have more than charts and stethoscopes in their hands, right? They prescribe pills, so why not write that into the Notepad?

THE GARDENS 1-2

Difficulty: 1	Par: 3	Possible Words:

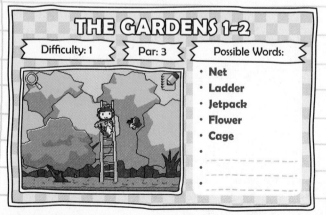

Possible Words:
- Net
- Ladder
- Jetpack
- Flower
- Cage

To unlock the Starite in this puzzle level, you must capture the butterfly that flutters overhead. Obvious solutions are nets. The handheld net works up close, so Maxwell needs to get up to the butterfly to use it. A ladder works well, as does something mobile, such as a jetpack. A heavier object, such as a traditional net, will weight the butterfly to the ground, too, where Maxwell can easily pick it up and release the Starite.

CAUTION

Do not use a weapon to bring the butterfly down—Maxwell must catch the butterfly alive.

CRAZY SOLUTION

Instead of going up to get the butterfly, why not pull it to you? Try the grappling hook here. Write it in and then fire it at the butterfly. Reel it to the ground and then grab the butterfly to release the Starite.

THE GARDENS 1-3

Difficulty: 1	Par: 2	Possible Words:

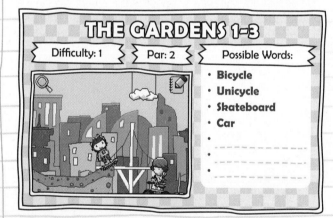

Possible Words:
- Bicycle
- Unicycle
- Skateboard
- Car

Maxwell stands at the top of a very long ramp. A rival stands triumphantly at the bottom, looking up at the little hero. You need to get Maxwell down the slope and over the rival to claim the Starite. Conjure up a vehicle, such as a bicycle, skateboard, or car, to easily clear the rival's record. The gravity of the ramp helps out, too.

You don't need to limit yourself to even-numbered wheeled vehicles. It turns out Maxwell is an expert unicyclist.

CRAZY SOLUTION

You just need to get Maxwell over the rival. The hint never said anything about wheels. Horses like to jump, too, you know.

THE GARDENS 1-4

Difficulty: 1	Par: 4	Possible Words:

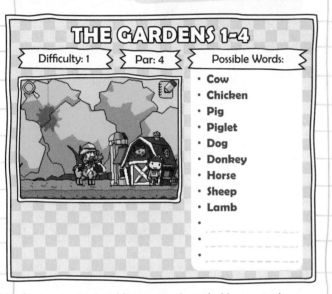

- **Cow**
- **Chicken**
- **Pig**
- **Piglet**
- **Dog**
- **Donkey**
- **Horse**
- **Sheep**
- **Lamb**
-
-
-

The farmer in this level has a simple wish: He wants three farm animals. All you need to do to get the Starite is to give the farmer three animals that you would find on a farm, such as a horse, a cow, a chicken, or a pig. You can also use the youth of many of these animals, such as a calf or a piglet. The larger animals take up a lot of space, though, so make sure the farmer rides the horse or cow.

CRAZY SOLUTION

Stumped for more farm animals? Think outside the fence. Try something like an ox or a goose to fill out the roster of farm animals needed to complete this level for the fourth time.

THE GARDENS 1-5

Difficulty: 1	Par: 2	Possible Words:

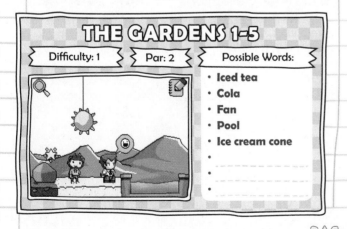

- **Iced tea**
- **Cola**
- **Fan**
- **Pool**
- **Ice cream cone**

This poor fellow is stuck in the desert, parched beyond belief under a sweltering sun. To earn the Starite, Maxwell must give this man something refreshing. Your first instinct might be to go for a cool beverage, such as a cola or an iced tea. Those are good choices, but perhaps the gentleman might like a breeze from a fan or a dip in a pool?

CRAZY SOLUTION

In the desert, nothing would be more refreshing than some ice. Take it to the extreme and offer the man an entire iceberg. There's not much room to drop the iceberg into the level, but he won't care if you lean it up against him. The first touch of the iceberg releases a Starite.

THE GARDENS 1-6

Difficulty: 1	Par: 2	Possible Words:

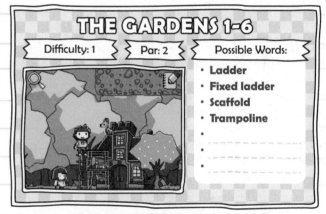

- **Ladder**
- **Fixed ladder**
- **Scaffold**
- **Trampoline**
-
-
-

The little girl's kitty-cat is stuck on the roof of her house. She really wants you to get it down. Be a dear and climb up to the roof with a ladder to rescue the kitten. Pick up the kitten and then bring it back down to claim the Starite. As you know, cats love to keep getting stuck in high places, so keep coming back to try new methods like a scaffold or a personal vehicle, such as the jetpack, to reach the kitten.

CRAZY SOLUTION

There are many ways to get up to the roof via climbing, but why not bounce up there on a trampoline? Or you could even bring the kitten to you with a grappling hook.

THE GARDENS 1-7

| Difficulty: 1 | Par: 2 | Possible Words: |

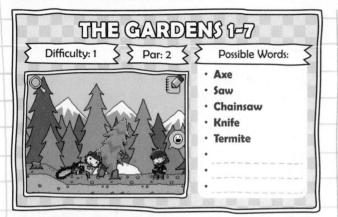

Possible Words:
- **Axe**
- **Saw**
- **Chainsaw**
- **Knife**
- **Termite**

The lumberjack needs help chopping down the tree. (Why he doesn't already have an axe, who knows?) You need to cut through the trunk of the tree, so write a sharp object into the picture, such as an axe, a handsaw, or a chainsaw. Carrying the utensil, walk into the tree to chop it down and put a smile on the lumberjack's face.

CRAZY SOLUTION

Want the Ingenious merit? Conjure up nature's solution to trees: a beaver. The beaver gnaws through the tree trunk without you or the lumberjack lifting a finger!

THE GARDENS 1-8

| Difficulty: 2 | Par: 3 | Possible Words: |

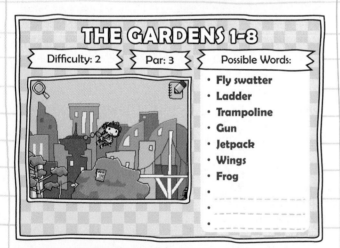

Possible Words:
- **Fly swatter**
- **Ladder**
- **Trampoline**
- **Gun**
- **Jetpack**
- **Wings**
- **Frog**

This do-gooder level tasks Maxwell with cleaning up the park and disposing of a pesky fly in order to earn the Starite. There are three pieces of trash that must be thrown into the can: a candy wrapper, a magazine, and cola bottle. The wrapper and bottle can be picked up. But the magazine is stuck up in a tree. Use something like the jetpack or wings to get to the magazine. A ladder or trampoline works, too.

The fly does not hurt Maxwell. He can just pick up the fly and stuff it in the trash can like garbage.

Now to deal with that fly. A regular fly swatter makes short work of the nuisance, but sometimes a little overkill is fun, too. Write in a gun for Maxwell to shoot the fly. Or go for the organic solution: a frog.

CRAZY SOLUTION

Try writing a fire and placing it under the tree. The whole tree goes up in smoke, taking the magazine with it. Plus, the fire can be picked up once the tree is ablaze and placed under the fly to incinerate it, too.

THE GARDENS 1-9

| Difficulty: 1 | Par: 2 | Possible Words: |

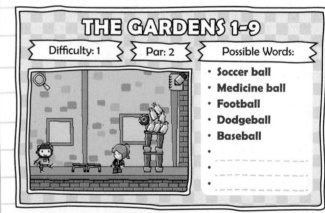

Possible Words:
- **Soccer ball**
- **Medicine ball**
- **Football**
- **Dodgeball**
- **Baseball**

This level re-creates that classic carnival game where you must knock down a stack of milk bottles. The catch here is that you may not use any weapons, such as a gun, to shoot the bottles. You must use something like a ball to throw and knock down all of the milk bottles. You can throw the ball as many times as necessary to drop the whole stack. Try different kinds of balls, such as a football or a baseball, to complete the level four times.

CRAZY SOLUTION

Although you cannot use guns to knock down the bottles, you can still be a little destructive. Use an axe to chop down the legs of the stool holding up the milk bottles. Or try a fire to burn the stool and drop the bottles.

THE GARDENS 1-10

Difficulty: 2	Par: 3	Possible Words:

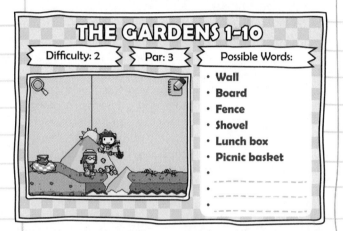

- **Wall**
- **Board**
- **Fence**
- **Shovel**
- **Lunch box**
- **Picnic basket**
- ·
- ·
- ·

There is a sandwich sitting on a small hill in the center of the level. From each side, two ants approach, for a total of four marching menaces. You must save the sandwich to earn the Starite. Sounds simple, right? Just bust out some swords and guns and save that sandwich? Not so fast, Sir Triggerhappy McBlastBlast. There's a hippie on the scene that will not relinquish the Starite if a single ant is harmed. So, you must use alternative methods to save the sandwich. Try digging holes with a shovel on each side of the sandwich to make trenches the ants cannot cross. Erect walls or fences to block the ants. Jot down a lunch box to place the sandwich inside. The ants cannot penetrate the lunch box.

CRAZY SOLUTION

You can actually solve this level without writing down a single object. Stay three under par by just walking up to the sandwich and picking it up. Hold it while the ants mill around the hill for a few moments. The hippie then awards the Starite.

THE GARDENS 1-11

Difficulty: 2	Par: 4	Possible Words:

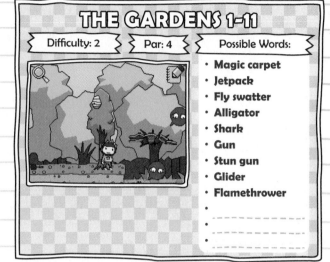

- **Magic carpet**
- **Jetpack**
- **Fly swatter**
- **Alligator**
- **Shark**
- **Gun**
- **Stun gun**
- **Glider**
- **Flamethrower**
- ·
- ·

To earn the Starite in this level, all Maxwell must do is collect three flowers and place them in the basket of a comely young maiden. Complicating matters: An angry bee is guarding the closest flower, a piranha is patrolling the waters below the second flower, and the third flower is located on a high ledge on the far side of the water. Thankfully, you have par 4 to get all three flowers—but you can definitely solve this level with only three objects.

The first thing you must do is eliminate the bee to get at the first flower. A fly swatter will take out the bee, as will any sort of gun. Watch out for bigger weapons, such as a flamethrower, which could possibly burn the flower. After securing the first flower in the basket, neutralize the piranha to collect the second flower. An attack creature in the water, such as an alligator, will destroy the piranha. After getting rid of the piranha, be sure to dispose of the attack creature so Maxwell can actually get in the water himself.

CAUTION

Do not use an electrical object to zap the piranha in the water. The shock will also burn the flower, ending the level.

Use some means of flight to cross the water and ascend the ledge to get the farthest flower. A helicopter or glider works well after you've used objects such as a jetpack or a magic carpet.

CRAZY SOLUTION

Some attack animals can actually serve dual purposes and thus save you an object. The bear is a great animal to introduce to this level. The bear can easily destroy the bee that hovers over the closest flower. But when dropped into the water, the bear is powerful enough to eliminate the piranha, too.

ACTION LEVELS

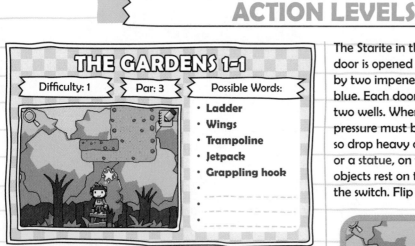

THE GARDENS 1-1

Difficulty: 1 | Par: 3 | Possible Words:

- Ladder
- Wings
- Trampoline
- Jetpack
- Grappling hook

This action level has a very simple goal: Collect the Starite at the top of the tall tree. All Maxwell needs to do is get up to the Starite and pick it up. A ladder (either a normal or a fixed ladder) will do the trick. Flight via a jetpack or a set of wings will also work quite well. You can also pull the Starite out of the tree with the grappling hook.

CRAZY SOLUTION

If you are going to fly up to the Starite, why not fly in style—mythological style? The friendly sphinx welcomes Maxwell on its back and will confidently fly right up to the Starite.

The Starite in this level is hidden behind a red door. The door is opened via a red switch, but that switch is protected by two impenetrable doors. The two doors are green and blue. Each door is controlled by a button at the bottom of two wells. When the button is pressed, the door opens. The pressure must be constant to keep the door open, though, so drop heavy objects, such as a rock, an anvil, a dumbbell, or a statue, on the buttons from a modest height. The objects rest on the buttons, opening the doors that lead to the switch. Flip the switch and collect the Starite.

This level can also be solved without writng in a single object. Walk into the rocks at the top of the wells to push them down on the buttons and collect some extra Ollars for not using any objects.

CRAZY SOLUTION

Heavy objects are required to press the buttons that open the doors. Get clever with the definition of a heavy object. You don't always have to go with something inanimate. Drop a walrus down there to open a door, and whistle a little "goo-goo-g'joob" while collecting the Starite.

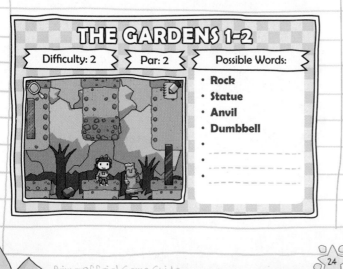

THE GARDENS 1-2

Difficulty: 2 | Par: 2 | Possible Words:

- Rock
- Statue
- Anvil
- Dumbbell

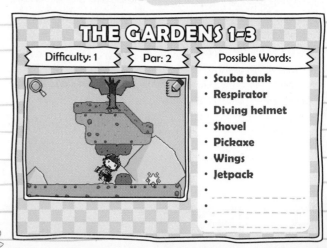

THE GARDENS 1-3

Difficulty: 1 | Par: 2 | Possible Words:

- Scuba tank
- Respirator
- Diving helmet
- Shovel
- Pickaxe
- Wings
- Jetpack

The Starite in this one is sitting right out in the open; all Maxwell has to do is walk up to it and pick it up to solve the level. However, before he can make that little walk, he needs to swim underwater, tunnel through soft dirt, or fly over a tall ledge to reach the Starite's perch. The dirt is easily chewed through with a shovel, a pickaxe, and any handheld earth-moving equipment. Wings or a jetpack will get Maxwell over the tree and down to the other side of the level. Getting through the water requires an object that allows underwater swimming, such as a diving helmet, a respirator, or a scuba tank.

CRAZY SOLUTION

Friendly sea life are also good objects to conjure up when Maxwell needs to get through an underwater passage. Ride a cute dolphin beneath the island to reach the Starite!

CRAZY SOLUTION

Get extra Ollars by conjuring up creative objects to perform tasks. Yes, pegasus is a pretty cool ride for flying, but everyone wishes they could ride a pterodactyl, right?

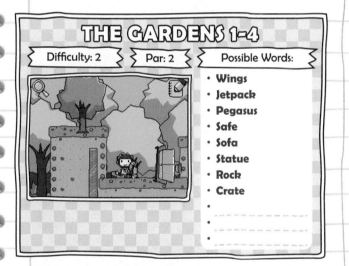

THE GARDENS 1-4

Difficulty: 2	Par: 2	Possible Words:

Possible Words:
- **Wings**
- **Jetpack**
- **Pegasus**
- **Safe**
- **Sofa**
- **Statue**
- **Rock**
- **Crate**
-
-
-

The Starite in this level is protected behind a heavy blue door. The door cannot be broken through, but there is a blue button at the top of the level that controls the door's position. Maxwell must fly up to the button and then push something against it to keep the door open. Use something to fly up there, such as a jetpack, a set of wings, or a flying creature like a pegasus.

Once up there, use something heavy and tip it into the button, such as a sofa or a statue. You need to make sure it is something that can be tipped and then stayed tipped. A small object, such as a log, is very difficult to position. As soon as the door is open, return to the ground level and pass through the door to collect the Starite.

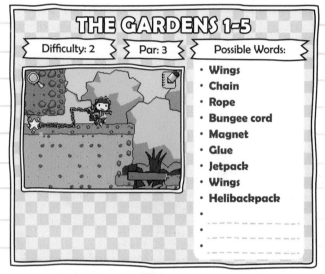

THE GARDENS 1-5

Difficulty: 2	Par: 3	Possible Words:

Possible Words:
- **Wings**
- **Chain**
- **Rope**
- **Bungee cord**
- **Magnet**
- **Glue**
- **Jetpack**
- **Wings**
- **Helibackpack**
-
-
-

The Starite is this level is in a low-ceilinged tunnel up on a high ledge. That tunnel is blocked by a metal crate. The ledge next to the crate is directly above a hole in the ground, covered only by a narrow wooden plank. Maxwell must find a way to get the crate out of the way and pull the Starite out of the tunnel. Traditional means of getting up to the platform work well, such as wings or the helibackpack. Once there, Maxwell can attach a length of rope to the crate. Fly away from the ledge to pull the crate out of the way. Use the rope to pull the Starite out of the tunnel.

TIP

Alternatively, Maxwell can use other rope-like objects, such as a chain or two bungee cords connected together.

The magnet that pulls aside the crate can also be used to coax the Starite out of the tunnel. Attach glue and a piece of metal to the Starite. The magnet pulls the metal, which in turn yanks the Starite toward Maxwell.

CRAZY SOLUTION

There are many ways to pull the Starite out of the tunnel, as described here. To prove yourself a prodigy, write in a tractor beam. This sci-fi device slowly draws an object toward it. The only catch with the tractor beam is that it is huge. You must clear the ledge of the crate to use it, although repeatedly balancing it on the edge will eventually pull the crate out of the way.

THE GARDENS 1-6

Difficulty: 2 | Par: 3 | Possible Words:

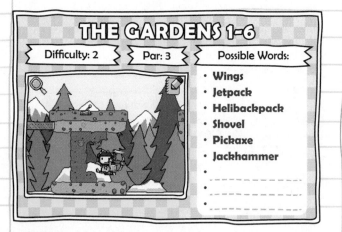

* Wings
* Jetpack
* Helibackpack
* Shovel
* Pickaxe
* Jackhammer
* ____
* ____
* ____

The Starite is located at the bottom of this level, just beyond two obstacles: a wall of dirt and a metal door. The metal door is opened via a switch. The switch is at the top of the level and accessible only by flying up to it. The vertical shaft is fairly narrow, so it will require a small flying machine, such as a jetpack. A plane is just too large.

After throwing the switch to open the door, Maxwell must burrow through the soil wall to reach the Starite. A shovel or pickaxe is an obvious tool for the job, but objects such as an auger or a jackhammer will also break through the dirt. Then it's just a short hop down to the Starite.

CRAZY SOLUTION

You've dug through dirt walls with shovels and whatnot—maybe it's time to really move some earth. Use a bomb or dynamite to blast through the soil and access the Starite. After placing the explosive, use a fire source, such as a campfire, a lighter, or a torch, to ignite the fuse. Get out of the way, because the explosion is powerful enough to rock Maxwell...and not in a good way.

THE GARDENS 1-7

Difficulty: 2 | Par: 4 | Possible Words:

* Wings
* Jetpack
* Helibackpack
* Sphinx
* ____
* ____
* ____

All that stands between Maxwell and the Starite is a tornado—a giant tornado. The tornado moves back and forth in the center of the level, directly beneath two small alcoves. Maxwell is small enough that he can fly through the narrow space between the top of the tornado and the alcove on the right using flying objects like wings or a jetpack. Just time the flight so Maxwell squeezes through as the tornado reaches the farthest point on its trip to the right. Then it's smooth sailing right to the Starite.

CRAZY SOLUTION

Circumventing the tornado by flying over is the obvious route, but what if there was a way to either minimize the tornado or destroy it altogether? Blast the tornado with a shrink ray to make it small enough to pass over or under. Or, drop a black hole in the path of the tornado to eliminate it from the level.

THE GARDENS 1-8

Difficulty: 2 | Par: 4 | Possible Words:

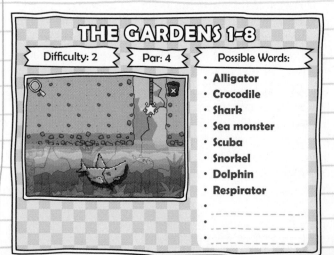

* Alligator
* Crocodile
* Shark
* Sea monster
* Scuba
* Snorkel
* Dolphin
* Respirator
* ____
* ____
* ____

The Starite dangles over pirahna-infested waters, attached to a rope. That rope is tied to the underside of a rickety board that spans a well. Maxwell must somehow clear the water of the dangerous fish before knocking the Starite into the drink. When the Starite swims, Maxwell needs to dive in after it. Getting rid of the piranha requires a bigger, nastier animal, such as a shark or an alligator.

Don't use an object to break the board and drop the Starite. Just kick it to the side by walking into it. The Starite will then drop into the water.

When the Starite is in the water, Maxwell needs the means to dive in after it. Jot down a respirator, scuba gear, or a snorkel. Even a dolphin is a good ride for Maxwell on his quest to nab the Starite.

CRAZY SOLUTION

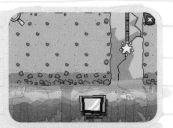

Remember all those public service announcements you saw as a kid about not using electronics near water? Well, they weren't kidding. Drop a toaster or TV into the water and watch the piranha pop and sizzle like bacon in a frying pan. After a brief moment, the water is then safe for Maxwell to dive into.

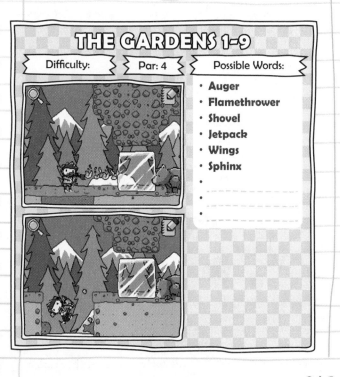

THE GARDENS 1-9

Difficulty:	Par: 4	Possible Words:

- **Auger**
- **Flamethrower**
- **Shovel**
- **Jetpack**
- **Wings**
- **Sphinx**
-
-
-

What's worse than a Starite protected by an angry bear? A Starite protected by two angry bears, that's what. At least these bears aren't just miffed at Maxwell—they are not terribly fond of each other, either. Maxwell can use that to his advantage, but first he must free the bear at the top of this level. A flamethrower will melt the ice block and push the big gray bear off the ledge to the right. Or Maxwell can burrow through the loose soil to the left of the ice block with a pick, an auger, or a shovel while wearing a jetpack. Once the hole in the floor has been dug, free the bear and then fly up so it marches right through the hole. The bears will then commence their fighting. Expect the big polar bear to win every time.

Once the bear on the top level has been dealt with, Maxwell must fly down to the Starite. The sphinx works well because it can hover. If Maxwell is using a jetpack or wings, let him fall down to the ledge with the polar bear and then immediately take flight over to the Starite. Trying to fly down the right side of the level puts Maxwell in danger of petering out too soon and dropping into a bottomless pit.

CRAZY SOLUTION

The polar bear can be defeated so the bottom tier of the level can be used as a safe staging ground for flying over to the Starite. The flamethrower alone only pushes the bear back. Place an explosive, such as a bomb or dynamite, near the bear, though, and you have the makings of a real party. Pop the bear and fly for the Starite.

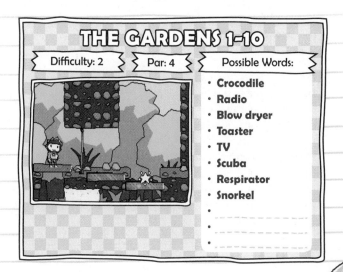

THE GARDENS 1-10

Difficulty: 2	Par: 4	Possible Words:

- **Crocodile**
- **Radio**
- **Blow dryer**
- **Toaster**
- **TV**
- **Scuba**
- **Respirator**
- **Snorkel**
-
-
-

This level is a funny little trap. There are two tripwires that control access to the Starite. The first tripwire near the starting point must be touched so the Starite itself drops down to the middle area of the level. The second tripwire is halfway down a vertical well below Maxwell's feet, under a wooden plank. When the plank is pushed down the well, it triggers the tripwire that drops the Starite down to the bottom of the level.

A shark patrols the waters that Maxwell must swim through to reach the Starite. Fry the shark with electronics, such as a TV, a toaster, or a microwave.

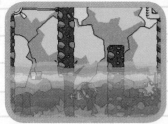

Use diving equipment, such as a diving helmet, to swim through the water and collect the Starite.

CRAZY SOLUTION

Maxwell does not need to trigger the tripwire in the well to complete this level, but it does require using an extra object than the previous methods. Glue something, such as a log, to the metal square next to the tripwire. Drop down to the log (or fly down) and then burrow through the sand with a digging utensil, such as a pickaxe.

The Starite is being held at the top of this level behind a steel beam. The beam cannot be destroyed, only moved aside by stepping on a button on a small platform in the middle of the multi-tiered level. At the very bottom of the level, a shark patrols the waters. And as if this isn't enough, several spikes poke out of the walls around the Starite, as well as one directly below it. If the Starite is not shielded from the spike, it will break on contact and end the level.

Maxwell can fly up to the ledge beneath the Starite and stand just to the side of the spike. Drop something heavy on the button (such as an anvil or a coffin) and then get ready to walk toward the Starite as it falls from its resting place. Other things can be stacked on top of the spike, such as boards and mattresses, to break the fall. If you attempt this route, be sure to frizzle the shark in the water with electronics, such as a TV or a radio, so it does not attack Maxwell when he dives for the Starite. A sea monster like the kraken is another way to get rid of the shark.

CRAZY SOLUTION

Bypass the shark altogether by making sure the Starite never even touches the water. Place floating objects such as a rowboat and a canoe in the water. These will catch the Starite once it bounces off of whatever you place on the spike to keep the Starite from hitting it.

THE GARDENS 1-11

Difficulty: 3 | Par: 3 | Possible Words:

- Lamp
- TV
- Radio
- Dumbbell
- Helibackpack
- Coffin
- Anvil
- Pegasus
- Kraken
- Jetpack

WORLD 2: METRO

PUZZLE LEVELS

METRO 2-1

| Difficulty: 1 | Par: 2 | Possible Words: |

Possible Words:
- **Bat**
- **Billy club**
- **Yardstick**
- **Wooden sword**
-
-
-

Maxwell has been invited to a party. There's a clown there, but none of the children are smiling. What's up? It seems there is no way for the kids to break open the piñata dangling in the center of the level. Write down a stick, a bat, a billy club, a yardstick, a wooden sword...whatever. Then hammer away at that piñata to get at the candy—and a Starite.

CRAZY SOLUTION

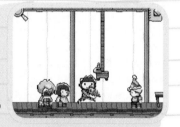

Sure, you could swat away at the piñata with bats and sticks. But why not get the candy out of that festive horse the way kids in 2231 will: using lasers. Give Maxwell a laser pistol and target the piñata to fetch the candy.

METRO 2-2

| Difficulty: 1 | Par: 2 | Possible Words: |

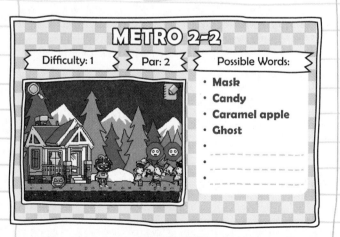

Possible Words:
- **Mask**
- **Candy**
- **Caramel apple**
- **Ghost**
-
-
-

This is Halloween, this is Halloween! There are three trick-or-treaters at Maxwell's door. Show them a good time, and you are rewarded with a Starite. Write down objects related to the spooky holiday, such as a mask or candy. At first sight of the Halloween-related object, Maxwell gets his Starite.

NOTE

If you provide a costume for Maxwell, you must actually place it on him to solve the level. Just conjuring candy earns the Starite.

CRAZY SOLUTION

Why not focus on the front half of the phrase "trick or treat"? You can write in something scary, such as a ghost, that will freak out the kids and reveal the Starite. But in this age of spare-no-gore horror, try reminding these kids what it means to be truly afraid. Jot down a huge monster, such as a hydra or the elder god Cthulhu, who sleeps no more.

METRO 2-3

| Difficulty: 2 | Par: 2 | Possible Words: |

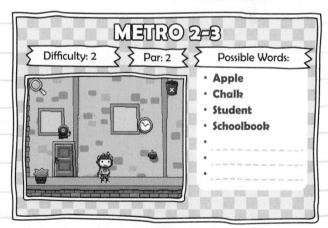

Possible Words:
- **Apple**
- **Chalk**
- **Student**
- **Schoolbook**
-
-
-

School's out, and the teacher is left behind in her classroom, all alone. If Maxwell gives the teacher something for the classroom, she will award him a big gold star—a Starite, to be exact. So, write down objects that belong in a classroom and give them to the teacher. An apple, a schoolbook, chalk...think of things you have seen around a classroom while in school and start jotting them down. The smaller objects must be given directly to the teacher to get the Starite. Larger things can just be placed near the teacher.

CRAZY SOLUTION

Take a hint from the beginning of the level. The teacher wistfully watches the students leave the classroom. So, give her what she really misses: another student. Write student in the Notepad and then place her at a desk. The overjoyed teacher gives Maxwell a Starite.

METRO 2-4

Difficulty: 1	Par: 2	Possible Words:

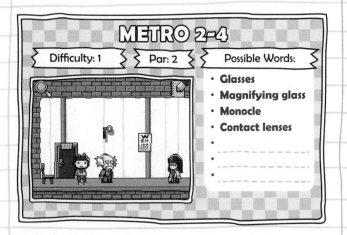

- **Glasses**
- **Magnifying glass**
- **Monocle**
- **Contact lenses**
-
-
-

Oh, flibbertigibbet! The old man at the center of this level needs some new eyewear so he can see. Thusly, he's visiting the optometrist. To solve this level, you need to write down a handful of objects that will help the old man see. Because this is an eye doctor's office, go for classic eyewear such as glasses and contact lenses. But consider other types of lenses, too, such as an old-school monocle or a magnifying glass.

CRAZY SOLUTION

The key here is lens, so you do not necessarily have to limit yourself to glasses and similar eyewear. Give some binoculars or a telescope to the old man. He's thrilled to be able to see through those, and you are awarded a Starite—with the Genius merit, to boot.

METRO 2-5

Difficulty: 1	Par: 4	Possible Words:

- **Dress**
- **Hat**
- **Shoes**
- **Robe**
- **Slippers**
- **Pants**
- **Shirt**
- **Sandals**
- **Blouse**
-
-
-

Maxwell is moonlighting as a fashion designer in this level. He stands in a room with a naked mannequin in front of him. His job is to dress the mannequin. The mannequin needs three articles of clothing to be considered "dressed," so start writing down some duds. Any article of clothing works here, such as a dress, pants, a blouse, socks, sandals, a robe, or shoes. But you need to make sure the clothing goes on separate parts of the body. One outfit might consist of a dress, a hat, and shoes. The next might be pants, a shirt, and socks.

CRAZY SOLUTION

Nobody said exactly what kind of store this mannequin is going into... so why not dress it up as if it will be on display at the local magicians' emporium. Toss a cape and a wizard hat on the mannequin. Or assemble an outfit from unexpected clothes, such as a barrister's periwig (fancy!) and a chasuble.

METRO 2-6

Difficulty: 2	Par: 3	Possible Words:

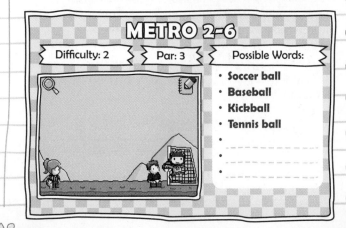

- **Soccer ball**
- **Baseball**
- **Kickball**
- **Tennis ball**
-
-
-

What a lovely day for a bit of sport. Maxwell takes to the field with a goalie and a referee. To earn the Starite, Maxwell must score a goal by getting a ball into the net. Just throwing the ball at the net will cause the goalie to block it. Maxwell can bypass the goalie, though, and deliver the ball to the net on his own. Jot down any kind of ball—tennis ball, baseball, soccer ball—and hoof it into the goal to score.

CAUTION

You cannot attack the goalie. Pull a sword on the field, and the referee calls a foul, ending the level.

CRAZY SOLUTION

There are more sports than just football, soccer, and baseball. Try to think of any sport that involves getting a ball into a net and then write down that object. Rugby ball, lacrosse ball, hockey puck—all of these will work in this level.

METRO 2-7

Difficulty: 2	Par: 3	Possible Words:

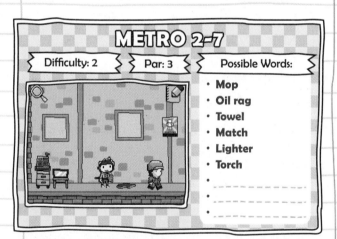

Possible Words:
• **Mop**
• **Oil rag**
• **Towel**
• **Match**
• **Lighter**
• **Torch**
• _____
• _____
• _____

There's a spot of oil in this mechanic's garage, and he needs your help cleaning it up. In addition to cleaning up the oil spill, the mechanic also needs you to throw away some trash on the right side of the garage. Tossing the trash is simple—just pick it up and throw it in the bin right next to it. Getting rid of the oil isn't too tough, either. Use some cleaning objects, such as a mop, a rag, or a towel, to soak up the oil.

CRAZY SOLUTION

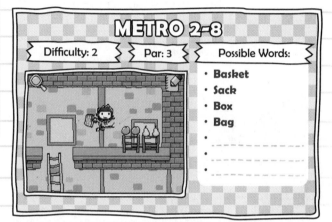

There is another way to get rid of the oil besides just mopping it up. Oil is flammable. If Maxwell burns it, that's as good as mopping it up. You can torch the oil spill with a match or a lighter. Or pretend to be a crazed medieval warrior and strike it with a fiery flamberge. This fire sword gives Maxwell all the fury of an avenging archangel but none of the responsibility.

METRO 2-8

Difficulty: 2	Par: 3	Possible Words:

Possible Words:
• **Basket**
• **Sack**
• **Box**
• **Bag**
• _____
• _____
• _____

Maxwell is hungry and needs to hit the grocery store for some grub-grabbin'. To satisfy his hunger, you must pick up a drink, vegetable, and fruit. The store has all of this stuff out on display: pears, oranges, milk, cola, heads of lettuce, and potatoes. All Maxwell must do is place one of each group into a container and then pay at the register to earn the Starite.

CAUTION

If you interact with the clerk, Maxwell will inadvertently empty his basket, sending the food objects flying.

To collect the groceries, give Maxwell a sack, a bag, a basket, or a box. Even a wooden crate will do the trick, although he cannot carry the crate with him as he shops. When one of each group has been placed inside the container—and this step is critical—Maxwell must interact with the register to pay for his food. That's when the checkout clerk offers up the Starite.

CRAZY SOLUTION

Maxwell needs a container to hold his stuff. Containers come in all shapes and sizes. Technically, a fish tank is a container and can be used to collect groceries. This will earn you a Prodigy merit, too.

CRAZY SOLUTION

Think of breakfast items from around the world when feeding the little girl. Not everybody has a bowl of cereal for breakfast. And have a little fun waking the boy. When you hear your alarm clock go off in the morning, does it sound like a gong to you? Then why not use an actual gong and bang that thing to rouse the sleepyhead?

METRO 2-9

Difficulty: 2	Par: 3	Possible Words:

- **Muffin**
- **Pancakes**
- **Egg**
- **Yogurt**
- **Drums**
- **Trumpet**
- **Tuba**
-
-
-

METRO 2-10

Difficulty: 2	Par: 4	Possible Words:

- **Fish**
- **Pot roast**
- **Pizza**
- **Lasagna**
- **Milk**
- **Cola**
- **Milkshake**
- **Cookie**
- **Cake**
- **Pie**
-
-
-

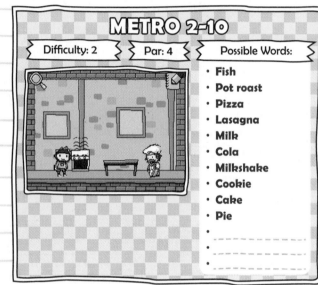

Some households just have a little trouble getting going in the morning. Maxwell is here to help! To earn the Starite, he must wake the sleeping boy upstairs and feed the little girl in the kitchen. Once both have been satisfied, the Starite appears in the center of the level. Feeding the girl is easy stuff: Just conjure up a breakfast item, such as a muffin, pancake, eggs, or yogurt.

To wake the boy, Maxwell needs something that will make a lot of racket. Drums certainly do the trick. But so does a stereo or a tuba. Just create the object and then interact with it to produce sound.

CAUTION

Just make sure the object is harmless. Thunder would wake the boy, but the lightning strike that comes down from it is no good.

The chef in this level wants Maxwell to prove himself in the kitchen. He has a simple menu to follow: a hot meal, a beverage, and something sweet. The catch is that you must actually cook something to make it a hot meal. It is not enough just to conjure up a casserole or a pot roast. It must be placed in the oven. Once the object has been dropped into the oven, interact with the oven to turn it on and start heating the food.

When the hot food is cooking, it's time to give the chef something to quench his thirst, such as milk, cola, or tea. Finally, the meal must end with a dessert. Cookies, cake, and pie are all agreeable to the chef.

A milkshake qualifies as both a drink and a desert, allowing Maxwell to come in way under par on this level.

CRAZY SOLUTION

Think about all of the different foods around the world you can call upon to complete the chef's menu. This is a great way to earn merits
for using objects for the first time. Instead of relying on a standby dessert, such as pie, feed the chef a portion of the sticky-sweet dessert baklava. Try different world cuisines in this level and bank those Ollars!

A cat is the natural solution to most of the rats, except one. The dog will attack the cat if you use it to get rid of the rat at the top of the level. However, if you place a wall between the rat and the dog, the cat can then safely devour the rat.

A bird of prey, such as an owl or a hawk, will attack the rat without hesitation and does not bother any of the other folks in the joint, such as the criminal or the chef. The dog could care less about the bird, too.

Just drag the bird to each rat and then release it. The bird automatically swoops down and finishes off the rat.

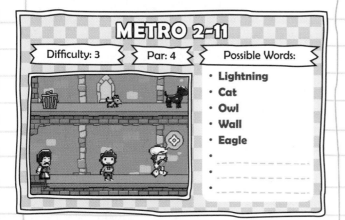

METRO 2-11

Difficulty: 3	Par: 4	Possible Words:

- **Lightning**
- **Cat**
- **Owl**
- **Wall**
- **Eagle**
- ⋅ _____
- ⋅ _____
- ⋅ _____

This speakeasy is infested with rats! And not the kind that squeal on the gangster's wrongdoing to the police, but real rats. Maxwell must dispose of the four rats in the level to earn the Starite, but there are two complications. One, the chef's dog cannot be injured. Two, the gangster near the front door is armed. If Maxwell walks out with a gun to shoot the rat by the gangster, the criminal will open fire.

CRAZY SOLUTION

This alternate method will get rid of the rats well under par, but it takes a bit longer to do the job. Write lightning. The cloud can be placed over a rat.
A few lightning strikes eliminates the rat. Then, just drag the cloud over another rat. Be careful to keep the cloud clear of the dog and the gangster, though. After a few moments, the rats are gone, and the Starite is yours.

ACTION LEVELS

METRO 2-1

Difficulty: 3	Par: 3	Possible Words:

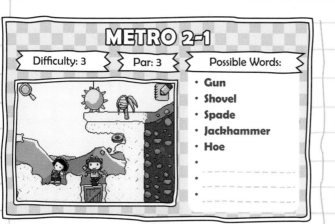

- **Gun**
- **Shovel**
- **Spade**
- **Jackhammer**
- **Hoe**
- ⋅ _____
- ⋅ _____
- ⋅ _____

The Starite is tucked in a wooden crate and buried in the desert just ahead. You must dig up the crate with the Starite, but the desert is not barren. There is a junkyard dog that gets upset if you start digging around his sandy

backyard with the shovel that was conveniently left out. (Seriously: Do not touch the shovel unless you want that dog to go berserk on you.) A bee to the right of the desert is upset if you stir the nest. And if that wasn't enough, there is a land mine buried in the sand that pops if Maxwell touches it.

The easiest way to get at the Starite is to use a digging tool, such as a shovel, a spade, a jackhammer, a hoe, or an auger. Just burrow straight down into the sand and aim for the wooden crate
directly below the land mine. Dig to the side of the land mine and then under it so you have some dirt over your head that keeps the land mine safe.

NOTE

Many of the crates are filled with objects. Dig around them as they are released.

CRAZY SOLUTION

Traditional digging tools are fine, sure. But sometimes it is satisfying to break out the bigger toys. Write down a **bucket excavator** and roll it across the desert, then burrow into the sand to wrench the Starite out of its wooden crate.

METRO 2-2

Difficulty: 2	Par: 3	Possible Words:

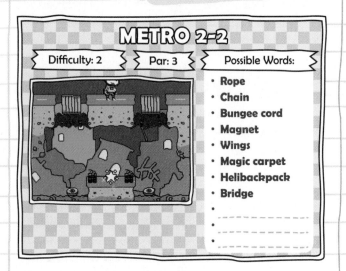

Possible Words:
- **Rope**
- **Chain**
- **Bungee cord**
- **Magnet**
- **Wings**
- **Magic carpet**
- **Helibackpack**
- **Bridge**
- _____
- _____
- _____

The Starite is located at the bottom of the mine, flanked on both sides by sticks of dynamite. The dynamite is then flanked by land mines, which will not only set off the dynamite and blow up the Starite, but will also destroy the soft soil beneath it, creating bottomless pits that swallow up objects written into the level. Before you can even get down into the mine, though, you need to move solid steel crates from soil patches on the surface—that just so happen to be directly above the land mines.

Use a **chain** or a **rope** to pull the crates out of the way. A **magnet** also works in Maxwell's hands, as it pulls the metal crates into the air. When the crate is gone, dig through the dirt patch with a **shovel** or another digging tool. Now you can try to fly down and pick up the Starite with some **wings** or a **magic carpet**, but watch out—if Maxwell accidentally pushes a stick of dynamite off the pedestal into a land mine, the explosion will destroy the Starite. You can also link ropes and chains together and then yank the Starite out of the mine.

Completely cover one of the land mines with a **bridge** so that you don't have to worry about the dynamite striking a land mine.

CRAZY SOLUTION

Sometimes you just need to call in the professionals to do the hard jobs. Summon a **bomb disposal expert** and place him near one of the land mines. The expert takes out the land mines, all right. Too bad he buys himself a dirt nap in the process. Or write in a **zebra** and place it over the Starite. The zebra kicks the dynamite into land mines and then absorbs the explosions from the mines. Of course, this is kind of rough on the zebra....

METRO 2-3

Difficulty: 2	Par: 3	Possible Words:

Possible Words:
- **Doughnut**
- **Kitten**
- **Puppy**
- **Dynamite**
- **Bomb**
- **Match**
- **Torch**
- **Axe**
- **Lighter**
- **Jetpack**
- **Wings**
- **Pegasus**
- **Wall**
- **Chain**
- _____
- _____
- _____

Starites are indeed precious. In this level, the Starite is so valuable that it has been assigned a security detail complete with armed guards and a camera. If Maxwell crosses the security camera's line of sight, a wall is immediately erected, blocking off his access to the Starite from the left. The key to solving this level is to somehow subdue the guards or at least lure them into positions where they cannot hurt Maxwell. But you should also avoid hurting the guards. The guard on the bottom floor is less of a concern because he only carries a nightstick. Block him off from Maxwell with a wall or link him to the security camera with a chain or a rope so he cannot chase you.

Fly into the upper guard's sight line and then lead him off the ledge so he drops down. Then, he does not bother Maxwell for a while.

There is a buildup of furniture and objects in the vertical shaft leading down to the Starite. You can burn it away with fire, a torch, or a bomb. Or, chew it to splinters with an axe.

TIP

You can also destroy the furniture with a termite or a beaver.

CRAZY SOLUTION

There are several ways to distract the guard upstairs who is holding a gun. Why not get the guard to drop his weapon by putting something far more happy in his hands? Jot down a puppy or a kitten and hand it to the guard. He drops the gun, which Maxwell can then pick up and use to shoot up the furniture. Maxwell can also give the guard a doughnut. Actually, better make it three doughnuts. After the guard polishes off the third doughnut, he falls asleep.

METRO 2-4

Difficulty: 3	Par: 4	Possible Words:
		• **Wall**
		• **Stove**
		• **Oven**
		• **Jetpack**
		• **Haystack**
		• **Boulder**
		• _____
		• _____
		• _____

Maxwell sets foot into a dangerous bomb factory in order to claim the next Starite. Two bomb-making machines drop

rolling bombs into the level, right on top of downhill slopes so they drop on Maxwell as he tries to fly to a switch on the other side of the room. That switch pulls back the metal panel that protects the Starite. To stop the bombs, Maxwell needs to place heavy objects in their path, right at the edge of the slopes. A wall will work. So will a stove, an oven, a sofa, or a boulder.

After halting the bomb runs, use a flying object, such as wings or a jetpack, to zoom over to the switch. Now return to the start of the level to collect the Starite.

CRAZY SOLUTION

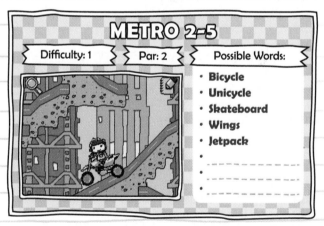

Stopping the rolling bombs requires a heavy object. But by no means are you limited to jotting down an inanimate object, such as furniture or a rock. Pick a largely immovable creature, such as the shoggoth (hello, H.P. Lovecraft fans!), to stand in the way of the bombs and clear a path for Maxwell. When the bombs stop rolling at the monster's feet, trash it so it does not attack Maxwell during his flight to the switch.

METRO 2-5

Difficulty: 1	Par: 2	Possible Words:
		• **Bicycle**
		• **Unicycle**
		• **Skateboard**
		• **Wings**
		• **Jetpack**
		• _____
		• _____
		• _____

Ready to race? When the level opens, Maxwell is standing behind a door at the very top of several ramps. He needs to get to the bottom of this level to grab the Starite, which dangles at the end of a rope. But the wall door will not open unless you jot down a wheeled vehicle. As soon as he's placed on a bicycle, a motorbike, a skateboard, or a unicycle, the door rises, and you can race down the series of ramps to get the Starite.

NOTE

Make sure to keep the wheeled vehicle small. A car is not maneuverable enough for this level.

However, Maxwell needs to be moving at full speed to launch off the final ramp and grab the Starite. If he misses the Starite, you need to give him something like a jetpack so he can zip up and grab the prize.

CRAZY SOLUTION

Maxwell needs wheels to get through the door, right? Think of all the different things with wheels on them that Maxwell can ride—or at least be strapped into. Give Maxwell a set of roller skates and send him careening down the ramps.

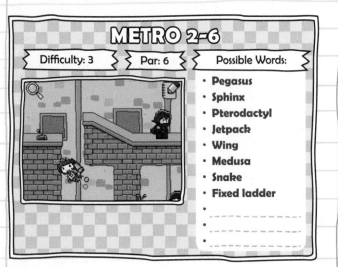

METRO 2-6

Difficulty: 3	Par: 6	Possible Words:
		• Pegasus
		• Sphinx
		• Pterodactyl
		• Jetpack
		• Wing
		• Medusa
		• Snake
		• Fixed ladder
		•
		•
		•

When Maxwell enters this level, he can see the Starite just a single floor above him. It's behind locked doors, though—and it's guarded by a ninja. There are several switches around the level that adjust the doors, but the one that automatically clears a path to the Starite is in the upper-left corner of the level. Just fly up to it and throw the switch to open the way to the Starite.

Of course, there is still the matter of those ninjas. Before flying around, you can summon a monster and place it next to the ninjas. Something like a medusa, a snake, or a bear will eliminate them. (The monster cannot shoot, though, or else you risk losing the Starite in the gunfight.) With the ninja near the Starite down, Maxwell can then fly down to fetch the Starite.

CRAZY SOLUTION

The pterodactyl is not only a good way to fly up to the switch, but this dinosaur is pretty ferocious. Use the pterodactyl on the ninja near the Starite to drop him and then pick up the Starite. Not only did you solve this action level Jurassic-style, but you did it with just a single object! That will help you finish this world under par.

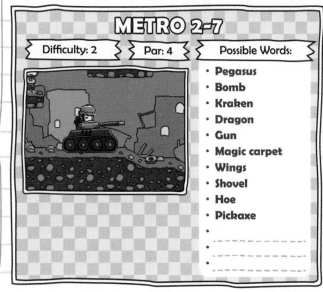

METRO 2-7

Difficulty: 2	Par: 4	Possible Words:
		• Pegasus
		• Bomb
		• Kraken
		• Dragon
		• Gun
		• Magic carpet
		• Wings
		• Shovel
		• Hoe
		• Pickaxe
		•

War! What is it good for? Getting Starites, it looks like. Allied tanks roll onto the scene just as the level begins, eliminating enemy troops. Unfortunately, a tank runs into a land mine and is destroyed just at the start of the battle. This leaves behind a handful of enemy troops that will shoot on sight.

An object that can fly without needing a cool-down period, such as a sphinx or a pegasus, is ideal for this perilous trip over the battlefield. Stick close to the top of the tunnel and then fly right into the Starite to collect it. If you need to use something more traditional, such as a magic carpet or a helicopter, to reach the Starite, you need to clear out the enemy soldiers first. Arm Maxwell and go to town on them with a bomb or a gun.

 TIP

Act fast! Disable the land mine right away by dropping a rock on it, and the allied tank will survive to blast at the enemy soldiers.

Maxwell can avoid the battlefield altogether by shoveling through the sand at the top of the level and just flying over to the Starite.

CRAZY SOLUTION

In the future, all wars will be fought with dragons. Well, not really—but it sounds cool, right? Call forth this medieval beast of legend and set it upon the enemy soldiers to show them that their guns mean nothing against fire breath and razor claws.

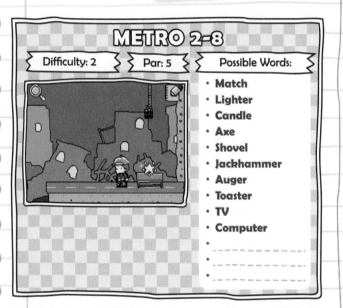

METRO 2-8

Difficulty: 2   Par: 5   Possible Words:

- **Match**
- **Lighter**
- **Candle**
- **Axe**
- **Shovel**
- **Jackhammer**
- **Auger**
- **Toaster**
- **TV**
- **Computer**
- ____
- ____
- ____
- ____

The Starite is in plain sight at this construction site. There's just one small catch. It's located on a table, directly below a wad of dynamite. If Maxwell trips either of the wires in this level, the dynamite will fall and destroy the Starite on impact. The site is also filled with construction workers who will pretty much keep to themselves, unless they perceive a threat—so weapons are out of the question. And finally, there is a crocodile in the water below the site, ready to pounce if Maxwell dips a toe into the water to cross over to the side of the level with the Starite.

The first thing you should do is neutralize that dynamite. Any small flame source released next to the dynamite, such as a match or a candle, will ignite the dynamite. Just make sure

you grab the fire source with the stylus before it falls on the Starite. With the dynamite out of the way, the tripwires are no longer a problem.

Dig through the hard soil to the right with a jackhammer or an auger.

Drop something into the water to clear out the croc. Anything electronic will zap the crocodile, but you can also fight off the creature with a sea monster.

CRAZY SOLUTION

That dynamite is a problem. Make it a problem for another dimension, though. Install a black hole next to the dynamite and pull it into the Great Unknown. Just make sure the black hole is not too close to the Starite!

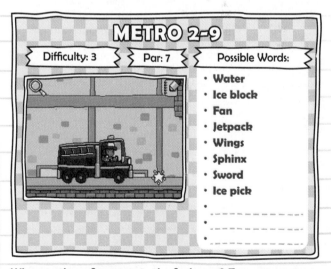

METRO 2-9

Difficulty: 3   Par: 7   Possible Words:

- **Water**
- **Ice block**
- **Fan**
- **Jetpack**
- **Wings**
- **Sphinx**
- **Sword**
- **Ice pick**
- ____
- ____
- ____

Why are there fire vents in the firehouse? For some reason, three bursts of flame are cooking the narrow tunnel along the top of this level, blocking Maxwell's path from the start of the level to the Starite, which is resting in front of a fire truck to the east. To escape with the Starite, Maxwell must put out those flames. There are actually two ways to go about this.

Put out the fire vents with water or ice. The ice block can be moved over each vent to immediately extinguish the flames. If you use water, though, you need three puddles—one to put out each vent.

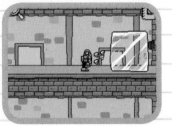

There are two buttons in this level that put out the fires, too. The ceiling button near Maxwell extinguishes the center vent. The button in the upper-right corner puts out the outer two vents. Fly Maxwell into the first button. He does not need to hold it to keep the fire out. Just a single press will do it. There is a large ice block in front of the second button. Push the ice block into the button with a fan. Now all three vents are out.

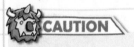 **CAUTION**

If you use the sphinx to fly up through the corridors, be sure to put out the fires first. The sphinx is afraid of fire and reacts poorly to it.

CRAZY SOLUTION

An ice block will put out all the fire vents, whereas water only does one vent before it turns into steam and evaporates. What other frozen objects could be used to put out the fire? How about that iconic holiday cheer-spreading snowman? Just write down a snowman and place it on each vent to put out the flames and let Maxwell safely soar to the Starite.

METRO 2-10

Difficulty: 2   Par: 4   Possible Words:

- Friend
- Mother
- Brother
- Nun
- Gun
- Shotgun
- Bow and arrow
- Missile
- Helicopter
- Helibackpack
- Wings

It's the future we all worried about: Zombies have taken over the planet, one small town at a time. In this level, the zombie is guarding a Starite right in front of a gas station. No big deal, right? Look down. There is an underground city packed with explosives beneath the zombie's feet. If that stuff goes off, the gas station is going with it. The Starite will be consumed in the inferno. So, the first thing Maxwell must do is figure out how to get the Starite to safety.

Place a driver in the tow truck next to the gas station. The truck is attached to the Starite. Any normal human, such as a friend, a mother, a brother, or even a nun, will drive away from the zombie.

CAUTION

If you conjured a doppelganger of Maxwell, it will not drive the truck. The evil "you" is not afraid of zombies.

Now that the Starite is safe, it's time to set off those explosives. Use a gun to shoot the rope holding up the bowling ball near the start of the level. The bowling ball falls into the passage with the explosives,

setting off a chain reaction. The zombie usually survives the blast and falls into the water at the bottom. However, Maxwell has a gun and can shoot the zombie while he crosses toward the Starite.

Death from above! Write down a missile and then rotate it so the tip is pointing down. Drop the missile on top of the dynamite near the zombie and then enjoy the fireworks.

CRAZY SOLUTION

This solution needs a hero. Don't just entrust the getaway tow truck to any pal. Write down of the greatest American presidents: Abraham Lincoln. Beneath that stovepipe hat is a survivalist. At first sight of that zombie, the Great Emancipator hits the gas.

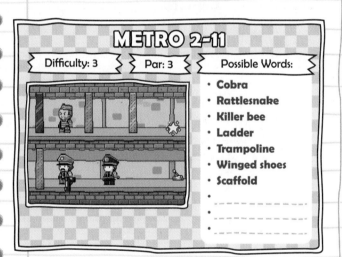

METRO 2-11

Difficulty: 3	Par: 3	Possible Words:

Possible Words:
- **Cobra**
- **Rattlesnake**
- **Killer bee**
- **Ladder**
- **Trampoline**
- **Winged shoes**
- **Scaffold**
-
-
-

How did Maxwell wind up in jail? No matter—let's bust him out! However, before throwing the switch in his own cell that will open all of the red doors, better take a look around. The red switch also opens two more cells—and they contain real criminals. If the red switch is thrown, the criminal in the cell at the top of the room is freed...but he lands right next to a machine gun. No good. You need to take care of the criminals before springing Maxwell.

Snakes. Why did it have to be snakes? Because they are small enough to fit in cramped cells and will drop the criminals with a single bite. Just move the snake around to all of the criminals.

Now, there are two more people in this jail: guards. They are both armed. One has a club while the other has a gun. Maxwell can race out and grab the machine gun in the middle of the level and open fire after throwing the blue switch that opens the guard door. Or, he can open the door and then run back into his own cell. Throw the red switch, and Maxwell is locked up all safe and tight. Drop something nasty into the main holding area to get rid of the guards. (The snake won't work—it's too small, and the guard with the gun will just shoot it.) Once the guards have been dispatched, run to the green switch they were protecting. This opens the path to the Starite. Use winged shoes or a trampoline to reach the Starite.

CRAZY SOLUTION

You need something big to get the two guards. Something that can withstand a bullet or two. Something like...a kraken!

WORLD 3: THE PEAKS

PUZZLE LEVELS

THE PEAKS 3-1

Difficulty: 1	Par: 2	Possible Words:

Possible Words:
- **Cookie**
- **Milk**
- **Elf**
- **Mistletoe**
- .....
- .....
- .....

Maxwell enters a rather festive scene. Santa stands beside his sleigh. Presents litter the icy ground of the North Pole. Nearby, a reindeer waits for orders to take flight. In order to earn the Starite, you must give Santa an object he would like but does not already have. Think of objects related to Santa and Christmas. A cookie, milk, mistletoe—even an elf. As soon as the object appears, Santa happily hands over the Starite.

CRAZY SOLUTION

You know what Santa loves even more than cookies, toys, and elves? The warm embrace of his beloved, Mrs. Claus. Jot down Mrs. Claus in your Notepad to put a smile on Santa's face and earn a Starite.

THE PEAKS 3-2

Difficulty: 2	Par: 2	Possible Words:

Possible Words:
- **Car battery**
- **Jumper cables**
- **Electrical cord**
- **Outlet**
- .....
- .....
- .....

Maxwell is not going anywhere in a car with a dead battery. To get that car to the house and earn the level's Starite, Maxwell must supply power to the automobile.

Once the car has been fully juiced up (the engine is no longer emitting little puffs of smoke), just drive it to the house to make the Starite appear. Naturally, you should try a car battery and a set of jumper cables. Just hook one end of the cables to the hood of the car and the other to the battery to power it. Try an electrical cord and an outlet, too. Despite not actually being on a wall, the outlet still sends a jolt of energy to the car via the cord.

That transformer on the power line produces electricity, too. Hook a chain up to the car and the transformer to send current into the car and get it started.

CRAZY SOLUTION

Let's get this car started Ben Franklin–style. Open the Notepad and write down a natural source of electricity: lightning. Position the storm cloud over the car. When lightning flashes over the vehicle, the battery is all charged up and ready to go.

THE PEAKS 3-3

Difficulty: 1	Par: 3	Possible Words:

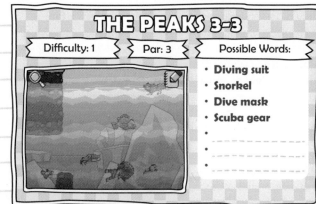

Possible Words:
- **Diving suit**
- **Snorkel**
- **Dive mask**
- **Scuba gear**
- .....
- .....

Everybody loves a penguin—and everybody is sad to see a hungry penguin. To solve this level, Maxwell needs to feed the hungry penguin on the rocks. The penguin wants the three smallest fishies in the water. Use the Notepad to conjure up something that will help Maxwell swim underwater: a diving suit, scuba gear, a snorkel, flippers. When Maxwell is fitted with the appropriate attire, he can

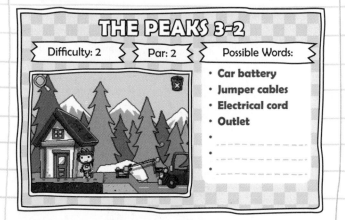

dive in and pick up the three small fish one by one. Just tap the small fish with the stylus and command Maxwell to pick it up. Then swim to the surface and tap on the penguin to hand it over. After the penguin's third helping, the Starite appears.

CRAZY SOLUTION

Go old-school when fishing for the penguin. How about a diving bell? Before the invention of scuba gear, these heavy bells were used to trap air and yet still sink, allowing divers to explore underwater. With the bell over his head, Maxwell sinks into the water and grabs fish but still has the strength to swim back to the surface and feed the penguin.

THE PEAKS 3-4

Difficulty: 1	Par: 4	Possible Words:

Possible Words:
- Snowball
- Ice ball
- Ice cream cone
-
-
-

Snowball fight! At the start of the level, three kids surround Maxwell and throw snowballs over his head. To earn the Starite, Maxwell must return the favor. (Except Maxwell should not miss.) This is a pretty simple level to solve. Just give Max three frozen things to throw at the three children. Snowballs and ice balls work well. But Maxwell can also hand each of them ice cream cones, too. The frozen treats make everybody happy, thus making the Starite appear.

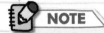
NOTE

To nail the kids standing on the ledges surrounding the level, stand back. If Maxwell throws the snowball too close, he'll just hit the ledge.

CRAZY SOLUTION

This level's par is 4, but with a little creativity, you can solve this level with a single frozen object: a snowman. Hold the snowman over each kid and then release it.

When the snowman drops on each kid, it is registered just like a snowball strike. After the third drop, the Starite appears.

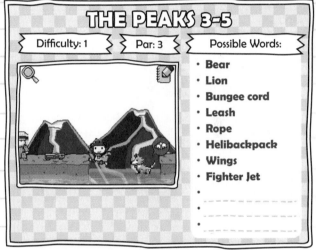

THE PEAKS 3-5

Difficulty: 1	Par: 3	Possible Words:

Possible Words:
- **Bear**
- **Lion**
- **Bungee cord**
- **Leash**
- **Rope**
- **Helibackpack**
- **Wings**
- **Fighter Jet**
-
-
-

A little lamb has been separated from its flock. Maxwell must return the lamb to the shepherd to earn the Starite, but he must get past a pool of water (the lamb cannot swim) and a hungry wolf. If the lamb is led down to the platform the wolf is on, the wolf will eat it. The wolf will also chase Maxwell if he gets too close. However, that is actually useful. Maxwell can lead the wolf into the water. Once the wolf is in the water, make Maxwell jump out. Then, because the wolf can also hop out of the water, drop some electronic in the water to make sure the wolf does not follow. A DVD player or VCR will suffice.

It is not entirely necessary to eliminate the wolf like this, but it does make getting the lamb to safety a touch easier. To cart the lamb across the level, fly it home. Attach one end of a rope or cable to the lamb and the other to Maxwell. Give Maxwell wings or a helibackpack, and he can fly the lamb home. Or, go full military and write down a fighter jet. A hot air balloon works, too.

CRAZY SOLUTION

The lamb cannot swim, but that doesn't mean you cannot lead it home over the water. The water is too wide for a bridge, and the par is too low to build one with glue and boards. Instead, place a rowboat in the water. Now, give Maxwell some clover (yummy for lambs) and lead the lamb across the rowboat to the rest of the flock. Hello, Starite.

THE PEAKS 3-6

Difficulty: 2	Par: 4	Possible Words:

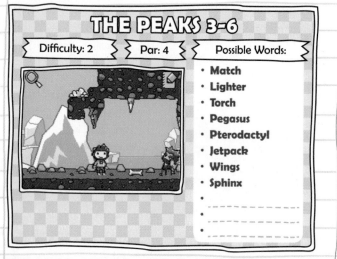

- **Match**
- **Lighter**
- **Torch**
- **Pegasus**
- **Pterodactyl**
- **Jetpack**
- **Wings**
- **Sphinx**
- ‒ ‒ ‒ ‒ ‒
- ‒ ‒ ‒ ‒ ‒
- ‒ ‒ ‒ ‒ ‒

It's hard to keep a caveman's belly full. The caveman in this level has a particular hankering for a dinosaur egg omelette, so you must break one of the eggs guarded by the two dinosaurs in this level. One egg is watched over by a raptor. The other is guarded by a pterodactyl. Now, the key here is omelette. That implies bird egg, so don't even bother with the raptor. You want to get the contents of the pterodactyl egg for the caveman.

Fly up to the pterodactyl. The pterodactyl is protective, so you will need a weapon of some sort—or a mount that will attack the pterodactyl on your behalf. Once the pterodactyl fights with something like another dinosaur or a pegasus, it turns tame and will not put up a fuss when Maxwell runs over and kicks its egg. Pick up the contents of the egg and then take them back down to the caveman. He's happy, but that's only half the solution.

The other requirement is to give the caveman fire. Something small, such as a match dropped on the log in the cave, works fine, but remember that cavemen did not always react well to fire.

The caveman actually fears fire, so if you light the log in the corner of the cave with a larger fire source, such as a torch, tether the cavemen to the cave ceiling first. Otherwise, he may attack you or the fire.

CRAZY SOLUTION

Match, torch, lighter, fire—you need to start thinking up new sources of flame so you can get additional merits for using new objects. Ever take a chemistry class? Remember what a chemist uses to heat the contents of a beaker? Conjure up a Bunsen burner and drop it on the log to start the fire.

THE PEAKS 3-7

Difficulty: 1	Par: 3	Possible Words:

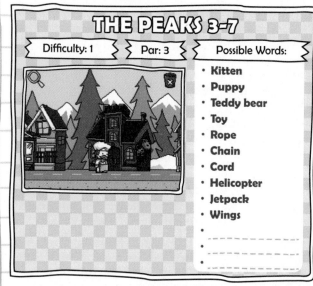

- **Kitten**
- **Puppy**
- **Teddy bear**
- **Toy**
- **Rope**
- **Chain**
- **Cord**
- **Helicopter**
- **Jetpack**
- **Wings**
- ‒ ‒ ‒ ‒ ‒
- ‒ ‒ ‒ ‒ ‒
- ‒ ‒ ‒ ‒ ‒

What's up with the traffic jam in this level? When you jump over the cars and trucks, you spy a cow standing in the middle of the road. It will not budge. Not even if you tie a rope to it and try to lead it off the road and into the field (where it wants to be) off to the right. What has this cow so spooked? It's the neighborhood butcher, standing just outside his house a little farther up the road. The butcher has a carving knife in his hand, so it's no wonder the cow will not move an inch. If you get rid of the knife, the cow is more amenable to moving. Get the butcher to give up his knife by handing him a teddy bear, a puppy, or a kitten.

Thar she blows! Place a whale in this would-be Ahab's path to stop the boat and solve the level.

TIP

The cow is still scared of the knife, even if the butcher is not holding it. Pick up the knife and place it inside one of the houses so it is completely out of sight.

Now it's time to get that cow to the field. Cows are vegetarians, so place some clover in Maxwell's hand and lead the cow to the field. Placing grass on the ground and moving it to lure the cow works, too. As soon as the cow enters the grassy field, the Starite appears—but it's back on the far side of the line of traffic. Fly over the cars and trucks with something like wings or a jetpack to retrieve the Starite.

CRAZY SOLUTION

The goal is to stop the boat from crashing into an iceberg, but there is no reason turning the ship into an iceberg itself is out of the question. Hand Maxwell the freeze ray and give him something to fly over the water on—a pterodactyl or a pegasus always works. Blast the ship with the freeze ray to stop the engines and turn it into an ice cube.

CRAZY SOLUTION

The cow is just too heavy for Maxwell to lift over the butcher with wings or a helibackpack. He needs something with a little more oomph. Try a helicopter or a UFO to yank the cow off the ground and zip it straight over to the field. When the Starite appears, just steer your flying machine back to the left and snag it.

THE PEAKS 3-9

Difficulty: 2	Par: 3	Possible Words:

- **Pegasus**
- **Pterodactyl**
- **Helicopter**
- **Bungee cord**
- **Rope**
- **Chain**
- **Leash**
- ⸱ _____
- ⸱ _____
- ⸱ _____

THE PEAKS 3-8

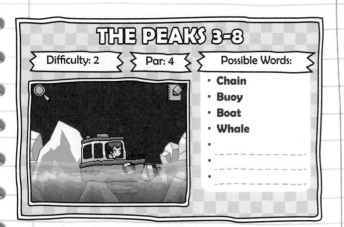

Difficulty: 2	Par: 4	Possible Words:

- **Chain**
- **Buoy**
- **Boat**
- **Whale**
- ⸱ _____
- ⸱ _____
- ⸱ _____

The penguins in this level have become separated due to the drifting ice. Maxwell must help the lone penguin on the ice floe to the left get back to its friends. However, the penguin must be kept out of the water. There is an orca under the ice—and orcas love to nosh on penguins. One of the stipulations of this level is that no harm can come to the orca, so Maxwell must stick to the surface (or above the surface) to reunite the penguin family. Hooking the penguin up to a flying object—a chopper, a pegasus, a jet plane, and so on—via a rope or other cord-like object will definitely get Maxwell the Starite.

A captain cuts through choppy seas in a sturdy vessel. The wind is at his back. But not all is well. Just beyond the captain's horizon is a giant iceberg. Maxwell must stop the boat from crashing into the iceberg in order to capture the Starite. The easiest thing to do is weigh down the ship with something like a chain. (An anchor is just too heavy and capsizes the boat, ending the level in failure.) Another solution: Place something in the boat's way that grinds it to a halt. (Not another iceberg, naturally.) A boat or a buoy makes the captain stop.

CRAZY SOLUTION

Create a bridge of sorts to get the penguin home. Drop two icebergs in the water. Now the orca cannot surface and get the penguin, even if it tries. Penguins love fish. Get the penguin to return to its friends by dangling some fish right in front of its beak. Lead the penguin across the two icebergs and back to its family.

CRAZY SOLUTION

Fight air with air! Install an air vent on the ceiling over the vent just in front of the lamp to create an opposing force. Now Maxwell can travel through the air without being blasted against the ceiling. Try some rope alternatives, such as hoses, to score more New Object merits.

THE PEAKS 3-10

Difficulty: 2 | Par: 3 | Possible Words:

- Rope
- Chain
- Hose
- Hammer
- Jackhammer
- Pickaxe
- _____
- _____
- _____

Welcome to a cave of wonders. Just beyond a rickety wooden bridge that spans a river of lava is a magic lamp. The sultan in the cave wishes for Maxwell to bring him the lamp. If Maxwell does so, the sultan will give him the Starite. There is just one catch, though. If Maxwell touches the lamp, the bridge over the lava vanishes. That's fine, right? A pair of wings will get Maxwell and the map to the sultan. Not so, due to the powerful air vent blowing straight down over the bridge that would push Maxwell right into the lava.

And that's not the last of the air vents either. There is another large air vent in front of the lamp that blasts air toward the ceiling. If Maxwell is caught in the air, he's pushed against the ceiling, between a pair of stalactites. A hammer or pickaxe gets Maxwell out of that pickle. But then there's the matter of getting the lamp back to the other side of the level without touching it. Ropes and chains work exceedingly well, allowing Maxwell to drag the lamp and earn the Starite.

THE PEAKS 3-11

Difficulty: 2 | Par: 4 | Possible Words:

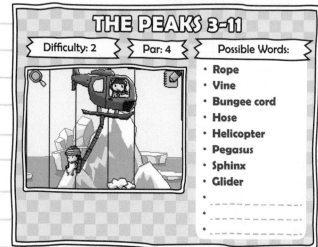

- Rope
- Vine
- Bungee cord
- Hose
- Helicopter
- Pegasus
- Sphinx
- Glider
- _____
- _____

The scene: base camp. The scenario: an ice hiker has been injured and requires immediate medical attention. There is a hospital at the top of the mountain. Maxwell must get the patient to the hospital to earn the Starite. Anything that flies can be used here. A helicopter and rope flies the patient right up to the hospital doors. So does a pegasus and a vine. Use any combination of tether and flying object to complete this level.

CAUTION

Steer clear of the mountainside. An angry polar bear lives in a cave halfway up the mountain. If the patient swings too close to the polar bear, it will swipe at her.

Use a jet so Maxwell isn't just dragging the patient through the air. Give them a little comfort when flying them up to the hospital.

CRAZY SOLUTION

Instead of just flying up the side of the mountain, scale it. Call upon a hydra or other monster to dispose of the polar bear in the cave halfway up the cliff face. Then install an air vent. Rope the patient to Maxwell and soar through the air. Keep moving the air vent up to the next level instead of creating a new one each time. When the pair reaches the polar bear's cave, place a crate under the air vent for the extra necessary height to reach the next ledge.

ACTION LEVELS

THE PEAKS 3-1

Difficulty: 2 | Par: 3 | Possible Words:

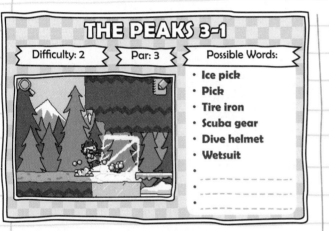

- **Ice pick**
- **Pick**
- **Tire iron**
- **Scuba gear**
- **Dive helmet**
- **Wetsuit**
- _____
- _____
- _____

The Starite is not only encased in ice in this level, but it's also submerged in the water. For Maxwell to retrieve it, he needs a means to break through the ice and swim under the water. An ice pick or sword makes short work of the large ice block that blocks access to the water. When that is gone, Maxwell then needs scuba gear or a wetsuit to slip under the waves and chisel the ice that holds the Starite.

CRAZY SOLUTION

Many animals can actually tear through materials such as soil or ice. Ride a dolphin underwater to reach the Starite and then break it open with the dolphin's rigid nose.

THE PEAKS 3-2

Difficulty: 3 | Par: 4 | Possible Words:

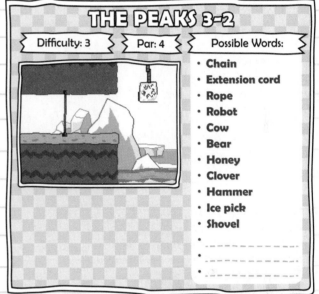

- **Chain**
- **Extension cord**
- **Rope**
- **Robot**
- **Cow**
- **Bear**
- **Honey**
- **Clover**
- **Hammer**
- **Ice pick**
- **Shovel**
- _____
- _____
- _____

The Starite is close enough to touch in this level. It's hanging by a rope. But that rope is dangling over a pit of lava. And if Maxwell tries to rush out to the Starite, he'll trigger a tripwire that severs the rope and drops the Starite into the lava. It doesn't matter that the Starite is encased in ice at that point. The lava will destroy it.

The trick is to secure the Starite before touching the tripwire. The tripwire only goes off if Maxwell touches it, though. You can use anything else around the tripwire without worry. Attach a chain to the Starite and the tripwire. When Maxwell hits the tripwire, just grab the chain and haul the Starite into the cave. Or, tether the Starite to a cow and tempt the cow with grass just beyond the tripwire. Then, when Maxwell triggers the tripwire, the cow runs for the grass and pulls the Starite into the cave. Chisel the Starite out of the ice to solve the level.

TIP

Almost every animal has something it likes to eat. Figure that out, and the animal will follow you anywhere.

Add a little danger to this level by using a creature that is hostile to Maxwell. Place a bear on the edge of the cave and tether it to the frozen Starite. Use honey to attract the bear and then immediately delete the bear as soon as Maxwell triggers the tripwire.

CRAZY SOLUTION

You've been experimenting with work animals. Now let's use some machinery. Tether the Starite to a robot. Pull the robot deeper

into the cave with a magnet or a tractor beam so when Maxwell trips the wire, the robot pulls the Starite to safety.

THE PEAKS 3-3

Difficulty: 2	Par: 4	Possible Words:

- **Jackhammer**
- **Ice pick**
- **Shovel**
- **Rope**
-
-
-

The Starite is in a pretty precarious spot at the start of this level. There is an old column holding up some rocks next to the Starite. However, between the column and the Starite is an explosive barrel. If the rocks drop on the barrel hard, the barrel goes off and destroys the Starite.

With a small tool, such as an ice pick, Maxwell can ease up to the column and nudge it so the rocks on top of it fall to the ground, but not hard enough to set off the barrel. Then, chisel apart the column and the rocks to get at the Starite. Hop over the barrel if it is not sitting right

next to the Starite. If there is no gap between the barrel and the Starite, Maxwell needs to create one.

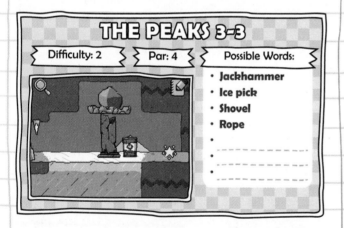

Use a rope or a chain to pull the explosive barrel away from the Starite.

NOTE

You cannot dump water on an explosive to diffuse it.

CRAZY SOLUTION

Feel like manipulating the very fabric of time and space? Use a black hole to inhale the column, rocks, and explosive barrel. The trick is to make sure it is far enough away from the Starite so it does not consume the Starite, too. Keep the black hole on the far side of the chamber with the Starite so the Starite is not picked up by its gravity.

THE PEAKS 3-4

Difficulty: 3	Par: 4	Possible Words:

- **Pterosaur**
- **Jetpack**
- **Helibackpack**
- **Chain**
- **Pegasus**
-
-
-

This level looks fairly simple at first glance. The Starite on the far side of the chamber is locked behind a red door. There is a red switch next to Maxwell. Flip the switch, open the door, and then fly over to the Starite, right? Not if those two giant spiked steel balls have anything to do with it. Air vents on the floor and ceiling cause the spiked balls to hover near the center of the room, making the flight over to the Starite tricky. Use a personal flying object, such as a helibackpack or pterosaur, to carefully avoid the spiked balls and grab the Starite.

CRAZY SOLUTION

Before turning on the air vents (and opening the door to the Starite), drop down to the bottom of the chamber. Tie the spiked balls together with a chain

so that when you do fly back up (perhaps on a sphinx?), they are caught on the rock in the center of the level. Now the path to the Starite is much clearer.

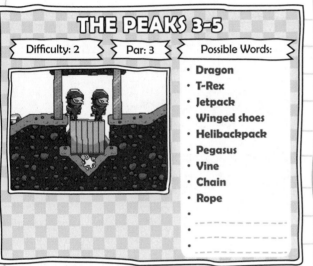

THE PEAKS 3-5

Difficulty: 2   Par: 3   Possible Words:

- **Dragon**
- **T-Rex**
- **Jetpack**
- **Winged shoes**
- **Helibackpack**
- **Pegasus**
- **Vine**
- **Chain**
- **Rope**
-
-
-

The Starite is at the bottom of the level, beneath a steel crate. That steel crate is beneath two red caps, which would chase down Maxwell if they weren't locked up by a green door and a blue door. There are two switches to open the doors on each side of the room. The green switch is closest to the blue door and vice versa.

Throwing a switch opens one of the doors. Now, Maxwell needs to cross the level and close in on the Starite. A personal flight object, such as winged shoes or a helibackpack, will get him across the room, but as soon as he crosses the center, the red caps march out of the small alcove above the Starite. Maxwell needs to destroy the red caps before he can get at the Starite. Call in a fearsome creature, such as a dragon, to get rid of the red caps. (Junk the creature as soon as the red caps are done for.)

Maxwell still needs to pull the steel crate out of the way. A rope or chain attached to the crate works, as does a magnet. Once the steel crate has been moved, flip the nearby switch to open the opposite door. Fly

back around the level and grab the Starite.

CRAZY SOLUTION

The red caps are dangerous foes. Are they more dangerous than whatever might pop out of a portal? If an alien drops out of the portal,

then yes. But if an ahool steps through to this world, then the red caps are in serious trouble.

THE PEAKS 3-6

Difficulty: 2   Par: 4   Possible Words:

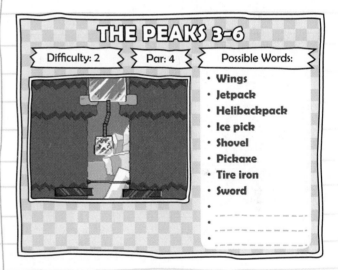

- **Wings**
- **Jetpack**
- **Helibackpack**
- **Ice pick**
- **Shovel**
- **Pickaxe**
- **Tire iron**
- **Sword**
-
-
-

The Starite is dangling above a deep pool of water. Between the water and the Starite is a tripwire. Maxwell must somehow protect the Starite from falling into the water. A red switch at the top of the chamber will close the doors beneath the Starite, but the switch is surrounded on both sides by spikes.

Use a small flying object to carefully avoid the spikes.

47

Now that the doors are closed, use a utensil, such as an ice pick or a pickaxe, to chop through the large ice block that's holding up the Starite. The Starite falls down the vertical shaft but is stopped by the red doors. Just drop into the shaft and carve the Starite out of the smaller ice block to finish the level.

CRAZY SOLUTION

If you use a sphinx, an archaeopteryx, or a pegasus and it touches the spikes, you can no longer ride it. So, cautiously position the creature so Maxwell can slide right between the spikes. Once the red switch has been thrown, though, he no longer requires a flying creature.

THE PEAKS 3-7

Difficulty: 2	Par: 5	Possible Words:

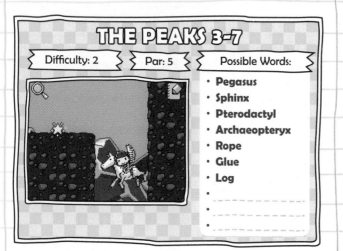

Possible Words:
- **Pegasus**
- **Sphinx**
- **Pterodactyl**
- **Archaeopteryx**
- **Rope**
- **Glue**
- **Log**
-
-
-

The Starite in this level is at the top of a very tall vertical shaft. Maxwell needs to fly up to it. Basic flight solutions, such as a pegasus or a sphinx, will get Maxwell to the top, where he can just pick up the Starite and complete the level.

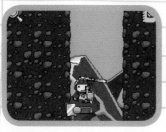

The shaft is too tall for wings and jetpacks to make it up without a spot to stop and recharge. Build a platform by gluing a log to the piece of metal sticking out of the side of the shaft. Attach a rope to the bottom so Maxwell can grab it. Then fly up and land on the log. Release the rope and continue flying all the way to the top.

CRAZY SOLUTION

This is one of those levels that has a solution so simple that you may not even think of it right away. Instead of building ledges and whatnot to scale the level, use a fan to push the Starite down to Maxwell. Position the fan so it blows the Starite into the shaft. The fan may need to be moved two or three times to finally nudge the Starite down.

THE PEAKS 3-8

Difficulty: 2	Par: 3	Possible Words:

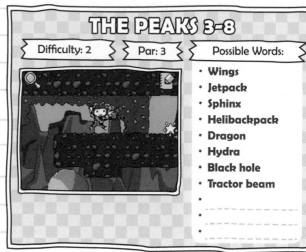

Possible Words:
- **Wings**
- **Jetpack**
- **Sphinx**
- **Helibackpack**
- **Dragon**
- **Hydra**
- **Black hole**
- **Tractor beam**
-
-
-

The Starite in this level is just above Maxwell's starting position. He is blocked from getting into the right half of the level by two large boulders, but he only needs a flying object and something that digs through the earth to fetch the Starite. Use a jackhammer or an auger to chew through the red dirt above Maxwell and pick up the Starite.

There are two elementals guarding a button on the right half of the level. That button moves the red door to the right of Maxwell's starting position. If he tries to get to the other side of the boulders, he'll need to open the red door to come at the Starite from the right. To dispose of the elementals, use a black hole or a dragon.

Drop an anvil or a heavy object on the button from afar to move the red door.

CRAZY SOLUTION

Do not neglect the powerful shrink ray. Use this weapon to blast one of the boulders that blocks the cavern where Maxwell starts the level.

He can then jump over the smaller stone and use a weighted object to open the door to the Starite. Just fly up on something like a pegasus or a pterodactyl and then remove the object from the button that moves the door.

THE PEAKS 3-9

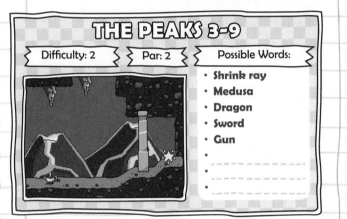

Difficulty: 2	Par: 2	Possible Words:

- Shrink ray
- Medusa
- Dragon
- Sword
- Gun
- _____
- _____
- _____

The Starite is just beyond a stone door that starts rising as soon as Maxwell steps toward the center of the room. However, there is a magic lamp in the middle of the room that will randomly release a creature. Every time Maxwell attempts this level, the creature might be different. Maxwell must find a way to defeat the creature so he can grab the Starite once the door is open.

If the lamp releases a medusa, just drop a mirror between the two of you. The mirror reflects the medusa's stone gaze and turns her stiff instead of you.

If the lamp releases a hydra, you can either attack it with something substantial, such as a bazooka or a missile launcher, or call in a large monster, such as a dragon, to deal with it. Or, try the shrink ray to reduce

the hydra to puppy size and just hop over it as you run for the Starite.

CRAZY SOLUTION

This level is all about the luck of the draw—and being ready for whatever pops out of that lamp. If Maxwell is truly lucky, the lamp will release...a kitten! All you need to do is walk by the kitty and wait for the wall in front of the Starite to rise high enough to slip under it and grab the prize.

THE PEAKS 3-10

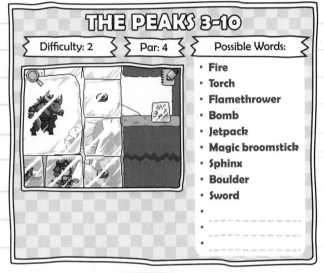

Difficulty: 2	Par: 4	Possible Words:

- Fire
- Torch
- Flamethrower
- Bomb
- Jetpack
- Magic broomstick
- Sphinx
- Boulder
- Sword
- _____
- _____

All that divides Maxwell and the Starite is a field of ice. However, frozen within that ice is all sorts of nastiness, such as land mines, bats, spike balls, and even a giant Minotaur. Maxwell must hack and melt his way through the ice cubes to reach the Starite and complete the level.

The Starite itself is encased in ice, but you can break it out with a fire source, such as a torch. Just lay the torch next to the ice, and when it breaks, quickly move the torch away. Use the torch or fire to melt the

ice blocks with the land mines so they drop and blow up, too. Dynamite or a bomb next to the Minotaur's block will dispatch the beast. You can keep using fire to melt through the blocks on the left side of the level, too.

There is a bat in a block directly beneath a spiked ball. Melt the spiked ball block first so it falls on the bat's block, crushing both the ice and the bat itself. Alternatively, you can chisel through the block with a sword or an axe and then slash the bat.

After clearing up the left side of the ice field, fly over to the right. If the ice blocks with the mines are still present, break them with your chiseling utensil or the claws of the animal you used to fly.

CAUTION

Be sure to move back the second a land mine is freed from the ice so you are not hurt in the resulting explosion.

CRAZY SOLUTION

The single spiked ball is actually a key piece of this entire level. If Maxwell drops the spiked ball to the ground, he can use it to chew up the rest of the ice field and clear a path to the Starite. Push the spiked ball to the right with a fan or an air vent. The spikes chew through the ice—and any creature inside of it.

THE PEAKS 3-11

Difficulty: 3	Par: 8	Possible Words:

Possible Words:
- Match
- Bomb
- Puppy
- Kitten
- Teddy bear
- Toy
- Snowman
- Ice block
- Ice ball
- Shotgun
- _____
- _____
- _____

This is the most complex level you have encountered thus far. Six colored doors separate Maxwell from the Starite. There are six switches in different chambers of this level that correspond to the doors. Throwing each switch warps Maxwell to the chamber with the next switch, working left to right through the six doors. The trick to solving this level is prep work. Solve problems in advance of actually reaching that chamber, and you can work through this level with relatively little threat.

First, give the warrior guarding the red switch beneath Maxwell something to hold other than his sword, such as a puppy or a kitten.

Next, drop a source of fire on the board to the east of Maxwell. You need to burn this board away so when Maxwell drops into the chamber, he falls directly onto the switch below. Otherwise, you must

conjure up an object to hammer through the board. Save the fire once you set the board ablaze in case you need it elsewhere, such as planting a bomb or dynamite next to any of the monsters in this level.

Extinguish the fire vent next to the green switch to the west. A snowman, an ice ball, or a snowball works.

After throwing the first red switch, Maxwell is moved to the chamber with the frozen pirate to the north. The pirate has a sword that will cut down Maxwell with just two hits. Keep the pirate at bay with a flamethrower and then shoot him with a gun. Or, destroy the pirate with a bomb or dynamite earlier in the level.

The first blue switch is guarded by a beast. A black hole makes short work of it, as does any large monster or a bomb.

TIP

If you quickly grab the black hole after the beast is pulled into it, you can move it over the dragon that guards the last switch and save yourself an object during one run through this level.

The final blue switch is guarded by a dragon. Take it down with another large monster (hydra, T-Rex), a black hole, or an explosive. Maxwell appears on the ledge above the dragon in this chamber, so a missile launcher or a bazooka works, too.

Throwing the final blue switch sends Maxwell to the chamber with the Starite. All six doors are open, so he can claim his prize.

CRAZY SOLUTION

There are any number of alternatives you can try in this action level. Explosives are great for eliminating any of the threats, from the pirate to the dragon. Try your luck with the portal and see what comes out. Maybe an ahool will show up, which makes short work of the swordsman or the pirate. Cthulhu or the shoggoth are good options to use against the dragon or beast. And never underestimate the power of the steel spiked ball. Roll that object into a creature with a fan or air vent and make mincemeat of the creature!

WORLD 4: ANCIENT

PUZZLE LEVELS

ANCIENT 4-1

Difficulty: 2   Par: 3   Possible Words:

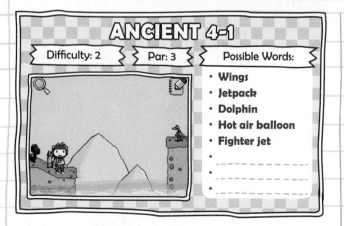

- Wings
- Jetpack
- Dolphin
- Hot air balloon
- Fighter jet
- _____
- _____
- _____

The poor ugly duckling has been separated from its fellow swans. Maxwell needs to somehow get the ugly duckling over to the left side of the level, but a black cat on the island will attack the duckling if it gets too close to the ground. Maxwell needs to either lift the ugly duckling well over the island or drag it beneath the waves to avoid the aquaphobic kitty. Any flight object will get the duckling to the left side of the level, such as wings or a jetpack. Just zoom over and grab the duckling or tether it to Maxwell with a rope.

 TIP

If you opt to go under the island, use a friendly creature, such as a dolphin, that will not try to attack the duckling.

CRAZY SOLUTION

Fly the ugly duckling to its mates in high style! Float over in a colorful hot air balloon or give it a lift in a plane. Just lower the plane on top of Maxwell and the duck. When it turns yellow and Maxwell is near the pilot's seat, both of them board the plane. Fly over the cat to collect the Starite.

ANCIENT 4-2

Difficulty: 1   Par: 3   Possible Words:

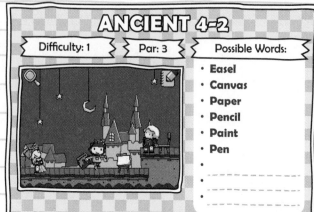

- Easel
- Canvas
- Paper
- Pencil
- Paint
- Pen
- _____
- _____
- _____

To collect the Starite in this level, Maxwell must paint a portrait to please the bourgeoisie. The solution here requires a surface that can be colored and some sort of artistic medium. Try an easel and paint to get things started. As soon as Maxwell touches the easel while holding the paint pot, the Starite appears. Use different art combinations, such as pencil and paper or pen and canvas, to keep collecting Starites.

CRAZY SOLUTION

These two asked for a portrait—they did not specific the medium, nor the time period. Let's show these fancy folks how we do it on the streets. Summon a wall and then hand Maxwell a can of spray paint. When Maxwell tags the wall, the Starite appears.

ANCIENT 4-3

Difficulty: 1   Par: 3   Possible Words:

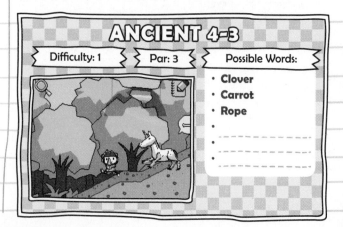

- Clover
- Carrot
- Rope
- _____
- _____
- _____

Standing before giant monoliths of millennia long gone by, Maxwell is asked by two people to fetch a unicorn. Maxwell does not need to write down a unicorn for them, though. There is one right at the top of the hill to the east. Maxwell just needs to lure the unicorn down to the standing stones to claim the Starite prize. Like horses, unicorns love to munch on clover and carrots, so place one of these objects in Maxwell's hands. Maxwell can then lead the unicorn down the hill. He can also drag the unicorn to the bottom with a rope or a vine.

CRAZY SOLUTION

This level does not necessarily need to be only about pulling—you can push the unicorn down the hill, too. Unicorns are frightened of fire, so pick up and drop any fire source, such as a torch or campfire, behind the unicorn until it is safely at the bottom of the hill.

This method is a bit slower, but you can also drop the same boulder over and over on the china. Just drop the china on the ground below the highest ceilings of the room and then release the boulder.

CRAZY SOLUTION

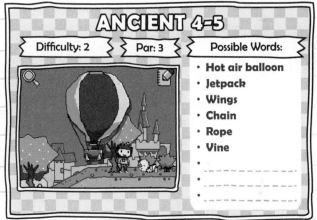

Let's clear this level in one big, beautiful explosion of broken glass. Stack as much of the china up in a pile as possible. Then, place dynamite in the pile and drop a match on it. Or, stand back from the pile and place a black hole just above the china. It is all pulled into the black hole and ruined.

ANCIENT 4-4

Difficulty: 1	Par: 3	Possible Words:

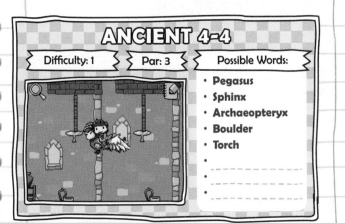

Possible Words:
- Pegasus
- Sphinx
- Archaeopteryx
- Boulder
- Torch
-
-
-

Maxwell is finally about to be rewarded for being a bull in a china shop! To earn the Starite in this level, all of the valuables in it must be destroyed. That includes pitchers, vases, plates, and glasses. There are several ways to shatter everything in the level, such as blasting away with bazookas and missile launchers. The baubles hanging by ropes from the ceiling can be clawed down by a sphinx or pegasus, too.

 TIP

The vases on the left side of the room can be broken just by picking them up and dropping them on the floor.

ANCIENT 4-5

Difficulty: 2	Par: 3	Possible Words:

Possible Words:
- Hot air balloon
- Jetpack
- Wings
- Chain
- Rope
- Vine
-
-
-

The royal family has lost its baby—the horror! The king and queen will give Maxwell a precious Starite if he can reunite them with their progeny. The baby is on the right side of the level, up on a small hill. The baby is too heavy for Maxwell to carry it to safety in his arms. He must devise the means for carting the baby back to the king and queen. A flying object is surely in order here.

Use a hot air balloon or a jet to quickly escort the baby to its parents. Tether the baby to the vehicle with a rope or another rope-like object.

CRAZY SOLUTION

What creature in the animal kingdom carries its young around with it all of the time? A kangaroo! Conjure up one of these adorable marsupials and place it over the baby. The kangaroo automatically picks up the baby. Now, lure the kangaroo over to the king and queen by holding clover in front of its face as you walk to the left.

CRAZY SOLUTION

The ancient Egyptians knew how to bury a body. Write sarcophagus and drop it in the freshly dug hole. Now, grab the body and place it in the sarcophagus. Do not mistakenly open the sarcophagus, though, or else an angry mummy pops out and chases Maxwell.

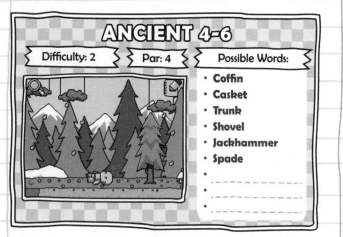

ANCIENT 4-6

Difficulty: 2	Par: 4	Possible Words:

Possible Words:
- Coffin
- Casket
- Trunk
- Shovel
- Jackhammer
- Spade

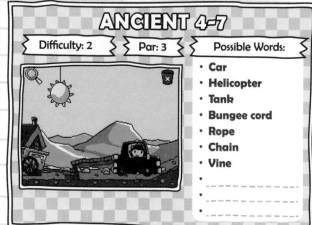

ANCIENT 4-7

Difficulty: 2	Par: 3	Possible Words:

Possible Words:
- Car
- Helicopter
- Tank
- Bungee cord
- Rope
- Chain
- Vine

Bad luck has befallen this traveler. Caught out in a storm, he was struck dead by lightning. Now Maxwell must put the body in a container and place it deep in the ground according to traditional funeral practices.

A knight at the top of a hill is guarding his castle, but he really needs that cart at the bottom of the hill. The knight cannot leave his post, so the job falls to you. Hoist the cart at the bottom of the hill to the knight. Maxwell is not strong enough to pull it via a rope all by himself. He needs something with a little more power. Mix eras here. Jot down a car, a helicopter, or a tank in the Notepad and use it to pull the cart to the knight and collect the Starite.

CAUTION

If you write down a container, such as a coffin, be sure not to accidentally open it. A ghost (or worse) will pop out.

CAUTION

Do not accidentally run into the knight or fire upon him. He will attack Maxwell without mercy if he feels threatened.

The first thing Maxwell must do is dig the hole for the body. The soil to the west of the cadaver is soft. Use the Notepad to conjure up a digging utensil, such as a shovel, a jackhammer, or a spade for Maxwell. Dig deep to the left in the soil patch, carefully creating stairs he can use to get out of the hole. (Otherwise, you must use an object to provide some wings.) Once the hole is dug, place a coffin, a casket, or a trunk in it. Fetch the body and carry it into the hole and then place it inside the box to collect the Starite.

CRAZY SOLUTION

These may be ancient times, but there are actually descriptions of flying saucers in ancient literature and art. So let's introduce a little sci-fi to this olden era by flying a UFO up the hill. Hook the cart to the UFO and fly it to the knight at the top of the hill. The UFO is powerful enough that the weight of the cart doesn't even slow it down.

ANCIENT 4-8

Difficulty: 3 | Par: 4 | Possible Words:

- **Dragon**
- **Tank**
- **Girder**
- **Glue**
- **Fan**
- **Tractor beam**
- **Wings**
- _____
- _____
- _____

Pull the wizard cage away from the lava with the tractor beam. Or tie an animal to the cage and place its favorite food almost within reach.

A wizard is trapped in a cage over a pit of lava. Okay, that situation sounds like something Maxwell can handle, right? Well, add two sleeping orcs to the equation. Now Maxwell must figure out a way to get rid of these creeps, because if he approaches the cage, they will wake—and attack. There has to be a way to use that lava against them....

CRAZY SOLUTION

The wizard is high enough off the ground that a ladder will work to reach him, but a little modern technology will not only grant Maxwell access to the wizard, but also provide a platform for the wizard to land on when he pops out of the cage. Install an elevator next to the cage. Ride it up to the second floor and interact with the cage to free the wizard.

A fan or air vent pushes the monsters into the lava without them even waking up.

TIP

Use a giant attack creature, such as like a dragon or a hydra, to eliminate the orcs. Simply place the monster near the orcs, and it will do the rest. Just be sure to dump the monster in the trash when the orcs are dead.

When the orcs are gone, Maxwell needs to figure out a way to get the wizard out of the cage. If Maxwell opens the door, the wizard pops right out. If the lava is uncovered, that's a real problem. Place something over the lava pit so the wizard does not fall to his death. A large vehicle, such as a tank, is wide enough to span the gap. Or glue two girders together to create a makeshift bridge. (An actual bridge is not wide enough, though a drawbridge or suspension bridge are.)

ANCIENT 4-9

Difficulty: 2 | Par: 4 | Possible Words:

- **Tank**
- **Jet**
- **Wall**
- **Jetpack**
- **Rope**
- **Freeze ray**
- **Wings**
- **Bungee cord**
- **Blue magic**
- **Carrot**
- _____
- _____
- _____

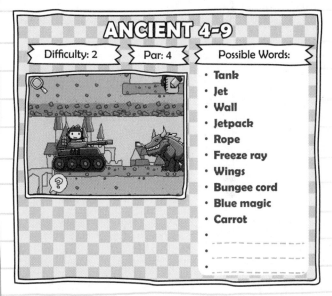

It's the classic fairy tale setup. A princess is trapped in a tower by a horrible witch. Her white knight must fight past a beast in order to even approach the tower, where he must still deal with the witch. It's up to Maxwell to make sure this fairy tale has a happily ever after. First things first: the beast. A missile launcher or a tank makes short work of the beast.

TIP

Maxwell can also lead the knight across the small pool of water, where he makes short work of the beast with his sword. The only catch, though, is that sometimes the knight falls back into the water and cannot get out. No worries: Just bring the princess to the pool.

www.primagames.com

When the beast is finished, the witch is next. Not so fast, hero. The witch cannot be harmed if you want the Starite. The witch has a magic wand that fires off a spell that turns its target into a frog. Fortunately for Maxwell, he is impervious to the spell. The princess and the knight, though, are not. So Maxwell must minimize their exposure to the witch. Place a wall next to the witch while she is closest to the tower on her patrol. All boxed in, she cannot fire magic spells very well while Maxwell flies the princess to safety. The freeze ray or blue magic also incapacitates the witch for a few moments, which is long enough to get a helicopter in and out of the tower area with the princess in tow.

TIP

Blue magic freezes enemies. What could red or green magic do?

CRAZY SOLUTION

If you're well read in Mother Goose (or the Brothers Grimm), you know what every princess needs: a fairy godmother. Place a fairy godmother next to the witch. The godmother gets scared by the witch, but not before turning her magic wand into a rose. Now the witch cannot hurl magical spells. The princess can be easily escorted to the knight below.

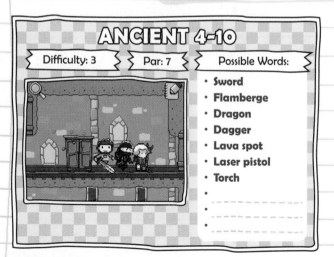

ANCIENT 4-10

Difficulty: 3	Par: 7	Possible Words:

- Sword
- Flamberge
- Dragon
- Dagger
- Lava spot
- Laser pistol
- Torch

The royal family is in danger from attackers. If you can make sure no member of the family is killed by the

encroachers—and that includes the knights—then you will be bestowed with the highest honor in the kingdom: a Starite. There are three human enemies in the castle: a ninja, a rogue, and an assassin. (Remember these three, because they may come in useful in other levels later, especially if you need a hired sword.) But there is also one more brute to deal with. A Minotaur downstairs is poised to rush the throne.

As soon as this level begins, a door in front of Maxwell lifts, and the ninja springs into action against an unarmed nobleman. After just a moment, the next door opens, and the rogue starts to attack either the nobleman from the first room or the knight in his area. The next door to open is downstairs, which allows the assassin to assault another knight. Finally, the door holding back the Minotaur rises.

Be ready to attack the ninja right away. A gun doesn't work very well because it is likelier to shoot the furniture than the ninja as he rushes past. A sword or a dagger is better suited to take down the ninja.

The knight in the next room can handle the rogue, so direct your attention instead to the Minotaur. No, it's not free yet. But you can guarantee that it never threatens the throne by placing fire to the left of the Minotaur. The Minotaur is afraid of fire and will not go near it.

Catch up with the assassin as the door to downstairs slowly rises. Drop down and stab the assassin. Now it's time to finish off the Minotaur. Both you and the knight make short work of it as long as it is cowering from the fire. If there is no fire, the Minotaur can kill you. Easily.

CRAZY SOLUTION

This clever trick requires a fast stylus, but with practice, you can pull this off. Write down black hole. Drag it next to the Minotaur. When the Minotaur is pulled into it, pick up the black hole again and pull it to the assassin. Then the rogue. You need to watch for when the enemy is pulled into the center of the black hole. As soon as you see the enemy flinch, it's toast. Move on to the next target. You can really come in under par in this level by using this trick.

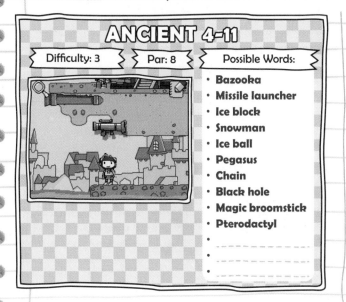

ANCIENT 4-11

Difficulty: 3	Par: 8	Possible Words:

Possible Words:
- **Bazooka**
- **Missile launcher**
- **Ice block**
- **Snowman**
- **Ice ball**
- **Pegasus**
- **Chain**
- **Black hole**
- **Magic broomstick**
- **Pterodactyl**
- _____
- _____
- _____

The Starite is awarded in this level when the king reaches his castle. But nothing is that easy. The king is riding a sheep. There are two fire vents in the king's path. There is a good-sized gap in the ground right in front of the castle. Oh, and the king is locked up behind a red door. And you might as well get the whole story up front: The switch for the door is guarded by a ferocious dragon. Another lazy day at the kingdom, right?

The first thing you need to do is get rid of that dragon. Another giant monster will work, but so will a bazooka or missile launcher. Once the dragon is gone, Maxwell can throw the switch and let the king out. But no so fast. There are still two more things to deal with in this level.

The two fire vents in front of the king must be extinguished. Drop water, an ice block, an ice ball, or even a snowman on the vents to snuff them out.

Now, you must create some sort of bridge for that gap in front of the castle. Glue two girders together and place them on the gap. This makes a good bridge. The sheep the king rides can perform little hops, so tying a chain to each side of the gap creates a makeshift bridge, too. You can also hold an air vent under the gap to push the sheep up and over.

TIP

If you need a little extra time, slow down the sheep by planting some grass along its path.

CRAZY SOLUTION

You can kill two birds with one stone by summoning a fighter jet. The dragon is flattened by the fighter jet's missiles. Just tap the dragon while in the jet and choose the attack option. The jet also makes a workable bridge for the king and his sheep. Just pilot the jet into the gap and face away from the castle so the knight guarding it will not perceive you as a threat. The king hops along the top of the jet and gets home safe and sound.

ACTION LEVELS

ANCIENT 4-1

| Difficulty: 2 | Par: 3 | Possible Words: |

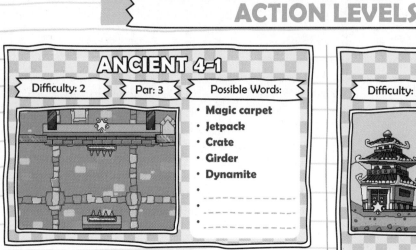

- **Magic carpet**
- **Jetpack**
- **Crate**
- **Girder**
- **Dynamite**
-
-
-

The Starite in this level is located behind two large red doors. There is a button on each side of the door that opens one of them—the door on the opposite side of the room. In order for Maxwell to get to the door opened by the button, he must fly through a gnashing set of metal teeth in the center of the room. You need a flying object to reach the button as well as to get through the teeth. How about a magic carpet ride?

Drop any object between the teeth when they are at their widest, and they slow down. Now you have enough time to slip through the teeth without getting injured.

⚠ CAUTION

If a pegasus, a sphinx, or any flying creature touches the teeth, it get hurt and will not let Maxwell ride anymore.

CRAZY SOLUTION

Place any object in the teeth to slow them down. This is a great place to get a New Object merit. Drop something unexpected into the teeth, such as a dodo. It really does not matter what is placed in there, just as long as it fits.

ANCIENT 4-2

| Difficulty: 2 | Par: 6 | Possible Words: |

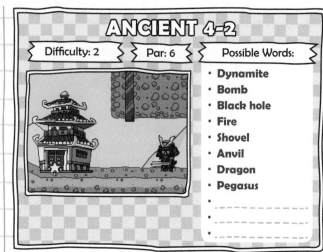

- **Dynamite**
- **Bomb**
- **Black hole**
- **Fire**
- **Shovel**
- **Anvil**
- **Dragon**
- **Pegasus**
-
-

The Starite in this feudal Japanese scene is located at the base of a pagoda at the very bottom of the level. Between Maxwell and the Starite are three samurai, each armed with a razor-sharp sword. There are essentially two ways to get to the pagoda. There is a dirt shaft to the right side of the level, but it is guarded by an angry oni demon. This soil shaft bypasses a sleeping samurai who is napping next to a button that raises a nearby door but slams shut another door by the pagoda. The button must remain pressed to clear the way to the pagoda and the Starite.

Try to clear out as many of the enemies as possible before putting Maxwell in harm's way. A black hole makes short work of the enemies. Dynamite and bombs also take out the oni, which is a much tougher customer than the samurai. The samurai can be eliminated with monsters much easier than the oni can. However, clearing out the oni opens the path to the soil. Digging through completely bypasses the sleeping samurai and the button that controls the pagoda door.

If you go the route of the sleeping samurai, be ready to replace the crate on the button. That button must remain pressed for the pagoda door to stay open. If the crate is destroyed, something else like an anvil or a rock must be placed on it.

CRAZY SOLUTION

Run roughshod over the samurai! Take down their medieval weapons with the might of the modern military. You can move a tank all over the area to blast enemies, from the oni at the top of the level to the two samurai in the tunnel next to the pagoda. Reusing weapons and vehicles whenever possible is good for coming in under par.

ANCIENT 4-3

Difficulty: 2   Par: 5   Possible Words:

- Pegasus
- DVD player
- Rock
- Boulder
- Balloon
- Air vent
- Fan
- Log
- Statue
-
-
-

The Starite in this lava-filled level is all the way to the right. Maxwell is stuck on a ledge next to a wide sea of lava that he cannot cross, not even with the help of a flying object with wings or a pegasus. He needs you to create some platforms for him. To help Maxwell across the lava, you must trigger the green and blue buttons above. Drop a rock, a boulder, or a DVD player on the blue button. Then, lift something up to the green button. A balloon floats right under it. An air vent or a fan will blow a small object into the button, too.

TIP

Because you cannot turn the fan on its back while placing the object, you must drop it on another object (such as a log) so it tips over on its own. The you can move it around while the air is gushing upward.

Once the two buttons have been pressed, run across the platforms and then give Maxwell the means to take flight.

Now Maxwell must manipulate the red button. Place something small on it so the vertical red door rises. However, this then blocks his path to the Starite. Step past the area where the red door drops and remove the object. The door slides back down, but the route to the Starite is open.

CRAZY SOLUTION

You do not need to keep whatever objects you place on the green and blue buttons there to have the platforms over the lava remain in play.

This is a good place to have a little fun with new objects. You know who would be a real pal and press that green button on the ceiling for Maxwell? George Washington, that's who. Place the first president of the United States on a trampoline and watch him bounce into the button.

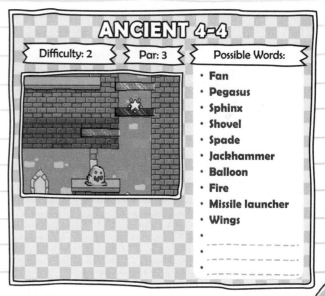

ANCIENT 4-4

Difficulty: 2   Par: 3   Possible Words:

- Fan
- Pegasus
- Sphinx
- Shovel
- Spade
- Jackhammer
- Balloon
- Fire
- Missile launcher
- Wings
-
-
-

59

The Starite in this action level is located on a red panel to the right of Maxwell's starting point. There is a red button on the wall next to Maxwell, but if he touches that right away, it just drops the Starite down into a monster-filled chamber. The Starite also falls on a blue button, which then blocks the upper route through the level. Because there are two potential ways to reach the Starite, consider trying both as you push on toward that fourth solution.

The ooze on the platform near the Starite is trouble. There are two ways to deal with it. Placing fire on the ooze instantly kills it. Blowing it off the ledge with a fan sends it to the monster below. The ooze is actually more powerful than the large monster below and will eliminate it for you. Now you can fly over the ooze at the bottom of the room. Just make sure you press the red button to drop the Starite down first.

If you do not sic the ooze on the monster, you can blow it up really well with a bazooka or a missile launcher.

The upper route is so much easier. You just need to be mindful of the red button. Fly up to the loose soil with a creature that can hover, such as the pegasus or the sphinx. Use a digging tool to burrow through the soil and drop down on the Starite. Or, if you are riding a sphinx, use its claws to burrow into the soil.

CRAZY SOLUTION

Explosives are good for moving earth, too. The trajectory of the howitzer is perfect for blasting through the soil without coming close to the red button. Set up the howitzer at the edge of the platform, aim for the soil, and then interact with the howitzer to open fire. A few shells ought to be enough to clear away the dirt and open a path for Maxwell to the Starite.

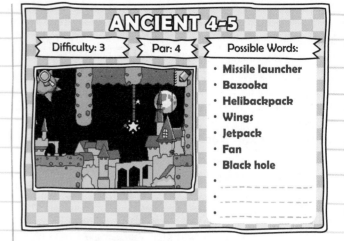

ANCIENT 4-5

Difficulty: 3	Par: 4	Possible Words:

Possible Words:
- Missile launcher
- Bazooka
- Helibackpack
- Wings
- Jetpack
- Fan
- Black hole
- _____
- _____
- _____

The Starite in this level is hanging by a thread over a pit of lava. Maxwell must figure out a way to reach the Starite without it—or him—falling into the molten earth. There are two routes through this action level. Each requires cleverness and cunning.

The upper route is guarded by a dark knight. This warrior will fall upon Maxwell with his giant sword if the hero gets too close, so stay back. Pepper the dark knight with attacks from afar via military tools, such as a bazooka, a missile launcher, or a laser pistol. Once the dark knight is gone, Maxwell can start digging through the soil to get at the Starite, but you must be careful. There is nothing below that last line of soil. If Maxwell breaks through without anything to break his fall, he drops right into the lava. It can be difficult to get wings or a helibackpack going in time before Maxwell drops—but it can be done by digging the last bit of soil out and then tapping the screen just above Maxwell. Now, fly down to the Starite.

The lower route is complicated by a pair of huge spiked balls that drop right in front of Maxwell if he triggers a nearby (and unavoidable) tripwire. After dropping the spiked balls, push them into the lava with a fan, a vent, or even a missile launcher.

CRAZY SOLUTION

This isn't so much crazy as it is necessary. Instead of trying to be brave and drop into the lava area with a helibackpack or a set of wings, use a sphinx.

The sphinx's claws dig through the soil like a jackhammer, too, which saves you an object and helps you come in under par in this level.

ANCIENT 4-6

Difficulty: 1	Par: 2	Possible Words:

- Tank
- Black hole
- Pegasus
- Sphinx
- T-Rex
- _____
- _____
- _____

There are three samurai on the ground between Maxwell and the Starite in this action level. However, when Maxwell steps toward the samurai, a giant enemy crab falls from the sky. It tears up the samurai before training its attacks on Maxwell. Maxwell must be ready to answer with an attack of his own—and it better be big enough to defeat the giant enemy crab and earn the Starite.

Monster-on-monster fights are always fun to watch.

CRAZY SOLUTION

Giant enemy crabs are no match for great old ones such as Cthulhu, the unbeatable elder god that tears up enemies with its massive claws.

ANCIENT 4-7

Difficulty: 2	Par: 4	Possible Words:

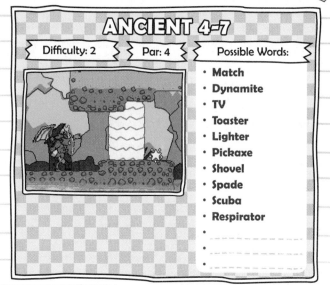

- Match
- Dynamite
- TV
- Toaster
- Lighter
- Pickaxe
- Shovel
- Spade
- Scuba
- Respirator
-
-
-

The Starite in this action level is located in a cave beneath the surface, where Maxwell mingles with centaurs. To retrieve the Starite, Maxwell must dive into the underworld. But he will not be alone down there. If he goes the water route and tries to swim up under the Starite, he must deal with a nasty gulper fish that has teeth like a bear trap. The land route isn't looking much easier. A large Jersey Devil is directly beneath Maxwell's feet and is ready to rip him to pieces if he tries to drop down and burrow to the Starite.

To reach the Starite via the Jersey Devil route, Maxwell must first burn through the bridge over the menace. Drop a match or a lighter on the bridge. It catches fire but will not burn right away. It takes a little time.

While the bridge burns, you can recycle the fire source as a means for setting off an explosive right in the Jersey Devil's face. Dynamite makes confetti of the devil. When the Jersey Devil is gone and the bridge burns,

just drop down with a shovel or a spade and burrow through the sand to access the Starite.

The gulper fish is fast and lethal. Take it out before dropping into the water by placing a large electronic object right next to the gulper. A TV has enough juice to fry the gulper. Now Maxwell can put on scuba gear or flippers and swim to the Starite.

CRAZY SOLUTION

The Jersey Devil will crush any small monster, but dip into your library of fierce creatures and conjure up some suitable candidates for the fight. The T-Rex will take down the Jersey Devil, as will a dragon or a hydra.

ANCIENT 4-8

Difficulty: 3	Par: 5	Possible Words:

Possible Words:
- Snowman
- Water
- Ice ball
- TV
- Cobra
- Wings
- Sphinx
- Whip
- Shovel
- Scuba
- Wetsuit
- _____
- _____
- _____

The Starite is not easy pickings in this action level. Not only is it sitting behind a fire, but it's also guarded by two violent shamans and a megalodon. Fortunately, Maxwell isn't alone in this conundrum. He has a familiar-looking archeologist on his side. The archaeologist is armed with a pistol and will attack the shamans if they drop off their ledge above the water and try to rush Maxwell.

The water route is the easiest way. Drop a TV or a DVD player next to the megalodon to snuff it out. Then, dig through the loose soil under the archeologist and swim through the water with the aid of flippers, scuba gear, or a wetsuit. Finally, extinguish the fire next to the Starite with something wet, such as a snowball or water.

The shamans are not big fans of snakes. Drop a cobra amongst them, and they try to attack, but the cobra (or any other poisonous snake, such as a rattler or an asp) will always get the best of one of them. You can clean up the pair with another snake.

The archeologist can also be enlisted to help with the shamans. However, that gun is pretty limited against two targets. If only there was a more appropriate weapon for the archeologist...such as a whip. Give a whip to the archeologist. He drops his pistol. Now, lure the shamans off the ledge and onto the archeologist. He whips them to death. Maxwell can then fly over the level and drop in on the Starite—after putting out the fire, of course.

CRAZY SOLUTION

The shamans are fearful of the gods. You can actually scare them away by placing Ra, the Egyptian sun god, in front of them. The shamans flee over the edge of the platform. If you get Ra right next to them, they will even run into the fire next to the Starite and, well, they are then on their way to meet whatever deity these shamans worship.

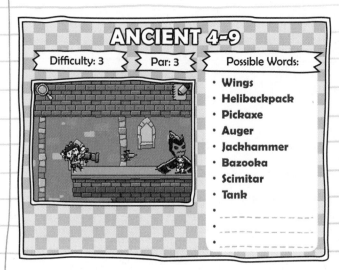

ANCIENT 4-9

Difficulty: 3	Par: 3	Possible Words:

Possible Words:
- Wings
- Helibackpack
- Pickaxe
- Auger
- Jackhammer
- Bazooka
- Scimitar
- Tank
- _____
- _____
- _____

This action level is a little tricky because, as the hint states, things are not necessarily as they appear. There is a green switch next to a Spring Heeled Jack (a really nasty fellow) that looks like it would clear a path to the Starite, but instead it drops spikes right on it. If the spikes hit the Starite, the level ends in failure. Maxwell needs to find a different way down to the Starite. But first, he needs to get rid of the Spring Heeled Jack. A missile launcher works, as do other powerful weapons, such as a laser pistol, a bazooka, or a scimitar.

Instead of throwing the green switch, dig through the gray soil behind the now-dead Spring Heeled Jack. Now Maxwell can drop right down on the Starite and finish the level.

CRAZY SOLUTION

The Spring Heeled Jack is not immune to mystic attacks, such as medusa's gaze. Place a medusa next to the Spring Heeled Jack. He will kill the medusa, but her head rolls to the ground. Give the head to Maxwell. Now, jot down a jackhammer and place it close to the Spring Heeled Jack. Fly up to the enemy and turn it to stone with the medusa head. Quickly give Maxwell the jackhammer and shatter the stone Jack.

While the leprechaun dawdles, you can rush to the right and close in on the Starite.

TIP

Roller skates or a unicycle help Maxwell go even faster.

If there is one thing a leprechaun cannot pass over, it is gold. Drop some gold right in front of the leprechaun, and he will freeze just so he can stare at it. Now, finish the race!

CRAZY SOLUTION

One place you can always count on finding a leprechaun and his pot o' gold is at the end of a rainbow. In this race, the leprechaun cannot help but stop in appreciation of the sudden appearance of a rainbow. Place the rainbow directly over a hole in the ground, and the leprechaun will become confused and fall right into the hole. Maxwell has no problem winning the race now.

ANCIENT 4-10

Difficulty: 4   Par: 3   Possible Words:

- Lava spout
- Skateboard
- Roller skates
- Unicycle
- Tiger
- Gold
- _____
- _____
- _____

Ready to race? The Starite is the prize for beating the leprechaun to the finish line at the end of this level. The leprechaun is nimble and fast, though. It will beat Maxwell every time unless Maxwell, well, cheats a bit. You must place things in the leprechaun's path that keep him from finishing the race. A lava spout or a tiger just as the leprechaun's path narrows will stop him for a few moments.

ANCIENT 4-11

Difficulty: 3   Par: 3   Possible Words:

- Sphinx
- Black hole
- Pegasus
- Pickaxe
- Jackhammer
- _____
- _____
- _____

Maxwell can see the Starite at the start of this action level—it's right behind the king's throne. But that's not the only thing visible. There is a tripwire directly in front of Maxwell that, if crossed, will drop boulders and spike balls into the throne room. If the king or queen is injured by the boulders or the spike balls, the level ends in failure. There is a long way around Maxwell can take on the back of a flying creature. If not on the sphinx, just give Maxwell a digging tool, such as a pickaxe, so he can push through the loose soil under the throne room.

Use a black hole to get rid of the boulders and spike balls after triggering the tripwire. Place the black hole above the objects so the king and queen are not threatened.

After the path is clear, just pick up the Starite from behind the throne.

CRAZY SOLUTION

After triggering the tripwire, you can clear an easy path to the throne with just a fan. As long as the spike balls fall to the right, you can blow the boulders to the left. The queen will move along with the boulders and not be injured. She cannot touch a spike ball, though, or she is instantly wounded. With just a fan, Maxwell can seize the Starite!

WORLD 5: SHORELINE

PUZZLE LEVELS

SHORELINE 5-1

Difficulty: 1 > Par: 2 > Possible Words:

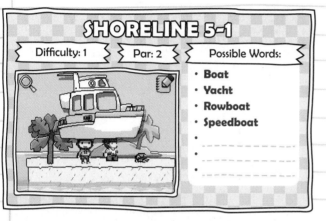

- **Boat**
- **Yacht**
- **Rowboat**
- **Speedboat**
-
-
-

This poor, stranded man has been marooned on this island for who knows how long. All he wants is the means to get off the island and back to civilization. If you give him a vehicle or an object that will help him leave the uncharted island, he will award you with a Starite. Write down all sorts of boats for the fellow, such as a rowboat, a yacht, or a lifeboat. He's just grateful for anything that gets him somewhere else.

CRAZY SOLUTION

This is one of those levels where you can really expand your vocabulary and think up a new object. The merit will result in extra Ollars for Maxwell's account. Try something new, such as a seaplane, to get the guy off the island.

SHORELINE 5-2

Difficulty: 2 > Par: 3 > Possible Words:

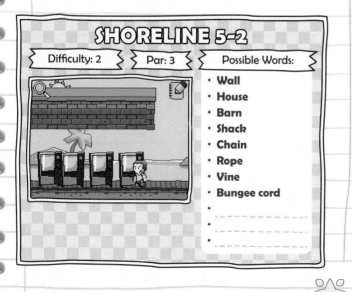

- **Wall**
- **House**
- **Barn**
- **Shack**
- **Chain**
- **Rope**
- **Vine**
- **Bungee cord**
-
-
-

At the start of this level, Maxwell meets a girl who just wants her favorite candy bar. Easy enough request, except that the four nearby vending machines are guarded by a total bully. This tough guy will attack Maxwell as soon as he tries to approach the vending machines, so you must come up with a way to keep the bully away from not only Maxwell, but also the girl while you, well, vend.

Tether the bully to an extra-large object, such as a wall, a house, or a barn. Then Maxwell can fly over to the vending machines and get the needed candy.

 TIP

The candy that the girl wants is in the second vending machine from the right.

CRAZY SOLUTION

You must contain the thug's movement to solve this level. You've already tethered the creep to a wall or a house. It's time to get creative. Give the bully some culture while he's all tied up by summoning a ziggurat into the level. That's heavy enough to hold back the bully.

SHORELINE 5-3

Difficulty: 1 > Par: 2 > Possible Words:

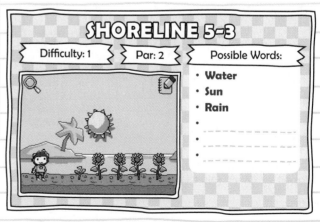

- **Water**
- **Sun**
- **Rain**
-
-
-

Maxwell approaches a neat row of sunflowers. One of the sunflowers has not yet bloomed, though. If Maxwell can make those petals peek, he earns a Starite. This requires a little green-thumb technique. Think of anything that would help make a plant grow, such as rain, water, or the sun. The sunflower instantly blooms, and the Starite appears for the taking.

CRAZY SOLUTION

Sometimes Maxwell needs to get his hands dirty for the good of the Starite. Hand the hero a bag of manure to sprinkle on the flower. The roots immediately react to what you're shoveling (probably a lot better than your friends do when you shovel some in their direction), and Maxwell gets the Starite.

SHORELINE 5-4

Difficulty: 2	Par: 2	Possible Words:

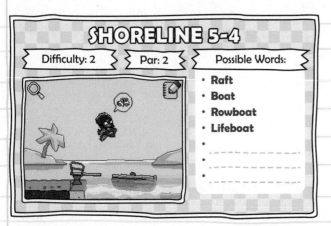

- **Raft**
- **Boat**
- **Rowboat**
- **Lifeboat**
- _____
- _____
- _____

As Maxwell begins this level, a diver is bouncing up and down on a springboard. The diver refuses to actually get in the water, though. It turns out the diver is not necessarily here for a swim. You need to jot down a boat or something that will lure the diver into the water. There are any number of boats you can write into the Notepad, such as a raft, a rowboat, or a lifeboat. When the boat is dropped into the drink, the diver dives onto it, and the Starite magically appears.

CRAZY SOLUTION

It is said that in the age of the Vikings, when a chieftain died, his body was set on a magnificent vessel, set ablaze, and then put to sea. Well, none of that grim pomp is necessary here, save for the elaborate Viking ship that lures the diver into the water.

SHORELINE 5-5

Difficulty: 2	Par: 3	Possible Words:

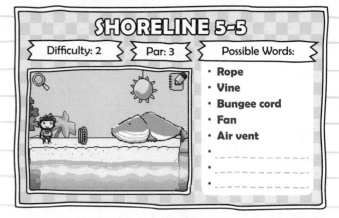

- **Rope**
- **Vine**
- **Bungee cord**
- **Fan**
- **Air vent**
- _____
- _____

There is nothing sadder than a beached whale. (Really, there isn't, if you think about it.) To earn the Starite in this level, Maxwell needs to get that whale back into the water so it does not dry out in the hot afternoon sun. Maxwell can drag the whale into the water with a rope or a cord. He can also give it a gentle push with a fan or an air vent. As soon as the whale slides into the water, the Starite appears.

⚠ CAUTION

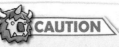

Don't be too brutish getting the whale into the waves. Any sort of sharp object will end the level in failure. No Starite for you!

CRAZY SOLUTION

That whale is pretty big. Write down a bulldozer and shove the whale in the water to earn another Starite in this level. Although you have a par three for this level, using single-object solutions such as this will help you finish the world completely under par and bank a sweet merit.

SHORELINE 5-6

Difficulty: 1	Par: 2	Possible Words:

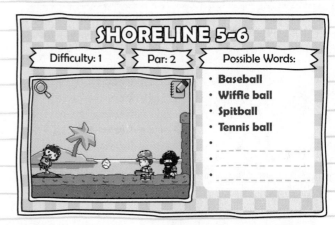

- **Baseball**
- **Wiffle ball**
- **Spitball**
- **Tennis ball**
- _____
- _____

Take Maxwell out to the ball game. If you help Maxwell put a heater over home plate, the batter and catcher in this level will hand over a Starite. All you need to do is write down a type of ball in Maxwell's Notepad, such as a baseball or a wiffle ball, and then hand it to the hero. Throw the ball to the batter, and the Starite bursts into the level.

CRAZY SOLUTION

You have to throw something round to the batter to finish this one. You're tried baseballs, tennis balls...all sorts of balls. Think off how the undead will play baseball after the zombie apocalypse. What will they use for balls? How about a skull? Morbid, yes—but Starite-approved.

SHORELINE 5-7

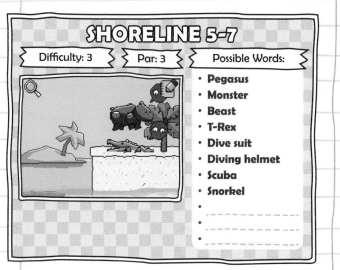

Difficulty: 3	Par: 3	Possible Words:

Possible Words:
- Pegasus
- Monster
- Beast
- T-Rex
- Dive suit
- Diving helmet
- Scuba
- Snorkel
- ....
- ....
- ....

As Maxwell steps into this level, he joins a pirate captain. The captain wants his watch back. He can even hear it ticking in the belly of a crocodile on the far side of the level. If you can collect the watch for the pirate, he will shiver his own timbers and hand over a Starite. You must eliminate the crocodile first. Use a fearsome creature to defeat the croc, such as a bear or a dinosaur. Sometimes the watch pops out of the croc and drops right on the beach. If that happens, just fly over and grab the watch.

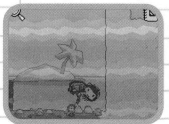

Occasionally, the watch drops out of the crocodile and slips under the surface of the ocean. Then, Maxwell needs some swim gear, such as a snorkel or a pair of flippers. Dive deep and pick up the watch.

CRAZY SOLUTION

Have fun with the crocodile. Drop all sorts of crazed monsters on it, such as a behemoth or a beast. As long as the creature is larger than the crocodile, the croc will give up the ghost—and the watch. Catch the watch on the deck of a boat if you can; otherwise, you need to get your feet wet and chase it down under the waves.

SHORELINE 5-8

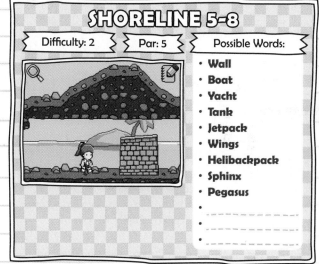

Difficulty: 2	Par: 5	Possible Words:

Possible Words:
- Wall
- Boat
- Yacht
- Tank
- Jetpack
- Wings
- Helibackpack
- Sphinx
- Pegasus
- ....

Maxwell finds himself in another race at the start of this level. The runner on the track below him is not only fast, but she also doesn't have to worry about falling spiked balls, boulders, and dynamite drops. Maxwell must figure out a way to slow the runner (preferably permanently) so he can avoid the dangers looming overhead and win the race. Once Maxwell reaches the finish line, the Starite appears. Place something in the runner's path she cannot get around, such as a wall.

TIP

You can also place a boat or a car in the way. The runner pushes it, but it gets stuck as her track narrows, making her stop in her tracks.

Once the runner has been stopped, Maxwell must negotiate his stretch of track. The first thing that falls from the ceiling as he runs to the right is a spiked ball. Drag the ball out of the way with a rope or a cord.

Then fly over it with an airborne object, such as wings.

Place an air vent directly under the spiked ball or boulder to keep pressed against the ceiling. When Maxwell runs over the vent, he barely breaks the stream, so the hazard remains aloft.

NOTE

The dynamite toward the end of the track sounds dangerous, but it's really not. As the dynamite falls, it explodes. This is designed to just freak Maxwell out a little and slow him down so the runner can win.

CRAZY SOLUTION

Okay, you've pushed some large objects in the runner's path and gotten her to stop. But there has to be something a little smaller that could do the trick, too. What would make you stop running (other than somebody offering you a free video game)? Drop a stinky skunk in the runner's path. She recoils in horror and refuses to move another inch as long as the skunk remains.

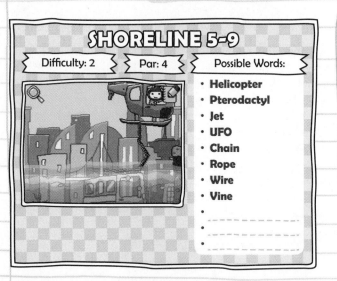

SHORELINE 5-9

Difficulty: 2	Par: 4	Possible Words:

- **Helicopter**
- **Pterodactyl**
- **Jet**
- **UFO**
- **Chain**
- **Rope**
- **Wire**
- **Vine**
-
-
-

When Maxwell begins the level, a student and a bus driver are looking wistfully at a river. It would seem that a school bus has plunged into the water. They need you to fish it out of the water and drag it back to dry land. If those four wheels touch the ground right in front of them, they will reward you with a Starite.

Maxwell is definitely not strong enough to lift a bus out of the water on his own. He will need some objects. Something heavy-duty and airborne will do the trick here, such as a helicopter or a UFO. (Even a pterodactyl is strong enough to hoist the bus out of the water.) Chain or rope that bus to the flying object and then return it to the driver and the student to claim the reward.

CRAZY SOLUTION

Now, although Maxwell is indeed not strong enough to pull the bus to land with his bare hands, he can walk it to shore by placing air vents underneath it. Just move the air vents along as Maxwell swims. The bus floats above the river like a balloon. When he finally reaches the riverbank, hop out and yank the bus onto solid ground.

SHORELINE 5-10

Difficulty: 2	Par: 6	Possible Words:

- **Shark**
- **Barracuda**
- **Piranha**
- **Hammerhead**
- **Vine**
- **Rope**
- **Chain**
- **Scuba**
- **Flippers**
- **Respirator**
- **Dolphin**
-
-
-

As the level begins, Maxwell stands on the shore of dangerous waters. Three nasty jellyfish flitter about in the river ahead, ready to attack if he tries to swim by. Maxwell must get the crate next to him to the other side of the river to earn the Starite, but something must be done about the jellyfish before he even slips into the river. A shark makes short work of the jellyfish. Smaller predators, such as piranha, work, too, but you may need to drop more than one into jellyfish central to clean out the pack.

Once the jellyfish are gone, Maxwell is free to swim the crate to the other side of the water. Tether the crate to Maxwell with a rope or a chain and place some diving gear on the little hero. (Maxwell can also ride a dolphin underwater to ferry the crate.) Dive in and pull the crate through the water. The nearby beluga whale is harmless. So is the octopus at the far side of the river, although it will start squirting ink as soon as Maxwell nears. The worst that can happen is Maxwell drops the cargo off on the shore covered in purple ink.

TIP

The beluga whale is too far away from Maxwell to ride without first conjuring up an object to swim. However, Maxwell can ride the beluga through the water to the jellyfish. The beluga will eliminate the jellyfish if you swim right into the thick of them. However, once the beluga has been attacked, Maxwell can no longer ride it.

CRAZY SOLUTION

Those jellyfish need to be taught some manners. Drop a giant kraken on top of them. The mythical sea beast thrashes about, eliminating the jellyfish without batting an eye.

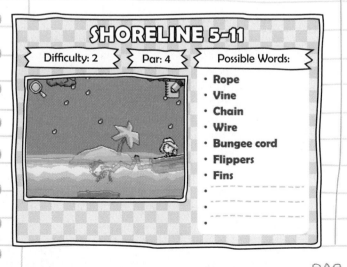

SHORELINE 5-11

Difficulty: 2 — Par: 4 — Possible Words:

- **Rope**
- **Vine**
- **Chain**
- **Wire**
- **Bungee cord**
- **Flippers**
- **Fins**

The sea is ruthless. It can turn on you in a heartbeat. In this level, a young woman has been trapped in a rowboat out at sea by a fierce storm. It is up to Maxwell to tow her back to shore. Maxwell must tether himself to the boat with a rope and drag the boat to the beach in order to earn the Starite. Above him, lightning crashes. If he does not hurry, he'll be zapped. Give Maxwell something to help him swim faster, such as flippers or fins, and pull the boat to the shore. Don't stop moving, lest the lightning strikes shock Maxwell.

TIP

If you hurry, you can get the girl to safety within just three lightning strikes. Anything more than that and you are courting trouble.

CRAZY SOLUTION

You don't actually need to pull the boat to shore. Maxwell is strong enough to push the boat as long as he has been given extra swim gear to move faster. A wetsuit lets Maxwell shove the boat to shore as if he himself has a little onboard motor.

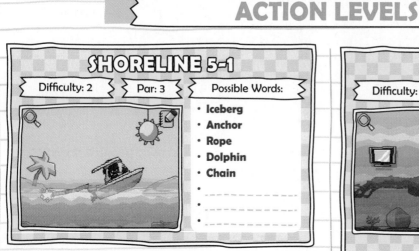

SHORELINE 5-1

Difficulty: 2	Par: 3	Possible Words:

- **Iceberg**
- **Anchor**
- **Rope**
- **Dolphin**
- **Chain**
- _____
- _____
- _____

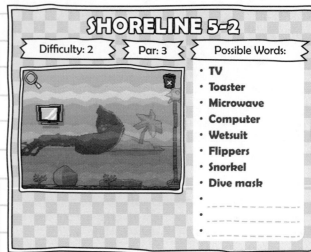

SHORELINE 5-2

Difficulty: 2	Par: 3	Possible Words:

- **TV**
- **Toaster**
- **Microwave**
- **Computer**
- **Wetsuit**
- **Flippers**
- **Snorkel**
- **Dive mask**
- _____
- _____
- _____

Quick, after that boat! A vandal is making away with the Starite in a speedboat. Maxwell must stop the boat before it reaches the far side of the level. The boat is pretty fast, so you only have about seven seconds to figure out a way to bring that boat to a full stop.

Drop something giant in front of the boat, such as an iceberg. The boat crashes into it and stops. You can also weigh down the boat with an anchor or a safe tied to a rope. Carry the object over to the boat and attach it to anything to pull the boat into the water and make it stop. Try gluing all sorts of heavy things to the boat.

CRAZY SOLUTION

Beach the speedboat on a volcano. Write volcano in the Notepad and then race ahead of the boat, dropping it on an underwater peak so the cone of the volcano is poking out of the water. The speedboat high-waters itself on the volcano. Now just swim out and collect the prize.

The Starite in this action level is just on the other side of the lake, tucked behind a heavy green door. The switch for the door is just below it, underwater. But whoever placed the Starite there left behind two security measures. First, Maxwell must get rid of a huge kraken. Shock the kraken with two electronic objects, such as TVs and computers. Or, drop a black hole next to the kraken to yank it out of the water.

Next, Maxwell must deal with the spiked ball floating right in front of the switch. If Maxwell tries to swim around the spikes, he will not make it. The spiked ball is kept floating right in front of the switch by a rope and an air vent. Grab the rope and pull it away from the switch. Then, swim below the switch and interact with it just as Maxwell is pushed by via the air-vent current.

CRAZY SOLUTION

Let's pop the spiked ball and the kraken with a single object. Place a sea mine in the water and let it float up into the spiked ball. The resulting explosion will eliminate not only the spiked ball, but also the kraken. If you cannot get the timing down just right, push the spiked ball toward the kraken with another air vent and then release the sea mine.

SHORELINE 5-3

Difficulty: 3 | Par: 4 | Possible Words:

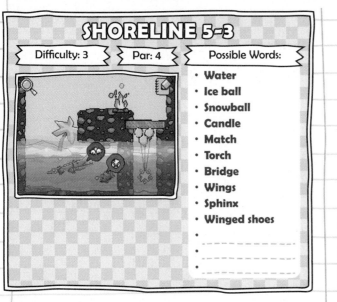

Possible Words:
- **Water**
- **Ice ball**
- **Snowball**
- **Candle**
- **Match**
- **Torch**
- **Bridge**
- **Wings**
- **Sphinx**
- **Winged shoes**
-
-
-

The Starite in this action level is tied to three balloons, held back by a blue door. The button that opens the blue door is in the water next to it, but it is guarded by a vicious piranha. However, that's not the end of the problems in this level for Maxwell. There is a bundle of dynamite just over the Starite that is also held back by a blue door. If the button is pushed and the Starite released, the dynamite will fall right on top of it.

Maxwell must first do something about that dynamite. You can set it off early with a match or a torch. Or, you can place an object beneath the blue door, such as a bridge, that will catch the dynamite.

⚠ CAUTION

The vertical shaft above the balloons has no ceiling. If you get rid of the dynamite and then press the blue button, the Starite will just float away unless you are right there to catch it.

Once the dynamite has been contained, you must press the button. Diving right into the water is out of the question, thanks to the piranha. You can drop a stronger creature into the water to get rid of the piranha and then swim to the button, but that will take a lot of extra time. Shocking the piranha with an electronic object is bad news, too, because the zap will also break the Starite. Instead, just get Maxwell close to the shaft the Starite flies through and extinguish the fire. Water-based objects will extinguish the fire—just release them above it. Then, place a floating object under the button and snag the Starite as it floats by.

CRAZY SOLUTION

Kill two birds with one stone by extinguishing the fire next to the Starite with an object that will also float in the water. The ice ball floats just like an ice cube in a glass of water. Carefully place the ice ball on the fire, and then under the button, shave off an extra object.

SHORELINE 5-4

Difficulty: 2 | Par: 4 | Possible Words:

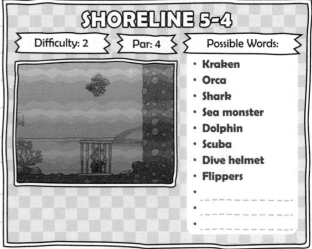

Possible Words:
- **Kraken**
- **Orca**
- **Shark**
- **Sea monster**
- **Dolphin**
- **Scuba**
- **Dive helmet**
- **Flippers**
-
-
-

There is a diver trapped in a cage at the bottom of the lake. Fortunately, she has more than enough oxygen to survive for a while. However, these are dangerous waters. A bullhead shark patrols above the cage, just waiting for its boxed lunch to finally be free. You must eliminate the bullhead and then swim down to the trapped diver. Open the cage, and the diver will release the door that blocks the Starite.

An electronic object is out of the question because the shock would hurt the diver. So, you must drop an attack creature on top of the bullhead to get rid of it. Any rival shark works well, such as a hammerhead or a great white. An orca can also take out the bullhead. (Yes, orcas are cute—but it's a trick to get you to come closer....)

As soon as the bullhead shark is gone, Maxwell can swim down to the trapped diver. The lionfish in the water isn't exactly pleased about the intrusion, but it will not attack Maxwell.

CRAZY SOLUTION

Lots of animals can swim—not just fish. Think about a fun match-up to take down the shark. How about bear versus shark? Who would win that fight? Fortunately for you, the bear wins this round.

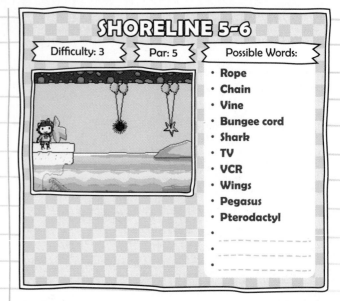

SHORELINE 5-6

Difficulty: 3	Par: 5	Possible Words:

- **Rope**
- **Chain**
- **Vine**
- **Bungee cord**
- **Shark**
- **TV**
- **VCR**
- **Wings**
- **Pegasus**
- **Pterodactyl**

SHORELINE 5-5

Difficulty: 2	Par: 4	Possible Words:

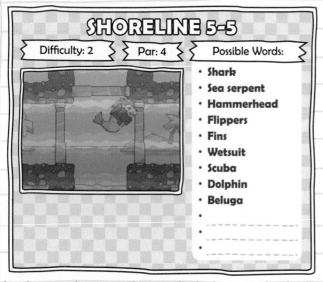

- **Shark**
- **Sea serpent**
- **Hammerhead**
- **Flippers**
- **Fins**
- **Wetsuit**
- **Scuba**
- **Dolphin**
- **Beluga**

Anything can be a mer-thing, really. In this action level, the Starite is guarded by two mer-lions. These half-fish/half-lions are ferocious. They are also locked up behind walls. However, in order to get into the water and swim down to the Starite, Maxwell must trigger a tripwire. This moves the walls. Now Maxwell must swim directly into the mer-lion den to reach the Starite.

Eliminate the mer-lions early by dropping a fierce creature next to them, such as a shark or a sea serpent. The mer-lion looks tough, but it wilts in the face of a really mean shark. Once the two mer-lions have been dispatched, strap on some scuba gear or a snorkel and dive down to the Starite.

CRAZY SOLUTION

Search your memory banks for nasty sea monsters you recall from your childhood. Use the mermaid in the water here as a hint. What kind of nastiness tormented a mermaid in recent memory? That's right—a sea witch. The half-witch/half-octopus makes short work of the mer-lions.

The Starite is locked up at the bottom of the sea. There is no key to open the door, nor is there an enemy to eliminate to force it open. Instead, this level is all about reuniting friends. There are three sea creatures trapped at the top of the level by balloons: a clam, a starfish, and a sea urchin. Maxwell must free these sea creatures and place them next to their friends down in the water. When all three pairs have been reunited, the door to the Starite opens.

Pop the balloons that hold up the sea creatures with a sharp object or the legs of a flying creature.

⚠ CAUTION

Do not use a jetpack or a helibackpack to reach the balloons in this level. The jetpack does not have enough power to last an entire trip up to the balloons, cut them, and get back to land before sputtering out. Once the jetpack or helibackpack falls into the water, it shorts out and cannot be used.

Just drop the sea life into their respective pairs to open the door to the Starite.

CRAZY SOLUTION

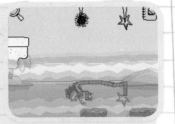

Try things in reverse. Instead of dropping the sea life and then carting them over to their mates, drag the sea life in the water directly under the match floating above. Pop the balloons, and the pairs hook up. The door opens, and the Starite is yours.

There are many ways to get to the Starite. You do not have to go down the right side of the level and work with the sea mine and the thresher shark. Dig straight down the left side of the level, carefully avoiding the shark. The smaller fish, such as the piranha, can be beaten with your digging utensil. Come at the Starite from the left to claim it.

CRAZY SOLUTION

Want to clear out the sea with as few objects as possible? Use the moving black hole trick. Create the black hole and then move it onto one of the two thresher sharks. As soon as the shark is pulled into it, grab the black hole and move it to the other shark. When that shark is yanked into the black hole, pick it up again and move on to the next fish. Can you get more than four fish with a single black hole?

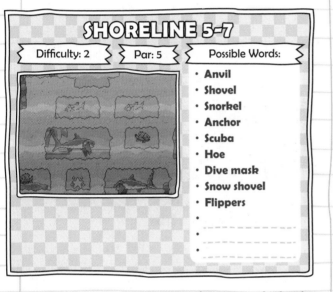

SHORELINE 5-7

Difficulty: 2	Par: 5	Possible Words:

- **Anvil**
- **Shovel**
- **Snorkel**
- **Anchor**
- **Scuba**
- **Hoe**
- **Dive mask**
- **Snow shovel**
- **Flippers**
-
-
-

The Starite is buried at the bottom of the sea in this level. No big deal, right? You just need some flippers and a shovel and dig it up. One problem...well, eight problems, to be exact. There are seven angry fish in air pockets surrounding the Starite. And to make matters worse, there is a sea mine on the ocean floor next to the dirt makeshift fish hotel. If Maxwell even touches that sea mine, it will blow up.

Use the sea mine to your advantage. Write down an anvil or a rock and then place it nearby. Dig the thresher shark out of the dirt and then drop the heavy object on the sea mine as the shark swims by.

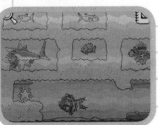

Once the path is clear, just dig into the dirt with a shovel or a spade and fish out the Starite.

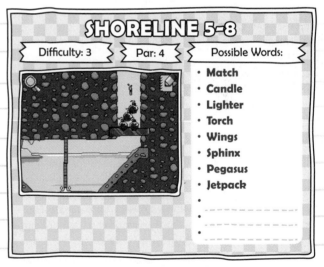

SHORELINE 5-8

Difficulty: 3	Par: 4	Possible Words:

- **Match**
- **Candle**
- **Lighter**
- **Torch**
- **Wings**
- **Sphinx**
- **Pegasus**
- **Jetpack**
-
-
-

This action level is a trap ready to be sprung. The Starite hangs from a rope, ready to be grabbed by Maxwell. It's just beyond a red door, controlled by a single switch at the bottom of the level. But the second he throws the switch, two additional doors open at the top of the level and release a load of bombs not only at Maxwell, but at the Starite, too. You must neutralize the bombs to get the Starite. A match or fire source on each stack of bombs cleans up the potential mess.

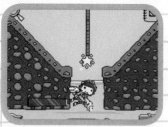

Once the bombs have been destroyed, you can fly right up and grab the Starite.

CRAZY SOLUTION

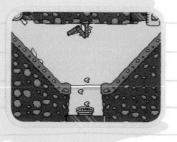

Try burning the rope holding up the Starite first. When the Starite drops to the red door above the water pool, place a large wall right above it. This will block the bombs from reaching the Starite.

CRAZY SOLUTION

Use animals to rescue the Starite. Hook the rowboat up to a cow or a horse with a rope or a cord. Then, place something yummy just beyond the reach of the animal. The animal pulls the rowboat to the side, thus moving the Starite away from the spiked balls. That way, when you trigger the tripwire, the boulders fall in the water and do not smash the Starite.

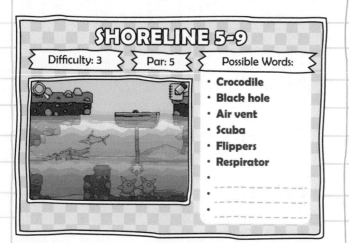

SHORELINE 5-9

Difficulty: 3	Par: 5	Possible Words:

- **Crocodile**
- **Black hole**
- **Air vent**
- **Scuba**
- **Flippers**
- **Respirator**
-
-
-

The Starite in this level is hanging directly above two spiked balls in the water. If Maxwell triggers the tripwire near his starting position, a bunch of boulders fall on a rowboat holding up the Starite. The Starite is then pushed into the spiked balls and ruined. Maxwell must stop these boulders from smashing into the rowboat—or pull the rowboat out of the way and then slip into the water to pick up the Starite. There is a swordfish guarding the Starite that will attack as soon as Maxwell enters the water.

Use a crocodile or a shark to get rid of the swordfish. Now it's time to preserve the Starite for when Maxwell triggers the tripwire. A black hole slipped between the boulders will consume them (but be careful—the black hole can be tricky to use and can end up consuming more than intended). You can also use an air vent in the water to push the Starite to the side of the spiked balls so it will not fall on them when the boulders hit the rowboat.

SHORELINE 5-10

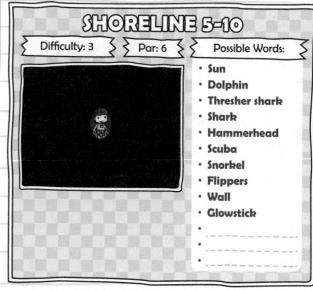

Difficulty: 3	Par: 6	Possible Words:

- **Sun**
- **Dolphin**
- **Thresher shark**
- **Shark**
- **Hammerhead**
- **Scuba**
- **Snorkel**
- **Flippers**
- **Wall**
- **Glowstick**
-
-
-

Hey, who turned out all the lights? This action level is bathed in darkness, making it difficult to see all of the angry creatures in the sea. And there are a lot of nasty fish down there, too. A hammerhead, a shark, a sea serpent, and more linger in the deep. There are a handful of lantern fish that do reveal a little bit of the environment, but for the most part, it is obscured. The Starite is located at the very bottom of the sea, under a lid.

Cast some light on things with the sun in your first attempt. The sun reveals much more of the environment than a lantern fish—and it can be moved around. This is a good way to see how the level is set up  for further runs. You can also give Maxwell a glowstick so he can see in the dark deep of the sea.

TIP

As you look around the level, drop creatures such as sharks into the water to clean up the nasty fish.

Once you reach the bottom of the level, you must remove the lid over the Starite. Tie a rope or a chain to the lid and then swim away to move it. Now you can release the lid and swim down to the Starite to finish the level.

CRAZY SOLUTION

Hammerheads and sharks are rough customers. A leviathan will survive almost any tussle in the deep.

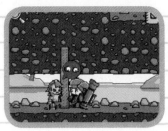

The switch for the green doors is guarded by two zombies. These zombies are tough enemies. Fortunately, there are two soldiers nearby to fight them. However, the zombies are stronger than the soldiers. You must give the soldiers better weapons. Write down a bazooka or a rocket launcher and hand it to one of the soldiers. Then, lift the door that divides the zombies and soldiers via the blue switch next to Maxwell. The soldiers will attack the zombies—and defeat them.

There is a curious archeologist near the soldiers. Once the door has been lifted and the zombies are gone, the archeologist will throw the green switch and allow access to the red buttons. Now, drop small items on the buttons, such as limes, oranges, and ice cream cones. The Starite then falls right in front of Maxwell.

 TIP

Reuse the same object for each red button to stay under par.

CRAZY SOLUTION

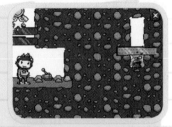

You can actually solve this level with a single object: a match. The match is small enough to fit between the doors and the red buttons. Just drop the match on each button and scoop up the Starite four under par!

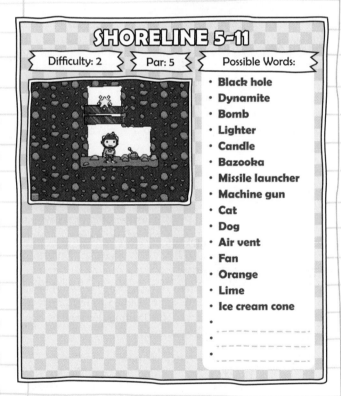

SHORELINE 5-11

| Difficulty: 2 | Par: 5 | Possible Words: |

Possible Words:
- **Black hole**
- **Dynamite**
- **Bomb**
- **Lighter**
- **Candle**
- **Bazooka**
- **Missile launcher**
- **Machine gun**
- **Cat**
- **Dog**
- **Air vent**
- **Fan**
- **Orange**
- **Lime**
- **Ice cream cone**
- •
- •
- •

The Starite in this level is locked right above Maxwell, behind two red doors. Each door is controlled by a red button. These buttons are in small chambers—one on each side of the Starite. Those buttons, though, are protected by green doors. You must remove those green doors in order to access the buttons.

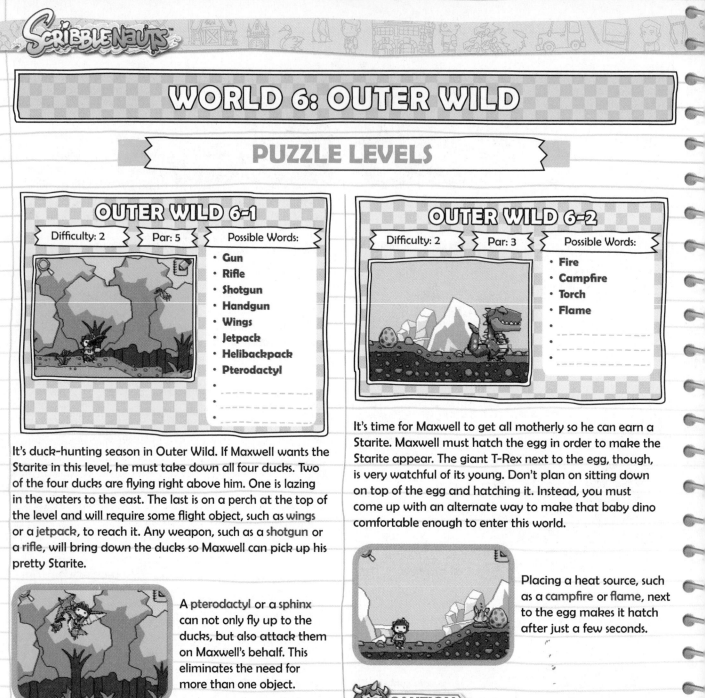

WORLD 6: OUTER WILD

PUZZLE LEVELS

OUTER WILD 6-1

| Difficulty: 2 | Par: 5 | Possible Words: |

- **Gun**
- **Rifle**
- **Shotgun**
- **Handgun**
- **Wings**
- **Jetpack**
- **Helibackpack**
- **Pterodactyl**

It's duck-hunting season in Outer Wild. If Maxwell wants the Starite in this level, he must take down all four ducks. Two of the four ducks are flying right above him. One is lazing in the waters to the east. The last is on a perch at the top of the level and will require some flight object, such as wings or a jetpack, to reach it. Any weapon, such as a shotgun or a rifle, will bring down the ducks so Maxwell can pick up his pretty Starite.

A pterodactyl or a sphinx can not only fly up to the ducks, but also attack them on Maxwell's behalf. This eliminates the need for more than one object.

CRAZY SOLUTION

You could hunt the ducks yourself, taking aim on them as they just try to enjoy a sunny afternoon. Or you could use something else to do your dirty work. A massive dragon or other such monster will clear out the ducks so you can maintain a clean conscience.

OUTER WILD 6-2

| Difficulty: 2 | Par: 3 | Possible Words: |

- **Fire**
- **Campfire**
- **Torch**
- **Flame**

It's time for Maxwell to get all motherly so he can earn a Starite. Maxwell must hatch the egg in order to make the Starite appear. The giant T-Rex next to the egg, though, is very watchful of its young. Don't plan on sitting down on top of the egg and hatching it. Instead, you must come up with an alternate way to make that baby dino comfortable enough to enter this world.

Placing a heat source, such as a campfire or flame, next to the egg makes it hatch after just a few seconds.

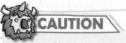 CAUTION

Do not force the egg open with a hammer or an axe. The egg must open naturally to solve the level.

CRAZY SOLUTION

Any small to midsize source of fire works in this level. But why not go large? Drop a lava spout next to the egg and hatch the baby dino. Just be sure to remove it right away so it doesn't burn up the Starite.

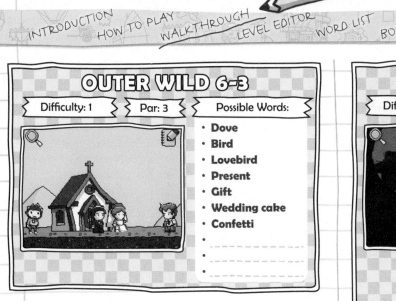

OUTER WILD 6-3

Difficulty: 1   Par: 3   Possible Words:

- **Dove**
- **Bird**
- **Lovebird**
- **Present**
- **Gift**
- **Wedding cake**
- **Confetti**
- _____
- _____
- _____

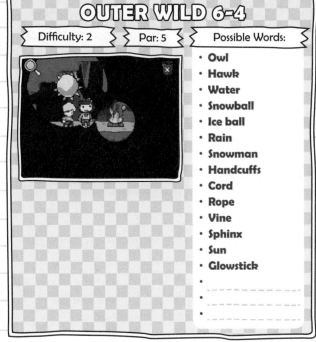

OUTER WILD 6-4

Difficulty: 2   Par: 5   Possible Words:

- **Owl**
- **Hawk**
- **Water**
- **Snowball**
- **Ice ball**
- **Rain**
- **Snowman**
- **Handcuffs**
- **Cord**
- **Rope**
- **Vine**
- **Sphinx**
- **Sun**
- **Glowstick**
- _____
- _____
- _____

Everybody loves a wedding—even Maxwell. To earn the Starite, he must celebrate the newlyweds by placing two celebratory objects in the level just as the couple exits the church. Think of any wedding traditions, such as a wedding cake, and jot them down so that Maxwell can get his Starite.

Here's a useful combo: dove and present. Just make sure you hand presents and gifts to a member of the couple.

CRAZY SOLUTION

Indulge in that tradition of the rattling newlywed getaway car. Tie a can or a shoe to the rear bumper of the nearby car with a rope or a cord. The car doesn't need to actually drive off for this gesture to register in the level.

When out in the wilderness, always stick together. This boy was separated from his father and is now lost. If Maxwell can return the boy to his father on the other side of the cave, he wins a Starite. However, there is some trouble in the cave. Bats flutter near the ceiling and will attack as Maxwell tries to lead the boy to safety.

First, add a sun to the level to illuminate Maxwell's surroundings. (In later runs through the level, you can also hand Maxwell a glowstick, although it is not as powerful as a sun.) A bird of prey, such as an owl or a hawk, will immediately attack the bats if summoned. But the bats are not the only problem. There is a hole in the ground that must be flown over. Tether the boy to Maxwell with a cord or some handcuffs and then fly him over the chasm.

As soon as the father lays eyes on his boy, he offers Maxwell the Starite.

CRAZY SOLUTION

The cave is dark, making it tough to see. You can use the sun to shed a little light on things, but that only works once. Use fire to illuminate the level.

However, fire freaks the sphinx and the pegasus you might use to cross the chasm. Here's a crazy tip: Write in a fire or a torch, but do not place it in the level. Leave it "in" the ground. You still get the benefit of the fire's light, but the sphinx can fly by it without getting spooked.

OUTER WILD 6-5

Difficulty: 2	Par: 3	Possible Words:

- **Drawbridge**
- **Iceberg**
- **Hay**
- **Clover**
- **Girder**
- **Glue**
-
-
-

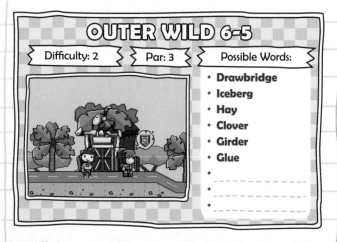

A giraffe has escaped the zoo and is wandering around the downtown area. The zookeeper cannot leave the park to fetch it, so she asks Maxwell to help bring the giraffe back. One problem, though: The road collapsed just as the giraffe walked by, so now the giraffe is trapped on the other side of a sinkhole.

Maxwell can create a bridge for the giraffe out of two girders or boards and some glue. The drawbridge or an iceberg is also wide enough to stretch across the gap. Now, just ride the giraffe home or lead it there with some clover or veggies.

CRAZY SOLUTION

Ever seen a flying giraffe? No? Well, today is your lucky day, then. Wing Maxwell and then place him on top of his long-necked steed. Fly the giraffe over the gap in the street and right down next to the zookeeper to earn a Starite.

OUTER WILD 6-6

Difficulty: 3	Par: 5	Possible Words:

- **Wall**
- **House**
- **Shack**
- **Rope**
- **Vine**
- **Bungee cord**
- **Sphinx**
- **Winged shoes**
- **Pterodactyl**
-
-
-

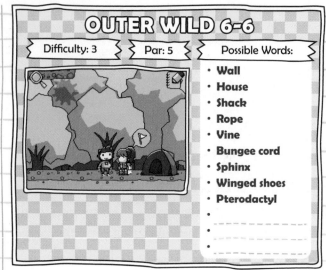

Nobody likes to go to the bathroom while camping. It's a necessary evil, though. The camper in this level was at least smart enough to pick a campsite near an outhouse. (No digging holes for her.) However, since setting up camp, a lion has moved in and now stands between her and sweet relief. Help her get to the outhouse without any bite marks, and she'll award you a Starite.

You must prevent the lion from storming the outhouse as you escort the camper. A basic wall between the lion and the outhouse works. You can also tie the lion to a heavy object, such as a house or a shack, to prevent it from lunging at the camper as she approaches the outhouse. Once the lion is tethered, fly over it with a pair of winged shoes or a jetpack to reach the outhouse.

NOTE

You cannot just write down another outhouse and place it next to the camper's tent.

There is also a monkey in this level that will harass the pair as well as steal any objects in Maxwell's hands. Feed the monkey a banana to make friends with it. The monkey will still follow you, but it will not slap or steal.

CRAZY SOLUTION

What could be more romantic than a sphinx ride through the jungle? Summon two sphinxes—one for Maxwell and one for the camper. When you take flight, the other sphinx follows. Lead the camper's sphinx right to the outhouse to nab the Starite.

OUTER WILD 6-7

Difficulty: 2 | Par: 5 | Possible Words:

Possible Words:
- Steak
- Meat
- Turkey
- Pork chop
- Hamburger
- _____
- _____
- _____

The ranger has lost a precious diamond while on his hike. Now, a pack of wolves has closed in behind him and surrounded the diamond. The ranger hopes Maxwell will fetch the diamond and bring it back. If he can, he'll trade one sparkly item for another.

It is imperative that you do not hurt any of the endangered wolves in this level. Instead, you must find a way around them. Create some meat objects, such as steak or pork chops, and place them near the deep trench in the center of the level to trap the wolves. Just keep dropping and moving the meat around the edge of the trench to lure the wolves inside.

Maxwell can make the jump across the trench without dropping down to the wolves. Pick up the diamond and cart it back to get the Starite.

CRAZY SOLUTION

The soil under the Starite is soft enough for Maxwell to tunnel to the Starite. It takes a little longer than just dropping meat for the wolves, but this will earn you the Genius merit and boost your Ollar count. Summon a spade or a shovel, hand it to Maxwell, and dig all the way to the bottom of the level so you can slip under the trench without breaking through it.

OUTER WILD 6-8

Difficulty: 2 | Par: 5 | Possible Words:

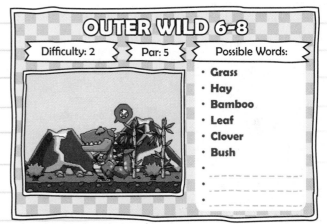

Possible Words:
- Grass
- Hay
- Bamboo
- Leaf
- Clover
- Bush
- _____
- _____
- _____

This level vaults Maxwell back a few epochs to the time of the dinosaurs. A mean T-Rex is hungry, but so are the three peaceful herbivores nearby: triceratops, charonosaurus, and brontosaurus. The level hint says you must feed all of the dinos to earn the Starite.

Give some grass or clover to the herbivores and place it right in front of each of them.

As soon as all three herbivores have been fed, approach the T-Rex. Using Maxwell as a lure, lead the T-Rex to the triceratops. The T-Rex gobbles up the triceratops, awarding you a Starite. Now, it does not necessarily have to be the triceratops every time. You can ride any of the peaceful dinosaurs close to the T-Rex and then lead the tyrant to its dinner.

CRAZY SOLUTION

The dinosaurs are vegetarian, so this is a good way to try some new objects you may not have thought about before and earn that New Object merit. Try vegetables, such as eggplant, and drop them in front of the dinosaurs. As long as it is a fruit or a vegetable, the dinosaur will merrily eat it and be satisfied.

CRAZY SOLUTION

The camper has intended to rough it a little during this trip, but he certainly will not turn down a brand-new RV. Write down an RV and drop it into the campsite. Now, you just need one more piece of gear. How about a compass?

OUTER WILD 6-9

Difficulty: 2	Par: 4	Possible Words:

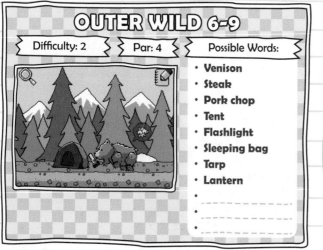

Possible Words:
- Venison
- Steak
- Pork chop
- Tent
- Flashlight
- Sleeping bag
- Tarp
- Lantern

OUTER WILD 6-10

Difficulty: 2	Par: 5	Possible Words:

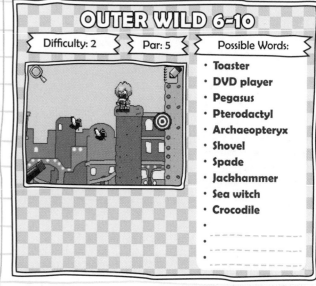

Possible Words:
- Toaster
- DVD player
- Pegasus
- Pterodactyl
- Archaeopteryx
- Shovel
- Spade
- Jackhammer
- Sea witch
- Crocodile

Oh no, a bear is tearing up this camper's equipment! Maxwell must help the camper by luring the bear away from the site and into a trench to the east. Then, the camper needs some new gear so he can still enjoy a night in the great outdoors. Fulfill these two desires, and the Starite is yours.

Use some type of meat, like steak or venison, to lure the bear to the right. Keep dropping the meat a little closer to the trench, but always pick it up just before the bear starts snacking.

Once the bear is busily tearing his dinner apart with those big ol' bear-sized incisors, start writing down new camping gear, such as a tent, a sleeping bag, a flashlight, and a tarp.

Welcome to the circus, Maxwell. The next act is a crowd favorite, the human cannonball. However, the target has been placed behind a tall pillar of soil, and several flies are in the path of the cannonballer. You must clear the area of these nuisances so the human cannonball can strike the target and release the Starite.

The first thing you must get rid of are the two flies buzzing near the clown on the soil column. Shoot the flies with a gun, swat them with a flyswatter, or use an animal, such as the pterodactyl, that is happy to nibble on the flies. When the flies are gone, you can concentrate on that pillar.

Give Maxwell a pickaxe or a shovel and tear through the pillar to make a path for the cannonballer.

CAUTION

There is a crocodile in the water just to the left of the pillar, so take it out if you are using a flying object that cannot maintain a steady altitude.

The soldier will instinctively follow Maxwell into battle. However, he only has a gun, not a magical stylus like you. You must keep him out of harm's way by tethering him to a tree on the beach.

Once things have been prepped, return to the cannon and interact with it. The daredevil erupts from the cannon and strikes the target.

One of the supply crates is in the water, but there are two piranha that will attack if you try to approach it. You cannot drop electronics into the water, or else they will damage the crate. Drop a creature or a monster into the water instead, such as a crocodile. The croc makes short work of the piranha but can then be dropped on the soldiers, too.

CRAZY SOLUTION

Use a single object to clear this entire level of trouble for the human cannonball: a howitzer. You must move the gun back and forth on the platform next to the cannon, but if you arc the first two shots just right, you can eliminate the flies. Then move it forward and dismantle the column to clear a flight path.

The soldiers cannot be reasoned with—you must employ violence. Shoot the soldiers as they near the edge of their base and set off some explosives (bomb, dynamite) to catch them in the blast.

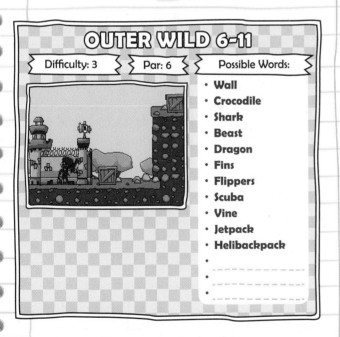

When the soldiers are down, collect the supply items from inside the two crates: map and toilet paper. You need to fly in order to fetch the toilet paper from the crate on the ledge, so summon some wings or a jetpack.

CRAZY SOLUTION

You've deployed dragons and T-Rexes to do your dirty work already, so call upon another fierce refugee from the Cretaceous period: the velociraptor. This predator is both fast and deadly, so you can use it on the piranha and the soldiers without any worry of it being erased. (Not to be confused with the philosoraptor, by the way...)

An allied supply drop has gone horribly wrong, and the needed supplies are now behind enemy lines. Maxwell must daringly slip into hostile territory and fetch the three supply items that are inside drop crates. When Maxwell has the items, he must bring them back to the soldier on the nearby beach (where Maxwell starts the level) to earn the Starite. This will not be easy. The enemy base is guarded by two soldiers who are crack shots.

OUTER WILD 6-11

Difficulty: 3   Par: 6   Possible Words:

- Wall
- Crocodile
- Shark
- Beast
- Dragon
- Fins
- Flippers
- Scuba
- Vine
- Jetpack
- Helibackpack

ACTION LEVELS

OUTER WILD 6-1

Difficulty: 2 | Par: 3 | Possible Words:

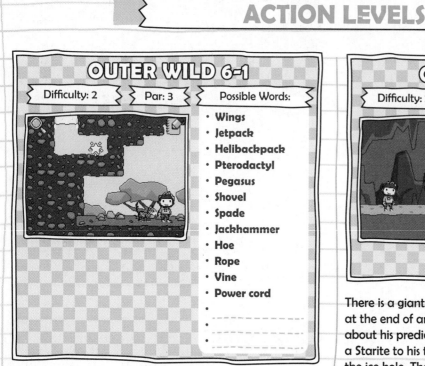

- **Wings**
- **Jetpack**
- **Helibackpack**
- **Pterodactyl**
- **Pegasus**
- **Shovel**
- **Spade**
- **Jackhammer**
- **Hoe**
- **Rope**
- **Vine**
- **Power cord**
- ⋯
- ⋯
- ⋯

OUTER WILD 6-2

Difficulty: 2 | Par: 3 | Possible Words:

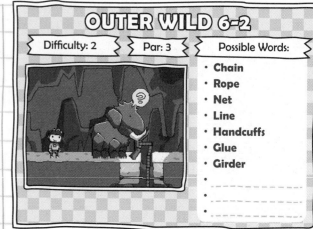

- **Chain**
- **Rope**
- **Net**
- **Line**
- **Handcuffs**
- **Glue**
- **Girder**
- ⋯
- ⋯
- ⋯

A tiger cub has been separated from its family and is stuck in a scary cave. Fortunately, Maxwell is on the scene to set things right. Maxwell just needs to get the cub to the family directly above him, but that means getting around a jackal in the cave first. Not only can no harm come to the cub, but none of the adult tigers can be injured either.

The tiger cub is small enough that you can just pick it up. You do not need to tether it to Maxwell or a flying object (pegasus, sphinx) to carry it home.

Carry the tiger cub straight to the family. If you linger near the edge, one the tigers might walk off. If the jackal is still alive, it will attack the tiger.

CRAZY SOLUTION

Punish the jackal for even thinking about hurting a harmless tiger cub. Conjure up a fierce mythological monster, such as a behemoth, and set it loose on the jackal. Just make sure to delete the behemoth before flying the tiger cub to its family.

There is a giant woolly mammoth in this level, standing at the end of an ice hole. The mammoth seems confused about his predicament—probably because somebody tied a Starite to his trunk. The Starite is too big to fit through the ice hole. There is also a tripwire near the ice hole that severs the rope holding up the Starite if the Starite crosses it. Maxwell must figure out a way to keep the Starite from falling into the abyss below the mammoth while staying within par.

You must do something to keep the Starite from falling when the original rope is cut. No matter what, that tripwire will be triggered, either by Maxwell going into the hole to fetch the Starite or by the mammoth trying to pull it out. There are two pieces of metal in the hole that can be used as anchors. Glue a girder to one of the pieces of metal or stretch a rope across the hole. This will create a safety net for the Starite.

📝 NOTE

The ice hole is too narrow for you to lower another rope down. You must work from within the hole itself.

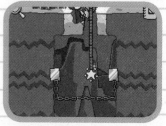

After you have created something to catch the Starite (two nets work well, too), you can either ride the mammoth and pull the Starite up, thus severing the rope, or burrow through the ice with a digging utensil and fall down on the Starite. As long as Maxwell grabs the Starite, it doesn't matter if he falls out of the screen.

CRAZY SOLUTION

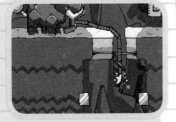

Use the tripwire itself as an anchor for grabbing the Starite. Stretch a bungee cord from the Starite to the tripwire. Attach the cord and then ride the mammoth to the right to cut the rope. Now Maxwell can burrow into the hole and grab the Starite.

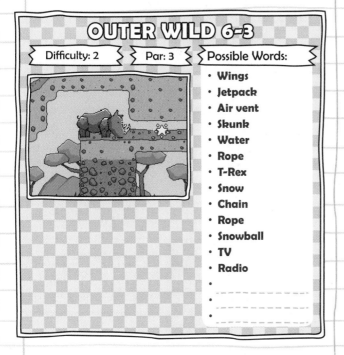

OUTER WILD 6-3

Difficulty: 2	Par: 3	Possible Words:

- **Wings**
- **Jetpack**
- **Air vent**
- **Skunk**
- **Water**
- **Rope**
- **T-Rex**
- **Snow**
- **Chain**
- **Rope**
- **Snowball**
- **TV**
- **Radio**
-
-
-

This level is a regular wildlife animal park. Rhinos, lionesses, and crocodiles—oh my! The Starite is right in the thick of the animals, too. There are two ways to get at the Starite. The first is to go over the small Starite chamber and drop down on the right side of the level. However, the lioness and a fire are along this route. The other method is to burrow through the loose soil to the left and come at the Starite from below. This way leads through shallow water, but it is inhabited by two crocodiles.

An air vent is a useful tool for moving both the animals and the fire. Blow the fire at the lioness to wound it and then blast it right back the other way to finish off the lioness. The air vent can also be used to push the Starite out of the tiny chamber next to the rhino and down onto the platform to the right.

TIP

If you try the lower route, be sure to drop an electronics object into the water to neutralize the two crocodiles.

If you cannot push the Starite out of the hole due to already using the air vent or fan, attach a rope (or chain) to the Starite. The weight of the rope slowly pulls the Starite out. From the platform to the right, wait until the rope or chain is low enough and then grab it. This will bump you right up to par, but it is effective for fishing the Starite out of its tiny nook.

CRAZY SOLUTION

You've used a lot of creatures and monsters to eliminate threats thus far. Time to reach deep into your bag of tricks and summon a new weapon-like object. Try out a vampire. Sure, it's the middle of the day, but this bloodsucker could care less about the position of the sun when it is about to slake its thirst on the veins of a crocodile or a lioness.

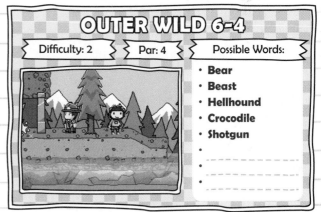

OUTER WILD 6-4

Difficulty: 2	Par: 4	Possible Words:

- **Bear**
- **Beast**
- **Hellhound**
- **Crocodile**
- **Shotgun**
-
-
-

No ranger likes a day like today. There are confirmed reports of three rabid animals in the park. Sadly, these animals must be put down for the safety of guests as well as other wildlife. It is up to you to carry out this grim deed with some form of killing object, such as a monster or a firearm.

However, there are more than three animals in the level, so which are rabid? After all, if you eliminate a healthy animal, the door next to the ranger that protects the Starite will not rise. Here are three rabid animals: the deer all the way to the right, the right-most fish in the water, and the eagle at the top of the level.

Drop a bear on the deer to eliminate it. The bear is a great animal to use because it can swim, too, making it ideal for removing the rabid fish in the waters below.

You can opt to handle this sad chore yourself by equipping Maxwell with wings and a weapon. A gun will take out the rabid animals, as will a sword.

CRAZY SOLUTION

As with Action Level 6-3, levels that require destruction are a good place to try out new objects that you haven't used before when setting

up contraptions or whatnot. Conjure up a devil or a demon here. The devil has no qualms about putting down these animals.

OUTER WILD 6-5

| Difficulty: 2 | Par: 7 | Possible Words: |

Possible Words:
- **Owl**
- **Snow owl**
- **Barn owl**
- **Hawk**
- **Sphinx**
- **Match**
- **Bomb**
- **Fire**
- **Chisel**
- **Ice pick**
- **Pickaxe**
- **Candle**

The Starite in this level is locked away, but not behind a door. The Starite is guarded by two frozen foes: a Yeti and a troglodyte. Both of them are a little cranky after their icy slumber, so be ready to take each of them on with a

weapon and an aggressive creature. But these monsters are not your only obstacles on the way to the prize. There are bats in the ice cave leading up to the frozen monsters. And the ground in front of the monsters is shaky at best. If you land too hard on it, it will shatter. That is a real problem after the first drop off because there is nothing beneath it. The second panel of crumbling ice is at least over water.

Use an owl or other bird of prey (snow owl, hawk) to get rid of the bats. You only need one owl. Just move it from bat to bat until the cave is cleared.

After flying down (remember, do not drop straight down to the lower level, or you will break the cracked ice), you must deal with the frozen monsters. The sphinx is a great solution because not only will its claws break open the ice, but it will also attack—and eliminate—the monsters.

If the troglodyte or Yeti gets a hit in on the sphinx, you can no longer fly it. Then, you need a weapon to deal with the recently thawed monster. Try a sword, a shovel, or an ice pick.

You can also kill two birds with one stone: Use explosives, such as bombs and dynamite, to eliminate the frozen monsters before venturing even an inch into the cave. Place dynamite right between the two

blocks and then set it off with a match or a lighter. The explosion will shatter the ice and eliminate the threats. Now you just need to deal with the owls and the precarious ground to capture the Starite.

CRAZY SOLUTION

How about a little sibling rivalry to get rid of the Yeti? Summon Bigfoot as soon as the ice is broken around the Yeti and turn it loose. If Bigfoot can get in the first hit, the Yeti will crumple to the ground. Bigfoot can also take care of the troglodyte.

You must place some type of bed on the vent so when the cow hits it, it can catch some shut-eye. This releases the Starite from the same pipe as the cows. Conjure up a bed and place it on the vent. As soon as the cow drops off the belt and touches it, the Starite appears. Now Maxwell just needs to fly up and capture it. Give him a magic broomstick or a jetpack to collect the Starite.

CRAZY SOLUTION

Everybody loves a quick nap, even ol' Bessie here. Jot down a sofa or a couch and lay it on the extinguished vent so she can catch a few Zzzs.

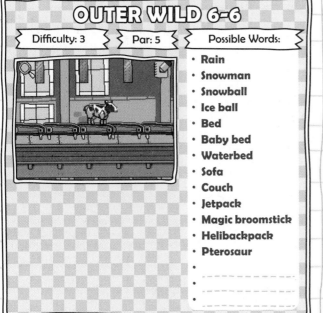

OUTER WILD 6-6

Difficulty: 3 | Par: 5 | Possible Words:

- Rain
- Snowman
- Snowball
- Ice ball
- Bed
- Baby bed
- Waterbed
- Sofa
- Couch
- Jetpack
- Magic broomstick
- Helibackpack
- Pterosaur
-
-
-

OUTER WILD 6-7

Difficulty: 2 | Par: 4 | Possible Words:

- Dragon
- Gun
- Magic carpet
- Sphinx
- Jetpack
- Pterodactyl
- Rope
- Chain
-
-
-

Welcome to a cattle-processing plant. There is a long conveyor belt that delivers cows to a fire vent. When a cow hits the vent, it is instantly turned into hamburger. There is no penalty for letting a cow be processed, but that will not release the Starite. The Starite is released when one of the cows is actually saved from burger-ization and given the nap it so deserves.

A few seconds after the level begins, a single cow is released from a pipe at the far end of the conveyor belt. This gives you plenty of time to make all the necessary preparations.

First, you must extinguish the fire vent. Rain works, as does ice. Use an ice ball, an ice block, or a snowman to put out the flames. Then, ditch it to clear the way for the next object.

High above this level, a pterodactyl flies with the Starite held firmly in its talons. Maxwell must get that pterodactyl to drop the Starite. The Starite can survive a long fall onto solid ground, but the huge lava spout near Maxwell's starting position will destroy the Starite if it lands in the flames. Maxwell could fly up and wrench the Starite from the pterodactyl's clutches, but a pair of phoenixes will attack if Maxwell enters their airspace.

The phoenixes can be shot down with guns or destroyed with a fierce creature, such as a dragon.

The pterodactyl at the top of the level will drop the Starite if it is significantly threatened. You can place a dragon or any other fierce creature in the pterodactyl's path as it flutters over the rock outcropping on the right side of the screen. Attacking the pterodactyl here is actually useful because it drops the Starite right onto the rocks without any risk of it hitting the fire below.

Alternatively, you can extinguish the lava spout and then give the pterodactyl something like a rope or a chain. The pterodactyl dips when the extra weight is added and drops the Starite. If the lava spout is out, you can just walk over and pick up the Starite.

CRAZY SOLUTION

If you know your mythology, then you know that the phoenix is a bird that self-immolates and is then reborn from its own ashes. Use this to your advantage. Fly up to the phoenixes to get their attention. When they give chase, lead them to the lava spout. They quickly lose their interest in you and hover around the lava spout like moths to a flame. Now you can concentrate on the pterodactyl.

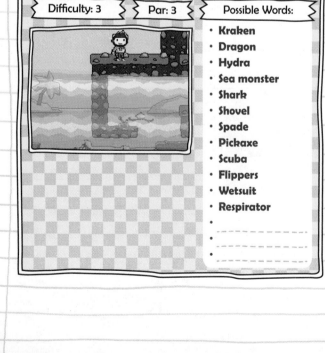

OUTER WILD 6-8

Difficulty: 3	Par: 3	Possible Words:

- **Kraken**
- **Dragon**
- **Hydra**
- **Sea monster**
- **Shark**
- **Shovel**
- **Spade**
- **Pickaxe**
- **Scuba**
- **Flippers**
- **Wetsuit**
- **Respirator**
- ⋯⋯⋯⋯⋯
- ⋯⋯⋯⋯⋯
- ⋯⋯⋯⋯⋯

The Starite in this level is just on the other side of the water. Oh, that water is patrolled by a sea serpent, shark, shocking jellyfish, and spiky blowfish—but Maxwell can handle all that, right? All he needs for you to do is clear a path to the red switch just below his starting position so he can open a route to the green switch, which is guarded by a hammerhead at the very bottom of the lake. Once that green switch is thrown, a door leading to the surface (and the Starite) is opened. But that red switch locked up the Starite...what to do?

The first thing you need to do is get rid of the jellyfish and blowfish. Any large, aggressive sea creature will do in this situation. The kraken has a tough time fitting, but it clears out everything. A dragon or a sea witch works, too. You must eliminate the blowfish under the nearby red door because they will float toward Maxwell as you steer toward the red switch needed to open the way deeper into the lake.

 CAUTION

Remember, after an animal eats three times, it must snooze. Because you have a limited par in this level, you just have to wait for the animal to wake back up.

The sea serpent near the bottom of the lake is tough. You need a large creature, such as a dragon, to take it out. The sea serpent will occasionally win fights against sharks.

Maxwell can actually handle the hammerhead at the bottom of the lake guarding the green switch. Give Maxwell a shovel so he can dig through the dirt. Then, tap the hammerhead and choose to attack it with the shovel. If Maxwell strikes first and fast, the hammerhead goes belly up, and Maxwell can easily throw the switch.

Now that the green door to the top of the water is open, Maxwell has two ways he can head up for the Starite. The catch, though, is the shark patrolling the waters near the surface. With the green door open, swim up and get the shark's attention. Then lead it down into the lake before ducking to the left and swimming up the middle of the level. Use the red switch again to reopen the door in front of the Starite and then jump out to claim the prize before the shark heads back up.

CRAZY SOLUTION

Did you ever have to read the Greek poet Homer in school? Homer's twin epics, "The Odyssey" and "The Iliad," are hugely entertaining—and in the case of this game, very helpful. Summon Charybdis, one of the sea monsters that attacked the hero Odysseus's ship, and use it to clear out almost the entire lake. The terrible creature doesn't blink as it chews up jellies, sharks, blowfish, and sea serpents.

OUTER WILD 6-9

Difficulty: 3	Par: 6	Possible Words:

- **Mongoose**
- **Devil**
- **Beast**
- **Cobra**
- **Match**
- **Lighter**
- **Candle**
- **Fireball**
- **Candle**
- **Jetpack**
- **Helibackpack**
- **Pegasus**
- **Winged shoes**
- ⋅ _____
- ⋅ _____
- ⋅ _____
- ⋅

Ah, the life of a rancher. Early mornings putting out hay and sun-soaked afternoons driving cattle around the pastures. But for Maxwell, his day on the ranch is complicated by needing to drive a cow and a bull from the ranch and into a series of caves to catch up with a rancher who has gotten a little ahead of himself. The cave is home to a snake, though, that would love to sink its fangs into some grade-A prime. You must deal with the snake before herding the cattle into the caves.

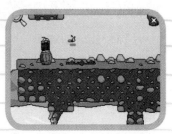

Take out the snake with a mongoose, a devil, a beast, or a cobra.

It turns out that the miners who dug these tunnels left behind some gear—some explosive gear. There are three small piles of gunpowder in the cave, located right next to a barrel and a bunch of

dynamite. You must do unto these explosives as you did to the snake—eliminate them. Drop a fire source, such as a match or a candle, onto the gunpowder to send the whole kit and caboodle up. Now the cave is completely safe for the cattle.

Now, you can either ride the cattle down into the caves one by one (a little fall will not hurt them), or you can lead them by flying in front of them with clover in your hand. A flying object like winged shoes lets you hover

over the edge of the tunnel and dangle the eats in front of the cattle. The cows eagerly pursue the tasty treat all the way to the rancher. The overjoyed rancher repays the favor with a Starite.

CRAZY SOLUTION

The snake at the bottom of the cave cannot be pacified, not even by a snake charmer. However, this particular snake charmer is not especially charming. It kills the snake!

OUTER WILD 6-10

Difficulty: 3	Par: 6	Possible Words:

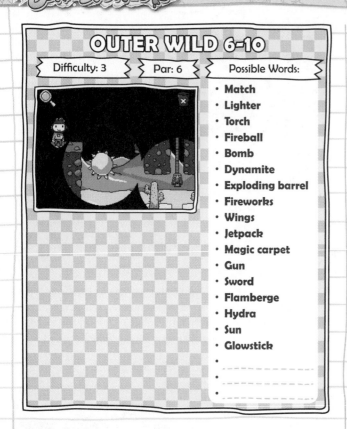

- **Match**
- **Lighter**
- **Torch**
- **Fireball**
- **Bomb**
- **Dynamite**
- **Exploding barrel**
- **Fireworks**
- **Wings**
- **Jetpack**
- **Magic carpet**
- **Gun**
- **Sword**
- **Flamberge**
- **Hydra**
- **Sun**
- **Glowstick**
- _____
- _____
- _____

This action level is bathed in darkness. Under the cover of night, many dangers lay hidden, such as angry vultures, pointy cacti, explosives, and even the fabled chupacabra. In your first trip through this level, use a sun so you can see everything you must deal with. It's a good way to scope out the trouble ahead for future attempts to grab the Starite.

The chupacabra near the fire vents to the east can be dealt with via explosives. Drop some dynamite or a bomb on the fire, and the blast drops the infamous "goat sucker."

CAUTION

The fire vents are easily put out with water or ice, but watch out for the red button on the floor between them. Stepping on it reignites the vents.

There are four vultures protecting the Starite in the upper-right corner of the level. They will attack as soon as you enter that section of the map. You must either take them out beforehand or enter the area with a weapon, such as a gun or a sword.

The lantern near the beginning of the level is hanging directly above some dynamite. Setting off this dynamite destroys the soil around it as well as some of the cacti below.

TIP

Before setting off the dynamite, use the match or torch to burn the cacti throughout the level. Not only will this eliminate obstacles, but it also creates multiple light sources.

The vultures are afraid of fire, so instead of shooting them with a gun or scratching at them with the claws of a sphinx, wield the flamberge. The fire on the blade not only makes them run, it also lights up the immediate area. Slash at the cowering vultures to clear the area and a path to the Starite.

CRAZY SOLUTION

The Starite is tough to reach without clearing out the vultures. Write in Death to send the vultures to their final resting places. The sphinx is also a great object because of its claws. But the sphinx is afraid of fire, so you cannot use it until you have eliminated the chupacabra and extinguished the fire vents with ice or snow.

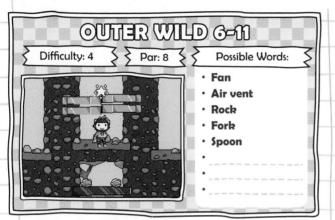

OUTER WILD 6-11

Difficulty: 4	Par: 8	Possible Words:

Possible Words:
- **Fan**
- **Air vent**
- **Rock**
- **Fork**
- **Spoon**
- _____
- _____
- _____

CRAZY SOLUTION

After using the fan and the air vent, how can you move the apples and the lettuce? Use the weight of small objects, such as forks and spoons, to nudge the produce left and right. The objects have just enough weight to push the produce as well as set off a button.

The Starite in this level is located directly above Maxwell, but it is locked behind two doors. There are no switches or buttons that open these doors. However, there is a row of buttons along the bottom of the level that open the green and red doors below Maxwell. Those doors prop up two apples and two heads of lettuce. You must feed these to the appropriate animals in the center of the level. The zebras want the apples, and the rhinos want the lettuce. You must properly divide the produce before dropping objects on the buttons and releasing the doors.

Use a fan or an air vent to push the lettuce to the left and the apples to the right. There is a hill just below the green door that will naturally divide the food for the animals, but the apples and lettuce must hit the ground just right for this tactic to work.

NOTE

You cannot just write down more apples and lettuce and feed them directly to the zebras and rhinos.

After pushing the produce, drop an object on two of each color of button. Start with red to drop the lettuce and then move on to green.

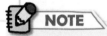

WORLD 7: STUNT PARK

PUZZLE LEVELS

STUNT PARK 7-1

Difficulty: 1 | Par: 5 | Possible Words:

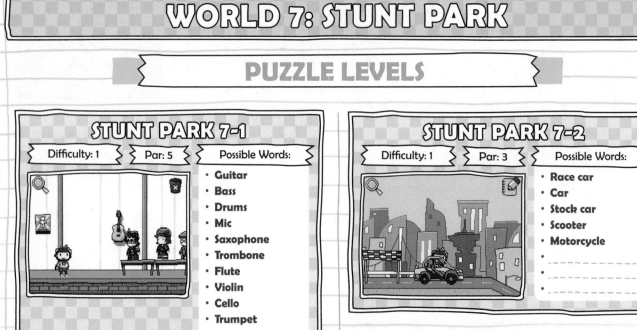

- Guitar
- Bass
- Drums
- Mic
- Saxophone
- Trombone
- Flute
- Violin
- Cello
- Trumpet
- ......
- ......
- ......

Maxwell arrives just in time for band practice. Four fellows stand on a stage. All that is missing are, well, instruments. Maxwell must come up with four instruments for the band. If he can turn them into a serious rock collective, they will award Maxwell a Starite. Jot down the obvious band instruments in your Notepad right off the bat to get the band started: guitar, bass, mic, drums. Once those are out of the way, start branching out into other types of musical instruments. Go for horns, such as the trumpet or a trombone. Or use some strings, such as a violin or a cello. Every four instruments you hand over result in a Starite.

CRAZY SOLUTION

Have fun thinking of instruments from around the world for this new band. Give them a fresh sound with a djembe, a congo, and a didgeridoo.

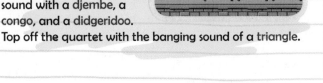

Top off the quartet with the banging sound of a triangle.

STUNT PARK 7-2

Difficulty: 1 | Par: 3 | Possible Words:

- Race car
- Car
- Stock car
- Scooter
- Motorcycle
- ......
- ......
- ......

This stunt track separates the drivers from the racers. The goal is to roar down a long ramp and launch a vehicle over two huge fire vents. As soon as the vehicle (and it has to be a ground-based vehicle, too—no planes or helicopters) clears the second fire vent, the Starite appears. Order a race car, a scooter, or a stock car for Maxwell. Place him in the driver's seat and then race down the ramp to arc over the fire and win the prize.

NOTE

Wheeled objects, such as bikes and roller skates, will not work. They do not get enough momentum by the bottom of the ramp to make it over the second fire vent.

When the Starite appears, just stop and let it fall right on top of Maxwell. Don't hop out of a car early and step right into the fire.

CRAZY SOLUTION

What goes better with a sweltering day at the stunt track than ice cream? Jot down an ice cream truck for Maxwell and race it down the ramp.

The truck is not the fastest vehicle you can create, but the momentum of rolling down the ramp gives it enough power to clear the second fire vent.

STUNT PARK 7-3

Difficulty: 2	Par: 4	Possible Words:

Possible Words:
- **Parachute**
- **Glider**
- **Hang glider**
- **Wings**
- **Torch**
- **Match**
- **Pterodactyl**
- **Pegasus**
- **UFO**
- **Magic carpet**
-
-
-

Can you fly, Maxwell? This level begins with Maxwell tethered to an airplane, high above the ground. To win the Starite, Maxwell must safely soar through a slalom course of flags on his way to terra firma. To accomplish this daring feat, you need to conjure up something that will slow Maxwell's descent enough so he may glide between the three sets of floating flags, such as a UFO.

NOTE

To disconnect from the plane holding Maxwell up at the start of the level, tap the helmet.

A parachute on Maxwell's back slows his fall. Now you can direct Maxwell's descent with the stylus.

If you use wings or a magic carpet to descend through the flags, you can actually fall through the first two. Just glide to the right as soon as Maxwell clears the first set of flags. However, to pass through the last set of flags, you must get back over to the left side of the level. Without slowing down, this is impossible. Because the wings and magic carpet only last for a short period before needing a recharge on solid ground, do not use them until you have passed through the second pair of flags. Then, tap above Maxwell to sail over to the left.

CRAZY SOLUTION

Give Maxwell a flying animal to ride through the slalom course. Since tapping the helmet would cause Maxwell to dismount, you must disconnect from the plane in some other way. Burn through the rope with a torch, a match, or a lighter while Maxwell sits on his airborne steed. Once the rope burns all the way through, you can fly right through the flags without any problems.

STUNT PARK 7-4

Difficulty: 2	Par: 3	Possible Words:

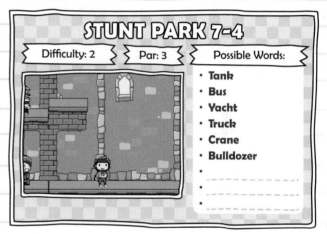

Possible Words:
- **Tank**
- **Bus**
- **Yacht**
- **Truck**
- **Crane**
- **Bulldozer**
-
-
-

Maxwell finds himself before a roaring crowd at the start of this level. What do these people want from him? That's when he sees the incoming giant. Stomping toward him, it becomes all too clear that this audience demands a show—a wrestling bout. To win, Maxwell must pin the giant. He's so much larger that any physical act of force will not cut it—and using a gun is totally out of the question.

To win the match, you must drop a heavy object on top of the giant. The object must also be large enough to knock the giant over. (The bigger they are, the harder they fall—and all that jazz.) Dropping a tank or a bus right on the giant's noggin rocks him back on his heels, making him pass out. Maxwell then wins the match.

CRAZY SOLUTION

Think of all of the different pieces of construction equipment you could drop on the giant, such as a dump truck or a steamroller. This is another great opportunity to try an unused object and earn that New Object merit.

CRAZY SOLUTION

You have par three to work with in this level, but the World Under Par merit is so tempting. So, try a flying animal, such as the archaeopteryx, and fly into the Starite to come in way under par.

STUNT PARK 7-5

Difficulty: 2	Par: 3	Possible Words:

Possible Words:
- Wings
- Jetpack
- Helibackpack
- Pegasus
- Pterodactyl
- ___
- ___
- ___

The Starite is not visible when this level begins. Maxwell must make it appear by throwing a switch. However, there is an entire line of switches that stretches across this level, and only one of them will make the Starite appear. Two of the switches even make the floor disappear. If Maxwell uses one of those switches while standing in the wrong place, he will fall into the abyss.

The fourth switch from the left (pictured here) makes the Starite appear.

Once the Starite is out, you need to actually throw one of the switches that makes floor panels disappear. Switches two and five (from the left) cause the panels to the left of them to disappear. Stand to the

right of them and then interact with them to flip the switch. Then use a flying object, such as wings or a jetpack, to fly down to the Starite.

STUNT PARK 7-6

Difficulty: 3	Par: 6	Possible Words:

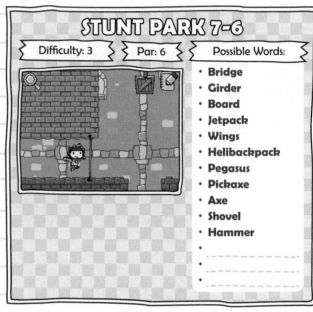

Possible Words:
- Bridge
- Girder
- Board
- Jetpack
- Wings
- Helibackpack
- Pegasus
- Pickaxe
- Axe
- Shovel
- Hammer
- ___
- ___
- ___

This level looks like trouble from the get-go. There are several crates hanging from the ceiling, each dangling by a rope over a lava pit. If Maxwell crosses the tripwire in front of him, all of the ropes break, and the crates drop into the lava. The Starite is in one of those crates, though, so you must write down some sort of plug for the lava pit below the correct crate. The Starite is in the fourth crate from the left.

You need to bridge the gap over the lava pit with something sturdy enough to hold the crate as it crashes down. An actual bridge works because it is just wide enough to span the gap. A tank is also wide enough.

Once the crate has been caught, you must fly out and break it open. Use an axe, a shovel, or a hammer to release the prize.

CRAZY SOLUTION

Catch that Starite in style. Summon a limo and stretch it across the gap. The roof is flat enough that the crate will not roll off of it into the lava. That's no reason to dawdle, though. Be ready to fly as soon as the crates drop by pre-equipping Maxwell with some wings and a sword.

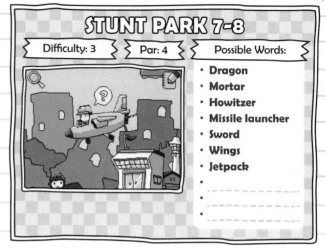

STUNT PARK 7-8

Difficulty: 3	Par: 4	Possible Words:

- **Dragon**
- **Mortar**
- **Howitzer**
- **Missile launcher**
- **Sword**
- **Wings**
- **Jetpack**
- _____
- _____
- _____

STUNT PARK 7-7

Difficulty: 3	Par: 4	Possible Words:

- **Hydra**
- **Dragon**
- **Scylla**
- **T-Rex**
- **Behemoth**
- _____
- _____

There is an out-of-control truck racing down a stretch of unfinished highway. Maxwell must stop the driver before he races right into the water at the abrupt end of the road. Just dropping something heavy in the path of the truck will not get the Starite, though. You must shock the driver into stopping the truck before he steers into the drink.

Maxwell has been charged with protecting an allied jet plane that is flying over a base. There are two enemy soldiers coming from the west, each armed with high-powered guns. A few shots from those guns will bring down the allied plane. Maxwell must stop those two soldiers from unloading their weapons on the place by attacking the enemy as soon as the level begins.

Drop a huge monster in the path of the speeding truck. A massive creature, such as a hydra or a behemoth, shocks the driver into slamming on the brakes. Something smaller does not necessarily work, so be sure to conjure up a major-league freak-out.

The enemy soldiers will turn those weapons on you if you get too close, so attacking from a distance is essential. Launching a volley from a mortar or a howitzer works, but make sure the plane is not in the arcing path of the shell. Alternatively, you can also drop a fierce creature, such as a dragon, on the soldiers. A giant monster easily overwhelms the soldiers and can withstand their gunfire.

CRAZY SOLUTION

This is a good chance to try out words you may not have used up to now. Think of monsters from local legends. The Mothman, spotted in West Virginia back in 1966, sufficiently spooks the driver into stopping. Release the Mothman right in front of the truck to earn the Starite.

CRAZY SOLUTION

Maxwell can attack the soldiers directly and solve the level with a single object: a dagger or a sword. Just wait until the plane is overhead. The enemy soldiers look up. That's when you need to strike. Rush it and run those soldiers through as their eyes are skyward.

STUNT PARK 7-9

Difficulty: 3	Par: 4	Possible Words:

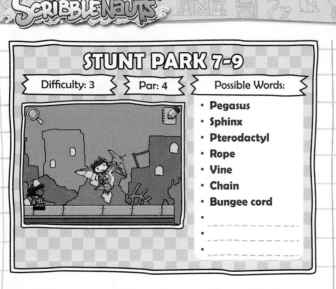

- Pegasus
- Sphinx
- Pterodactyl
- Rope
- Vine
- Chain
- Bungee cord
-
-
-

Three folks are stranded in a storm on pillars and columns. The firefighters and rescue workers do not have the means to travel to the folks who need help, though. So, it is up to Maxwell to fly out to the victims and bring them back to the rescue workers. There are storm clouds between each pillar that dump rain. That means Maxwell cannot use an electric flight device, such as a jetpack or a helibackpack. If those objects get a single drop of rain on them, they short out and drop Maxwell out of the sky.

Use an object that is not affected by weather. Place Maxwell on a flying creature, such as a sphinx, a pegasus, or a pterodactyl. None of these is bothered by rain at all. Attach a rope, a vine, or a cord to the person who needs help and then cart that person back to the rescue workers.

CAUTION

Although flying creatures are not affected by rain, duck out of the way of lightning strikes.

CRAZY SOLUTION

Try a flying vehicle, such as a UFO, to get through the storms. The UFO actually has a tractor beam on the bottom of it. Lower the UFO over the victim. He or she is pulled up toward the UFO. You can try to inch the UFO back to the rescue workers—but you'd better be slow about it. Sharp movements will drop the rescued person. If you need a little help, go ahead and write in a vine or a bungee cord.

STUNT PARK 7-10

Difficulty: 3	Par: 7	Possible Words:

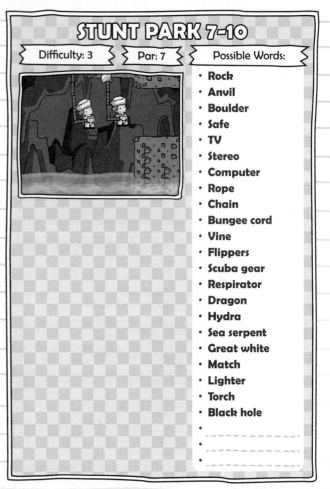

- Rock
- Anvil
- Boulder
- Safe
- TV
- Stereo
- Computer
- Rope
- Chain
- Bungee cord
- Vine
- Flippers
- Scuba gear
- Respirator
- Dragon
- Hydra
- Sea serpent
- Great white
- Match
- Lighter
- Torch
- Black hole
-
-
-

Two allied sailors have been strung up on ropes at the eastern edge of this level. Maxwell must save these sailors and bring them back to the left side of the level in order to earn the Starite. However, between here and there is a lot of trouble. Three sea mines, a submarine, a battleship, and a shark are all in the water. Before conjuring up some scuba gear or flippers for Maxwell so he can swim deep and get under a rock that blocks a surface path, all of these hazards must be addressed. And by addressed, we mean destroyed.

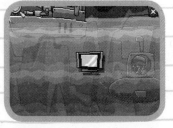

Electronics have helped you get rid of angry sea creatures, but you can also use them to attack ships and submarines. Place a large electronic object, such as a TV, between the enemy ship and the sub. The shock jolts the soldiers as well as the vehicles and removes them from the area. If desired, you can also use an electronic object on the shark directly below the sailors.

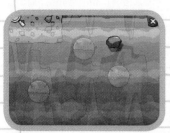

All you need to do to remove the sea mines is to touch them with an object. Drop a rock or another heavy object (safe, boulder) on the mines. The leftmost mine is far enough away that it will not blow up with the other two. It requires its own object. You must destroy all three. You cannot squeeze a sailor past that leftmost sea mine.

Cut down the sailors by burning the ropes with a match or a fireball.

If the sailor has some rope left on him, you can use it to drag the sailor to safety on the far left side of the level. If there is no rope, you must create some.

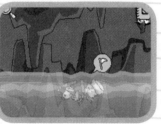

Don't forget to get rid of that shark! A dragon or a hydra works as well as a TV.

CRAZY SOLUTION

There remain few objects more powerful than the black hole. Don't be afraid to use it. The black hole is powerful enough to pull in the submarine, ship, and sea mines. Be wary of using it near the shark, though. The black hole is powerful enough to swallow the sailors.

STUNT PARK 7-11

Difficulty: 3	Par: 4	Possible Words:

Possible Words:
- **Dragon**
- **Hydra**
- **T-Rex**
- **Velociraptor**
- **Jenny Greenteeth**
- **Mothman**
- **Bigfoot**
-
-
-

For Maxwell to earn this Starite, he must take down three aggressive creatures. But he doesn't need to do it himself. He needs you to write down monsters that can handle these three creatures: a troglodyte, a griffin, and a behemoth. Each creature is tougher than the previous contender, so you'd better engage with a tough monster right up front—or a monster army that gets successively meaner as the threats grow in size.

The troglodyte is the lesser worry. It's the griffin that will draw first blood on whatever monster you put into play. A huge monster, such as a dragon or a hydra, can easily overpower the griffin and conserve health for the behemoth battle. That's when you can expect to really see some blows land on your big monster.

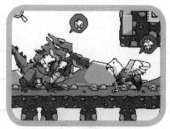

If you go the midsize-monster route, a hellhound or a Jenny Greenteeth (another wonderful regional legend like the Mothman) can at least take down the troglodyte and the griffin.

CRAZY SOLUTION

You know what would really inflict massive damage on that behemoth? A giant enemy crab. Jot down this Internet meme and drop it into the battle. Those huge pincers rip and tear through all of the monsters.

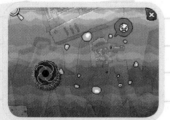

ACTION LEVELS

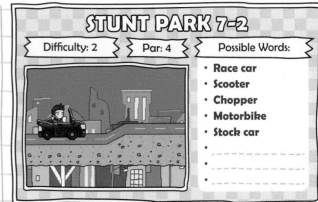

STUNT PARK 7-1

Difficulty: 2	Par: 4	Possible Words:

- **Wings**
- **Jetpack**
- **Helibackpack**
- **Pegasus**
- _____
- _____
- _____

The Starite is just within reach at the beginning of this action level. Easy peasy, right? However, as soon as Maxwell takes a step toward the Starite, it is pulled up into the ceiling. Maxwell needs to chase the Starite down as it is yanked out of reach. This requires a flying object, such as a jetpack or a pegasus.

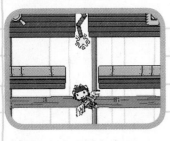

The Starite is pulled into the ceiling, but not entirely out of reach. Just fly up and grab it.

CRAZY SOLUTION

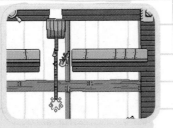

Instead of chasing the Starite, let it come to you. Burn the rope that yanks the Starite away with a torch, a lighter, or a match. The rope burns after a few moments and drops the Starite to the bottom of the room. Just pick it up to end the level in success.

STUNT PARK 7-2

Difficulty: 2	Par: 4	Possible Words:

- **Race car**
- **Scooter**
- **Chopper**
- **Motorbike**
- **Stock car**
- _____
- _____

Vroom, vroom, Maxwell. The little hero must race three of the game's developers across the level. Each of the developers is behind the wheel of a nice ride, so in order to reach the finish line on the right side of the screen, Maxwell needs some fast wheels, too. If Maxwell reaches the finish line first, the Starite appears in his lane of the track.

Conjure up a fast car for Maxwell, such as a race car or a stock car.

The track is not even. There are hills and gaps Maxwell must get across to reach the finish line, and these can actually trip him up. In a fast ride, such as the stock car, Maxwell can actually get going too fast and start to flip backwards after a ramp. So, keep up the pace, but mind your speed as you go off the hills and ramps.

CRAZY SOLUTION

Avoid the hills and ramps completely by ripping through the level in a spaceship. This vehicle leaves all of the developer cars in the dust with seconds to spare.

STUNT PARK 7-3

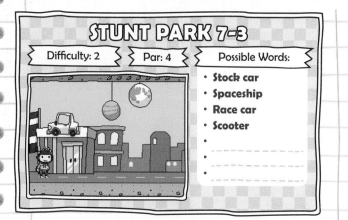

Difficulty: 2	Par: 4	Possible Words:

Possible Words:
- **Stock car**
- **Spaceship**
- **Race car**
- **Scooter**
- _____
- _____
- _____

The Starite is at the very end of the track in this level. It looks easy to pick up; just jot down a car and drive over to it, right? Not so fast, speedster. There are several pipes over the track that drop exploding barrels from the ceiling. Once the barrels start falling, they do not stop—so neither can Maxwell.

You truly cannot stop when you set off the barrels, so as soon as Maxwell is motoring, do not let the stylus off the right side of the screen until the Starite is in your grasp.

CRAZY SOLUTION

If you feel daring, try this level with a flying creature. Place Maxwell on a fast-moving pterodactyl. Duck into the gaps between the barrel-dropping pipes.

STUNT PARK 7-4

Difficulty: 3	Par: 3	Possible Words:

Possible Words:
- **Glider**
- **Parachute**
- **Pegasus**
- **Pterodactyl**
- _____
- _____
- _____

Ceiling Cat sees all. (*All*—so be good.) The omnipotent feline watches over a Starite located at the bottom of the level. Maxwell starts things on top of a rock outcropping,

overlooking a huge empty space. The Starite is there, though. It's just resting on a small column in the middle of a sea of lava at the very bottom. And if that wasn't dangerous enough for Maxwell, there are several spiked balls floating on top of the lava.

Maxwell must jump down to the Starite, but as in the flag slalom, he needs to slow his descent in order to safely grab the Starite. A parachute works well, as does a pegasus or a pterodactyl. Fly down to grab the Starite, but watch out for the spiked balls and lava.

CRAZY SOLUTION

Strap Maxwell into a glider. The glider slowly drifts down into view. Keep ahead of Maxwell by scrolling the screen down so you can track his position in relation to the Starite. Alternatively, you can also fly down with a helicopter and grab the Starite with a rope. Pull it back up to the rock outcropping at the top of the level.

STUNT PARK 7-5

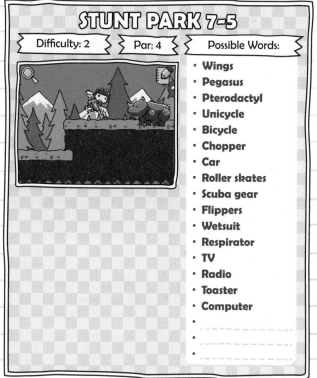

Difficulty: 2	Par: 4	Possible Words:

Possible Words:
- **Wings**
- **Pegasus**
- **Pterodactyl**
- **Unicycle**
- **Bicycle**
- **Chopper**
- **Car**
- **Roller skates**
- **Scuba gear**
- **Flippers**
- **Wetsuit**
- **Respirator**
- **TV**
- **Radio**
- **Toaster**
- **Computer**
- _____
- _____
- _____

Maxwell must perform in a makeshift triathlon in order to collect the Starite in this action level. Time is of the essence here. The Starite is slowly dropping down the right side of the level. If Maxwell does not reach the bottom of the level in time, it is lost. Here is how the triathlon works: Maxwell needs to avoid a bear that is on land, drive through a street scene, and swim underwater. You will need to use at least three objects to reach the Starite.

First, you need something that flies so you can make it over a bear as well as fly up a vertical shaft. There is a storm cloud at the top of the shaft that will short out any mechanical flight object, so look into something such as wings or a pegasus.

CAUTION

The bear is a fighter, so if you ride a sphinx or a pegasus, keep out of the way of the beast. If it successfully strikes the flying creature, you can no longer use the creature, and you must write in a new one.

At the end of the first stretch of the track, Maxwell runs into a wall. That wall will not move unless you give Maxwell something with wheels. Whether you choose a unicycle, a bike, or even roller skates, you must place them on Maxwell for the door to open. The door will not budge if you just place the wheeled object in the level.

Maxwell must jump over a cop car to finish the highway leg of the triathlon.

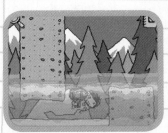

There is a shark in the water on the third leg of the event. You cannot slip past it. You need to eliminate the shark before getting too far into the water. Drop some electronics on the shark and then use water gear, such as scuba gear or a snorkel, to rush for the end of the level and claim the Starite.

CRAZY SOLUTION

You can actually use the pegasus for the majority of the level. Although you do need wheels to open the door, you can ditch them as soon as the door opens and give the pegasus back to Maxwell so he can fly over the cop car in the highway segment.

STUNT PARK 7-6

Difficulty: 3	Par: 7	Possible Words:

- **Winged shoes**
- **Jetpack**
- **Helibackpack**
- **Fan**
- **Air vent**
- **Sword**
- **Shotgun**
- **Gun**
- **Kitten**
- **Puppy**
- **Bear**
- **Lion**
- ⋯⋯⋯⋯⋯
- ⋯⋯⋯⋯⋯
- ⋯⋯⋯⋯⋯

A villain has made off with the Starite and is at his hideaway in a small chamber in the lower-right corner of the level. Some enemy soldiers are on his trail, but they don't know necessarily whodunnit, so they will try to attack Maxwell if they spot him, too.

And to give things even more urgency, a group of innocent civilians is trapped on a steel slab that is slowly moving to the right. When the slab has completely retracted into the wall, the innocents will be dropped into a lava pit. Maxwell must get to the Starite and stop the villain before the civilians perish.

You must get rid of those soldiers right away. A fan or an air vent blows them off their perches and into the abyss below. Alternatively, you can also install bears and lions right next to them and take them out organically. Or you can fly next to them and fire away with guns—pistol, shotgun, rifle, and so on.

The route to the villain is blocked by a blue door. The switch for this door is next to the lava pit.

The villain will not give up the Starite without a fight. Arm Maxwell as he descends the shaft on the right side of the level to close in on the Starite. The villain is unarmed but will take swings at Maxwell and overpower him unless Maxwell has the means to defend himself as well as fight back. A sword or a club works well because there is no chance of the Starite itself getting shot.

CRAZY SOLUTION

Roar! The same tiger that you can use to terrorize the enemy soldiers can double as an attack creature to use against the villain. Just make sure Maxwell is nowhere to be found when you drop off the big kitty. After eliminating the villain, the tiger is more than happy to go after the nearest live body.

STUNT PARK 7-7

Difficulty: 3 • Par: 5 • Possible Words:
- **Magic broomstick**
- **Wings**
- **Helibackpack**
- **Unicycle**
- **Roller skates**
- ....
- ....
- ....

The Starite in this action level is not far from Maxwell. It's just down a hill and on a ledge. But as soon as Maxwell starts walking toward it, a door in the ceiling opens, and a giant boulder starts rolling down the hill. Maxwell must keep ahead of the boulder or else get squashed. Stepping back is not an option, either. The floor just below Maxwell's starting position falls away as soon as Maxwell releases the boulder.

Gravity is on the boulder's side. To give Maxwell an edge, jot down some wheels, such as a unicycle or roller skates, so he can outrun the boulder.

There is a second boulder above the bottom of the hill. It drops just as soon as Maxwell reaches the lowest point of the level. With a par five on this one, you have enough spare objects to use some dynamite to explode the boulder or install a black hole to rip it into another dimension.

CRAZY SOLUTION

Avoid the first boulder by zooming up into the small corner right next to the drop spot. Use a magic broomstick or wings to get over the boulder and let it pass by harmlessly. The wings and broomstick are necessary anyway to reach the Starite on the ledge at the end of the level.

STUNT PARK 7-8

Difficulty: 3	Par: 3	Possible Words:

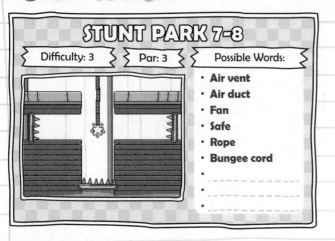

Possible Words:
- Air vent
- Air duct
- Fan
- Safe
- Rope
- Bungee cord
- ....
- ....
- ....

This action level is a spring-loaded trap. The Starite hangs from a rope in the center of the room. There are three panels surrounding the Starite, each baring sharp steel teeth. When Maxwell approaches the Starite, the teeth close in. A few more steps and the teeth slam into place, crushing the Starite. You must help Maxwell pull the Starite out of the trap.

An air vent or an air duct will push the Starite out of the trap. Gently place the vent on the bottom set of teeth. If you drop it, you risk destroying the object.

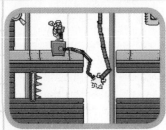

The platforms around the Starite are too small to use an animal to pull the Starite out of the trap. However, you can set up a contraption that does the same thing as a cow-and-clover combo. Place a safe next to the ledge. Attach a bungee cord to the safe and the Starite. Then, place a fan on the safe (as pictured). The current moves the safe to the right, pulling the Starite out of the trap. Now Maxwell can jump across the gap as the teeth harmlessly close in.

CRAZY SOLUTION

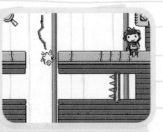

With just a single object, you can yank the Starite out of the dangerous trap. Conjure up a shrink ray and hand it to Maxwell. Shoot the rope. The rope shrinks, pulling the Starite away from the teeth. Now Maxwell can just walk over and pick it up.

STUNT PARK 7-9

Difficulty: 3	Par: 9	Possible Words:

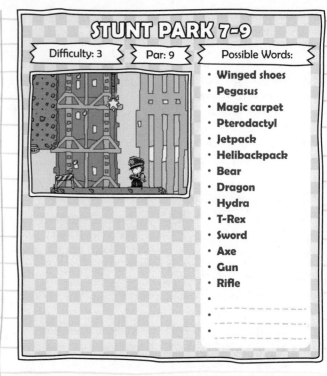

Possible Words:
- Winged shoes
- Pegasus
- Magic carpet
- Pterodactyl
- Jetpack
- Helibackpack
- Bear
- Dragon
- Hydra
- T-Rex
- Sword
- Axe
- Gun
- Rifle
- ....
- ....
- ....

Ever heard of parkour, the sport of urban acrobatics? Leaping from rooftop to rooftop. Vaulting over walls. Bounding across ledges. Usually the police frown on this sort of dangerous thing, and that's why Maxwell must contend with three officers as he bounces through this cityscape en route to the Starite. The officers will lash out when Maxwell gets too close, so Maxwell must be able to defend himself while flying through the level with winged shoes or on the back of a flying creature, such as a pegasus or a pterodactyl.

Maxwell can use a bat or a billy club to push back against the officers trying to stop his parkour special. Or you can nudge them off their ledges with fans and air vents. Just place the fan next to the officers and knock them off their perches.

The storm clouds above the city drop rain that shorts out jetpacks and helibackpacks. Watch out for those water drops!

You can also use winged shoes to fly around the level. Just watch out for the object to run out of energy. If it stops just as Maxwell flies over an abyss, Maxwell is in serious trouble.

There are lots of ledges for Maxwell to land on while moving around the cityscape. The officers are the far bigger threat. If you have already used a fan or an air vent to push the officers off the ledges, then call in bears or lions to attack them. Move the animal from officer to officer. Though the officers are armed with billy clubs, they are no match for a bear.

CRAZY SOLUTION

And nobody is a match against a dragon. Nobody.

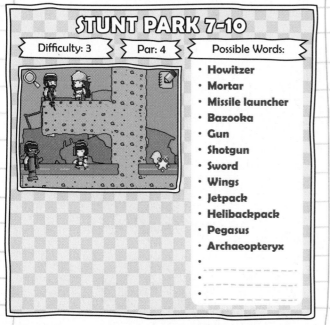

STUNT PARK 7-10

Difficulty: 3	Par: 4	Possible Words:

- **Howitzer**
- **Mortar**
- **Missile launcher**
- **Bazooka**
- **Gun**
- **Shotgun**
- **Sword**
- **Wings**
- **Jetpack**
- **Helibackpack**
- **Pegasus**
- **Archaeopteryx**
- _____
- _____
- _____
- _____

Guerilla fighters have taken a maid and a fortune teller hostage. Not only are they holding these innocents, but they are also blocking the path to the Starite. Maxwell must get through the guerillas without any injury to their hostages.

The Starite is in a well behind the guerillas, so Maxwell will need some means not only to cross a pool of water between him and the guerillas, but also to reach the top of the well.

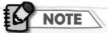 **NOTE**

Maxwell does not need to get rid of all of the guerillas to grab the Starite—it just makes the level a lot easier to finish, because the guerillas are armed.

Launch attacks on the guerillas from afar with a mortar or a howitzer.

There are many ways to get rid of the guerillas. Mortars and howitzers work, as do shotguns or rifles in Maxwell's hands. Because the guerillas are armed with weapons, too, they will return fire. You can fly close to the guerillas and lure them into the water. Or you can install a black hole near the center of the level. Just be sure to trash it before it sucks up the fortune teller and the maid, too.

After fighting through the guerillas at the top of the level, descend the back well to pick up the Starite.

CRAZY SOLUTION

How can you get rid of these guerillas without putting Maxwell in harm's way? Use a monster. However, you must rely on a smaller monster to make sure no harm comes to either of the innocents. The zombie is no good because it just turns whomever it touches into a zombie. But the ghoul does not. Plus, it immediately rushes whatever you set it next to. If you place it right next to a guerilla, the ghoul scares him. And then it kills him.

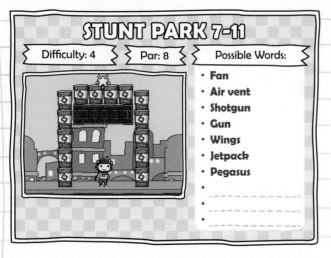

STUNT PARK 7-11

Difficulty: 4 | Par: 8 | Possible Words:

- **Fan**
- **Air vent**
- **Shotgun**
- **Gun**
- **Wings**
- **Jetpack**
- **Pegasus**

Huh. Now that's a predicament. Maxwell is surrounded by exploding barrels that go off if they are moved. The Starite located at the very top of the pile. If a single barrel goes off, the whole level goes up in flames and takes the Starite with it. This is a tricky level to solve at first glance, but the solutions for it are surprisingly simple as soon as you figure out how to keep the chain reactions in check.

Use a fan or an air vent to push the barrels away from the stack so they do not start a chain reaction.

CAUTION

You must step as far as possible to the opposite side of the stack when pushing the barrels out of the way. They invariably will explode. Stepping to the side keeps Maxwell out of the splash damage.

As soon as one stack of barrels has been cleared away, fly up to the top of the level and collect the Starite.

CRAZY SOLUTION

Feeling brave? You can set this thing off with a gun and not turn the level into an inferno. But it is a little tricky. As earlier, step off to the side. Then, give

Maxwell a gun. Shoot the third barrel from the bottom of the stack. This sets off a chain reaction but pushes the barrels away from the whole stack before the entire area explodes.

WORLD 8: FRONTIER

PUZZLE LEVELS

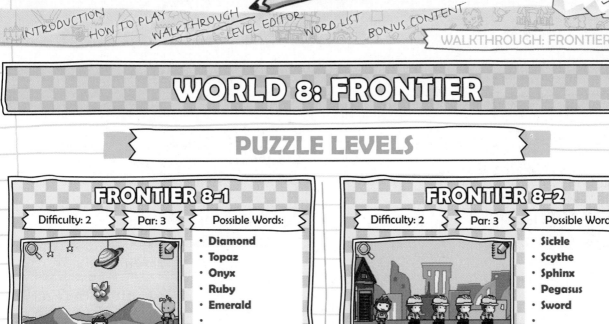

FRONTIER 8-1

Difficulty: 2   Par: 3   Possible Words:

- **Diamond**
- **Topaz**
- **Onyx**
- **Ruby**
- **Emerald**
-
-
-

FRONTIER 8-2

Difficulty: 2   Par: 3   Possible Words:

- **Sickle**
- **Scythe**
- **Sphinx**
- **Pegasus**
- **Sword**
-
-

Three Martians guard their precious soil samples. Maxwell needs to bring these soil samples back to the lander in order for science and progress to, well...progress. To earn the Starite, Maxwell must give these Martians something in exchange for each sample—something the Martians believe is of equal or greater value. There's no such thing as a free space lunch, you know. So, jot down some valuable minerals and stones, such as diamonds, topaz, rubies, and emeralds. Then, hand these stones to the three Martians.

The two soil samples at the bottom of the level require you to give Maxwell some wings or a jetpack. He needs to bring two of the soil samples back to the lander. Once Maxwell grabs the third sample (they are light enough to hold—you do not need a rope), the Starite appears in the center of the level.

CRAZY SOLUTION

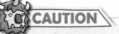

There are plenty of minerals and precious stones in the game for you to dig into and earn some great New Object merits. These Martians might like a moonstone or three. Ground control? Mission accomplished.

Aliens. They are already here. They have taken over the bodies of unsuspecting citizens and assumed their skins so they may walk among us undetected—studying, planning. Maxwell must find the masquerading alien in this level to earn the Starite. Which of these four construction workers is truly from out of town?

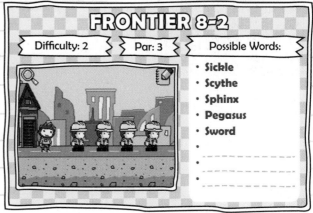

To determine the impostor, give the workers foods like pie or pizza. Everybody loves pie and pizza, right? Well, everybody but an alien. The worker that doesn't move to when you start handing out treats is the alien. To expose him, all you need to do is attack him. One thwack, and the alien sheds the disguise and reveals itself. Use a melee weapon, such as a club, a bat, or a sickle, to attack up close and make that alien molt. You can also use the attacks of a flying creature like a pegasus or sphinx to take care of the aliens.

CAUTION

Do not strike any of the other workers, or else the level ends in failure. For this reason, do not use any firearms to single out the alien.

CRAZY SOLUTION

Let's see how well this alien hides when Maxwell is whipping some sweet nunchucks around. Give the little hero a pair of the 'chucks and show that alien how we earthlings do things downtown.

FRONTIER 8-3

Difficulty: 2	Par: 4	Possible Words:

Possible Words:
- Beast
- Monster
- Devil
- Demon
- Behemoth
- Sword
- Planet
- Saturn
- Jupiter
- Pluto
- Mars
- Comet

FRONTIER 8-4

Difficulty: 3	Par: 4	Possible Words:

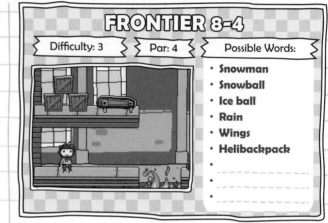

Possible Words:
- Snowman
- Snowball
- Ice ball
- Rain
- Wings
- Helibackpack

The pursuit of the origins of the universe is perhaps the greatest scientific endeavor of all. To know whence the universe was born is to understand the core of humanity—the cosmic marriage of science and the soul. Too bad this truth is put on hold for a skunk. Maxwell must make that skunk scat so the astronomer may gaze through his telescope. To make the little stinker vamoose, attack it with a sword or a bat. You can also go for pure, enjoyable overkill and conjure up a devil or a behemoth to take out the little woodland creature.

Once the astronomer is at his telescope, you must jot down a celestial body for him to gaze upon. Write down any of the planets in the solar system, such as Jupiter or Saturn, and then hang it in the sky. The overjoyed scientist rewards Maxwell with a Starite.

CRAZY SOLUTION

Dial the astronomer's focus a little closer to home and let him look at one of the most impressive heavenly phenomena within the Earth's atmosphere:

the aurora borealis. The crackling colors delight the astronomer and add one more Starite to your growing collection.

Who could possible be unhappy in a teddy-bear factory? Well, how about a little girl who is watching these teddy bears being accidentally fed into an incinerator? Maxwell must snuff out the flames and retrieve one of the teddy bears for the little girl. The overjoyed tot will grant a Starite reward for the good deed.

First things first: Put out the flames. Any decent-sized water source will do the trick here. It must be somewhat substantial, because the fire vent is so large. A snowman works, as does an ice ball. A little bit of water is just not enough. The fires burn too hot and turn the water into steam right away. A rain cloud, though, has means to extinguish the fire.

Once the fire is out, Maxwell just needs to grab one of the teddies coming off the conveyor belt and take it to the little girl. He will need some wings or a jetpack to fly over to the little girl.

CRAZY SOLUTION

With a single object, you can thwart the flames and take the teddy to the girl. Write down a ramp. The metal ramp cannot be destroyed by fire, and it

is wide enough to span the incinerator pit. The teddy rolls off the belt and down the ramp, right to Maxwell's feet. How's that for personal delivery?

FRONTIER 8-5

Difficulty: 3	Par: 7	Possible Words:

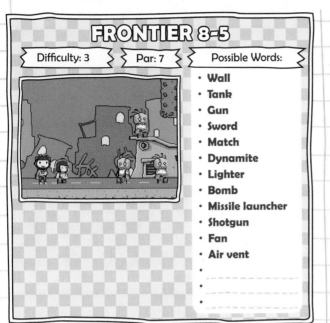

Possible Words:
- **Wall**
- **Tank**
- **Gun**
- **Sword**
- **Match**
- **Dynamite**
- **Lighter**
- **Bomb**
- **Missile launcher**
- **Shotgun**
- **Fan**
- **Air vent**

The zomb-pocalypse is finally here. The city is overrun by slavering horrors that hunger for the flesh of the living. A helicopter waits at the far end of the city to take survivors to safety. Maxwell must escort a girl through a gauntlet of zombies in order to escape with the Starite...and his life. However, if a single zombie touches the girl, her skin goes cold as she turns into one of the undead. So get to the chopper!

The zombies come at Maxwell and the girl from both sides at the start of the level. There is only one to the left of you and the girl. There are several to the right. You must prioritize here. Throw up a wall or a stack of two tanks to stop the advancing horde.

You can then take down the lone zombie with a gun or a sword.

The zombies demand brains. Give them what they want. Drop some brains or a body part into the throng of zombies. They descend upon it. While the mindless horde dines, drop some dynamite

(a bomb or gunpowder works, too) and a match into the mix. The explosion should eliminate all zombies in the immediate vicinity.

After erasing the zombies, run the girl to the chopper. If she has retreated to the left side of the level in fear, there is still a zombie in play. Neutralize it.

Try keeping the zombies at bay with a fan or an air vent. The gust of wind keeps the undead in check so you can handle them one on one.

CRAZY SOLUTION

You must protect the girl from the zombies. You can use a little tough love to get this job done. Shoot her with the freeze ray. While encased in the ice, the girl cannot be touched by the zombies. Now you can unleash h-e-double-hockey-sticks on them with a missile launcher or a monster.

FRONTIER 8-6

Difficulty: 3	Par: 5	Possible Words:

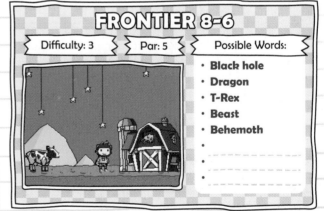

Possible Words:
- **Black hole**
- **Dragon**
- **T-Rex**
- **Beast**
- **Behemoth**

Why aliens seem to be interested in turning our cows inside out is a true mystery. But if Maxwell does not get this cattle mutilation problem under control, wholesale beef prices will skyrocket! There are four cows in this level. Maxwell must stop the alien before it abducts all of the cattle with its UFO. The tractor beam on the bottom of the ship lifts the cows into the sky.

A big monster, such as a dragon, will slam the ship and force the alien to consider vegetarianism. You can also summon a black hole and place it near the UFO to send the alien back to space...or the space between spaces.

CRAZY SOLUTION

Brute force works, too. Jot down a missile launcher and fly Maxwell right up to the UFO. Blast a rocket right up the alien's tailpipe to bring its cow-killing career to an abrupt end.

As soon as you push the alien onto the truck, the Starite appears.

CRAZY SOLUTION

It's time to play cowboys and aliens. Place Maxwell on a magic broomstick and give him a lasso. Once Maxwell ropes that frozen alien like a lil' doggie, he can easily spirit it back to the truck and bank the Starite.

FRONTIER 8-7

> Difficulty: 2 > Par: 4 > Possible Words:

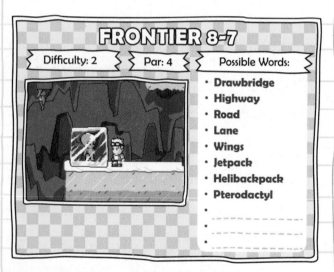

- **Drawbridge**
- **Highway**
- **Road**
- **Lane**
- **Wings**
- **Jetpack**
- **Helibackpack**
- **Pterodactyl**
- _____
- _____
- _____

FRONTIER 8-8

> Difficulty: 2 > Par: 3 > Possible Words:

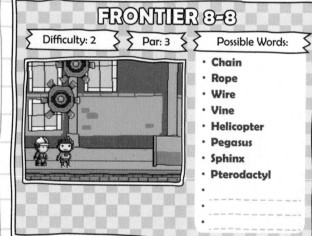

- **Chain**
- **Rope**
- **Wire**
- **Vine**
- **Helicopter**
- **Pegasus**
- **Sphinx**
- **Pterodactyl**
- _____
- _____
- _____

Somewhere in the frozen wasteland, scientists have discovered evidence of visitors long before the dawn of recorded human history. An alien is encased in a giant block of ice. You must get the alien-sicle off of its perch and to a waiting flatbed truck so it may be carted off to a black site and never seen again. One catch: There is a bottomless pit right below the frozen alien's ledge.

You must bridge the gap in the ground in order to push the alien to the truck. A drawbridge or a piece of highway works well. If you opt to pull it off the ledge with a flying creature (pterodactyl, pegasus) and some rope, just watch out for the stalactite. If the ice block slams into the stalactite, the block could crack open and drop the alien right into the abyss.

After dealing with aliens and zombies, it is a relief to be asked just a basic favor, such as lifting a giant pipe up to a ledge for some construction workers. Space inside the warehouse is limited, though, so you need to be mindful of using a large delivery vehicle to cart the pipe around.

A helicopter and a rope (or a chain) is a tight fit in this chamber, but it can be done.

A far better fit in the warehouse is a flying animal, such as a pegasus or a pterodactyl. Tether the pipe to the animal and fly it right up to the waiting worker. When the pipe touches down on the ledge, you win the Starite.

CRAZY SOLUTION

Lift the pipe to the ledge without even touching it. Create a forklift and then park it to the left of the pipe. Drop an air vent on the tines of the lift. The angled blast of air flips the pipe into the air and right on top of the ledge.

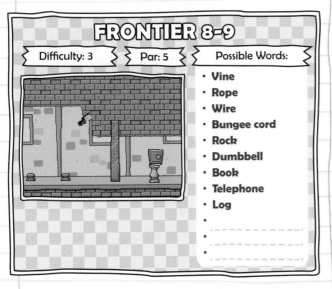

FRONTIER 8-9

Difficulty: 3	Par: 5	Possible Words:

- **Vine**
- **Rope**
- **Wire**
- **Bungee cord**
- **Rock**
- **Dumbbell**
- **Book**
- **Telephone**
- **Log**
- _____
- _____
- _____

Your mission—should you choose to accept it—is to break into a secret warehouse where a Starite is being held inside a safe. The safe is locked behind a blast-proof door that can only be raised by pressing three buttons at the same time. Those buttons, though, are closely watched by two security cameras. That video feed is then fed to a bay of monitors watched closely by an armed security guard.

What?

The security guard is asleep?

This is a perfect time to launch the mission. Get in there, Maxwell, and get to that safe so that your bank of Starites may grow.

As soon as you are spotted mucking with the buttons, the security guard wakes up. You must do something to keep the security guard busy while you open the door. Tether the security guard to the desk with a rope or a chain. That way, when the alarm sounds, the security guard is stuck just out of reach.

 CAUTION

Do not tie the security guard to one of the monitors. He will just pull that right off the desk as he pursues Maxwell.

 NOTE

You cannot kill the security guard in this level.

Once the security guard is tied up, place three objects—rock, dumbbell, orange, whatever—on the buttons. The door rises. Interact with the safe to open it and retrieve the Starite inside.

 TIP

Place a long object over the buttons to activate more than one with a single object. A girder, for example, will work on two buttons at once.

CRAZY SOLUTION

Because you cannot hurt the security guard, you must find another way to detain him. The freeze ray would be a good solution to this situation, but you cannot shoot the guard while he is asleep. You must wake him up and then hit him with the freeze ray. It's tricky because the guard is so close, but if you tap the guard as soon as the camera picks up your presence, you can nail him.

FRONTIER 8-10

Difficulty: 3	Par: 8	Possible Words:

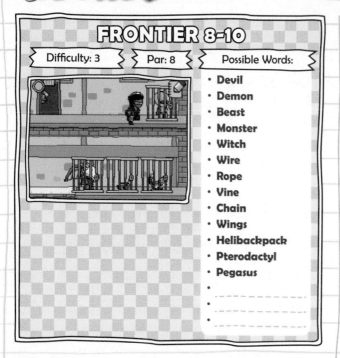

Possible Words:
- **Devil**
- **Demon**
- **Beast**
- **Monster**
- **Witch**
- **Wire**
- **Rope**
- **Vine**
- **Chain**
- **Wings**
- **Helibackpack**
- **Pterodactyl**
- **Pegasus**

The government has captured a live alien. Agents are holding the alien in a warehouse along with his UFO and a cool hologram machine they pulled out of his luggage. Maxwell must free the alien and get both it and the hologram machine to the saucer to earn the Starite. The alien and the hologram machine are guarded by agents, each armed with a stun gun. The path to the UFO is also under surveillance by security cameras. If Maxwell is picked up on camera with the alien or the hologram machine, soldiers enter the warehouse...and their guns are not set to stun.

This mission is much easier if you disarm the agents first. Give each agent a kitten or a puppy to hold. The agents immediately drop their stun guns. Now Maxwell can take them out with a gun or a sword or conjure up a monster to get its claws dirty on Maxwell's behalf.

A truly frightful monster, such as a devil, will scare the agent into not reacting right away.

Now that the agents are down, you need to keep the coast clear of any potential reinforcements. Drop a gun into Maxwell's mitts and shoot the security cameras. Once the cameras are down, no soldiers will appear.

Alternatively, you can destroy the doors the agents would come through with fire or explosions. But it is much easier just to shoot the cameras.

Use a flying creature, such as the pterodactyl, or wings to carry the alien and the hologram machine to the UFO. Tether the alien and the hologram machine with a rope or a vine and then fly them right up to the saucer to collect the Starite.

CRAZY SOLUTION

These agents are interested in alien technology, right? Well, give them an encounter of the ferocious kind. The robosaur is a vicious creature that is part metal, part dinosaur, but all violent. It takes out the agents regardless of whether they still hold their stun guns. When the agents are down, delete the robosaur.

FRONTIER 8-11

Difficulty: 2	Par: 4	Possible Words:

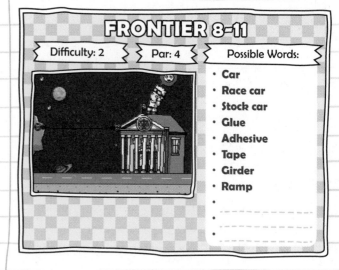

Possible Words:
- **Car**
- **Race car**
- **Stock car**
- **Glue**
- **Adhesive**
- **Tape**
- **Girder**
- **Ramp**

1.21 gigawatts! Maxwell must help a scientist on top of city hall perform an experiment in time travel. To do this, the little hero needs to touch a power cord stretched across a road just as lightning strikes. The power of the lightning provides enough juice to the reflexive contraptinator and pulls a Starite out of the future. However, Maxwell starts this level with nothing but the lint in his pockets. To assist the scientist, you must create a vehicle for Maxwell and then mod it up.

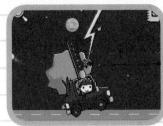

The vehicle hits the cord and lightning strikes, powering up the vehicle and revealing the Starite.

The power cord is high off the ground. Maxwell needs to make sure that something metal is attached to his vehicle so that when it hits the cord, the lightning strike is harnessed. Write down a car and then glue a girder to the roof. (A ramp on the roof works, too.) Then, hit the gas.

CRAZY SOLUTION

Speed is not the solution here—it's height. Maxwell must be in something metal that touches the cord. Create a mech and drop Maxwell into the pilot's chair. Lumber toward the power cord. The mech is tall enough that the cockpit touches the cord. Lightning crashes, and a Starite is born.

ACTION LEVELS

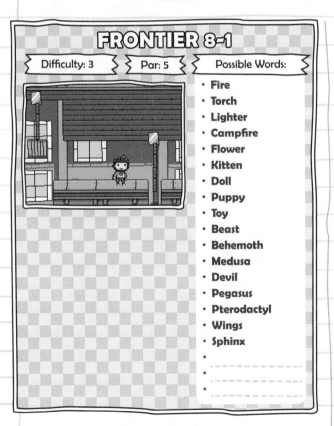

FRONTIER 8-1

Difficulty: 3	Par: 5	Possible Words:

- **Fire**
- **Torch**
- **Lighter**
- **Campfire**
- **Flower**
- **Kitten**
- **Doll**
- **Puppy**
- **Toy**
- **Beast**
- **Behemoth**
- **Medusa**
- **Devil**
- **Pegasus**
- **Pterodactyl**
- **Wings**
- **Sphinx**
-
-
-

The Starite is safe and sound on a ledge to the right as Maxwell begins the level. However, the path from here to there is far from safe. There are enemy soldiers and a phoenix standing in the way, and the floor is nothing more than a wide lava pit. Maxwell must fly through the level after disposing of all threats.

The phoenix near the Starite is easy to distract: fire. However, before dropping fire right next to the phoenix, use it to burn the ropes of the crates hanging from the ceiling, thus clearing a route. Once the ropes are ablaze, place the fire (or lighter or torch) near the phoenix. It becomes entranced and will not bother Maxwell for the remainder of the level.

The enemy soldier is well armed but has a soft heart. Offer the soldier a puppy, a flower, or a kitten. He drops his gun. Now he is much easier to defeat with an attack object or a monster.

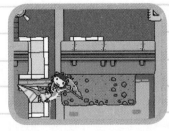

There is a storm cloud near the Starite. The raindrops will short out a helibackpack or a jetpack, so use wings or a flying creature, such as the pterodactyl.

NOTE

You can widen the lower route through the level by digging through the loose soil.

Watch out for lightning strikes from the storm cloud. If lightning hits a pterodactyl or a pterosaur, you might get dropped.

CRAZY SOLUTION

Once the soldier has been disarmed, you need to dispose of him or burrow through the dirt above him to widen the path. Conjure up a witch to cast a spell on the soldier. The witch's spell turns the soldier into a frog. Now you can flutter through here without worry.

FRONTIER 8-2

Difficulty: 2	Par: 4	Possible Words:

- **Black hole**
- **Dragon**
- **Pegasus**
- **Sphinx**
- **Pterodactyl**
- **Missile launcher**
- **UFO**
- **Glue**
- **Mortar**
-
-
-

Four fighter jets rule the night sky here. The lead jet dangles the Starite from a rope attached to the bottom of his plane. The rest of the squadron surrounds the hanging Starite, making it difficult to break through. Maxwell must use a flying object himself to mix it up with the fighters. But he needs to be careful with the lead pilot. Junk his craft, and the Starite goes down with it.

Destroy the three flanking aircraft with a black hole or a flying monster, such as a dragon. You can also arm a flying ship, such as a UFO, by gluing a mortar on top of it. A pegasus or a pterodactyl is a great option, too, because Maxwell can hold a weapon, such as a missile launcher, while riding it. As the enemy fighters come into view, tap them to release a rocket.

After the flanking jets have been destroyed, get under the lead pilot so he does not open fire on you. Come up from below and grab the Starite.

CRAZY SOLUTION

Feeling brave? Drop Maxwell in the pilot's seat of his own fighter jet and zoom straight into the thick of the squadron. The element of surprise works for you. The jets will not have time to open fire, and if they do, they are just as likely to shoot each other instead of you. Fly right into the Starite to grab it.

FRONTIER 8-3

Difficulty: 3	Par: 4	Possible Words:

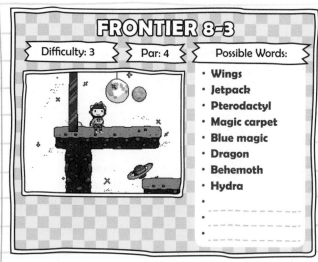

- **Wings**
- **Jetpack**
- **Pterodactyl**
- **Magic carpet**
- **Blue magic**
- **Dragon**
- **Behemoth**
- **Hydra**
-
-
-

This level is more of a cosmic maze than a battleground. There are two monsters in the maze—haetae and hellhound—but they can be completely circumvented on your way to the Starite, which is being guarded by the playful haetae. To get the Starite, you must open a series of doors by throwing the color-coded switches.

The green switch is below Maxwell's starting position. You can drop down to it, but you will need a jetpack or a magic carpet to fly out of the area.

The green switch opens the green door. Now Maxwell can fly to the blue switch in the upper-right corner of the level. Drop down on the switch to open the blue door near the hellhound. You can fly right past the hellhound and head down to the red switch.

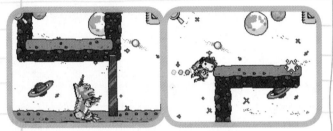

Wait a second—the red switch did not open the red door next to the haetae guarding the Starite. No, but it did open the red door in the upper-left corner of the level, near Maxwell's starting position. Fly back up there and drop down the tall shaft. The Starite is on the ledge closest to the bottom. By now, the haetae has dropped down to the ground floor (it started sniffing around while you were activating the red switch) and is a non-threat.

CRAZY SOLUTION

Although it is not necessary to eliminate the haetae or the hellhound, you can always conjure up a fearsome monster to eliminate them, such as a dragon or a hydra. Just make sure the Starite is not damaged in the process. Alternatively, you can also use Cupid's arrow on the haetae to make it like Maxwell and not attack.

FRONTIER 8-4

Difficulty: 3   Par: 6   Possible Words:

- **Stone**
- **Lime**
- **Cherry**
- **Orange**
- **Log**
- **Chain**
- **Rope**
- **Vine**
- **Pegasus**
- **Wings**
- **Jetpack**
- **Helibackpack**
- **Pterodactyl**
- _____
- _____
- _____

The Starite in this level is sitting on a blue door at the top of a shaft. There are three doors beneath it: one red and two green. These doors are all that stands between the Starite and an abyss. But these doors must be opened for Maxwell to reach the Starite. How can the Starite be propped up so it does not fall when the doors are systematically opened by using the buttons and switches around the level?

The doors will not remain open once a button has been pressed. If you place a rock on a button to open the door, removing the rock closes the door. Use this method to drop the Starite through the blue door. Once the Starite rests on the red door, tie it to the blue door with a rope, a chain or a vine.

Now, place objects on the red and green buttons (reuse the object from the blue button) to open the rest of the doors. The Starite dangles from the rope but is held firmly in place by the blue door. Fly up and

grab it on the back or a pegasus or a pterodactyl. There is no water in this level, so feel free to use a jetpack or a helibackpack, too.

CRAZY SOLUTION

You can propel the Starite to safety with an air vent. However, to use the air vent, you must prop it up so it does not fall through the green door when you

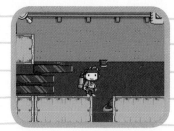

open it. Stretch a bridge across the hole. When the green door opens, the bridge is wedged into place. Now, place the air vent on the bridge, facing up. The burst of wind pushes the Starite up so it hovers in place as you open the red and blue doors and fly into the shaft to fetch it.

If you do move the red doors, the Starite falls. Now you must only touch the blue button on the way down to open a path into the area where the Starite fell. If you hit both buttons, the Starite falls.

CRAZY SOLUTION

Go for the red button. Keep your hands off the button by just floating a rock or a log up into it via an air vent. You have enough par to use this

method and have plenty of objects left over to hit the blue button (throw those rocks!) and open the way to the fallen Starite.

FRONTIER 8-5

Difficulty: 2   Par: 4   Possible Words:

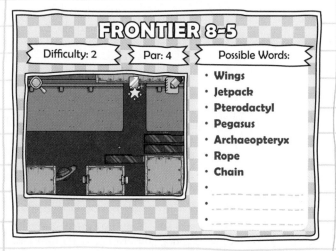

- **Wings**
- **Jetpack**
- **Pterodactyl**
- **Pegasus**
- **Archaeopteryx**
- **Rope**
- **Chain**
-
-
-

As in the previous level, the Starite dangles above an abyss. All that stands in the way are two red doors and a green door. These doors are controlled by buttons in the level. The red doors, though, are activated by a button on the roof of the level. When pressed, these doors slide to the left—quickly. If you try to fly up to the Starite and then brush against the blue or green buttons in the area right in front of the Starite, the remaining doors move, and the Starite falls into space.

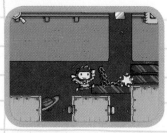

Try avoiding the red button at first. Instead, fly up to the red doors with wings or a jetpack. Attach a rope or a chain to the Starite. The weight pulls it off the ceiling of the room. Now attach the rope to Maxwell

and pull the Starite out of the small chamber and into his waiting hands.

FRONTIER 8-6

Difficulty: 3   Par: 5   Possible Words:

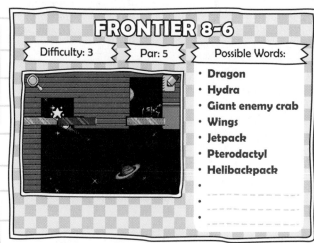

- **Dragon**
- **Hydra**
- **Giant enemy crab**
- **Wings**
- **Jetpack**
- **Pterodactyl**
- **Helibackpack**
-
-
-

The Starite here is held up by red and green doors. These doors are moved aside by throwing corresponding switches on the floor of the level. However, there are hostile robots—two androids and four nanobots—being held back by red and green doors, too. If you throw the switches, these beasties are released into the room. They will ignore the Starite, though. They would much rather pound on Maxwell.

Give Maxwell some wings or a jetpack so he can fly up to the ledge above the switches.

CAUTION

You may not have enough time to throw both switches in a single trip to the floor. The robots will be on you within seconds. It's okay to do this one switch at a time.

After throwing a switch and flying back to the ledge, drop a monster into the level to attack the androids and the nanobots. The bigger the beast, the better. The nanobots and androids will attack back.

CRAZY SOLUTION

There is only one thing robots fear: electromagnetic pulses. After releasing the army of androids and nanobots, create an EMP for Maxwell and set it on the ledge. When Maxwell sets it off, the blast temporarily disables the robots. Now Maxwell can run by them and grab the Starite.

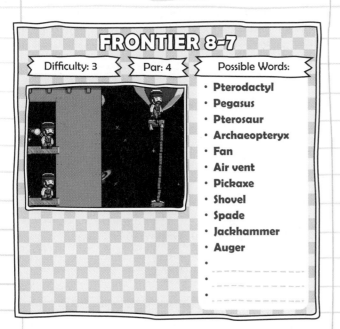

FRONTIER 8-7

Difficulty: 3	Par: 4	Possible Words:

Possible Words:
- **Pterodactyl**
- **Pegasus**
- **Pterosaur**
- **Archaeopteryx**
- **Fan**
- **Air vent**
- **Pickaxe**
- **Shovel**
- **Spade**
- **Jackhammer**
- **Auger**
- ⋅ _____
- ⋅ _____
- ⋅ _____

Four guerilla fighters guard the Starite in this level. One of them is piloting a hot air balloon that's holding up an exploding barrel. Maxwell must fly to the top of the chamber and throw the blue switch to free the Starite. However, this drops the Starite to the bottom of the room...

as well as the three caged guerillas. How can Maxwell get the Starite and avoid heavy battle with these tough guys?

First things first: Fly up the left side of the level with a pegasus, a pterodactyl, or a pterosaur.

Dig through the dirt wall in order to reach the blue switch and release the Starite and guerillas.

The guerillas on the ground are now susceptible to an attack from above. Time to make good use of that hanging barrel. Drop down on the hot air balloon and attack it with your shovel or jackhammer. The balloon

pops and drops the barrel. The explosion may eliminate one or two guerillas. The rest can be pushed away from the Starite with a fan or an air vent. Feel free to drop a bear on the guerillas, too.

Quickly drop to the bottom of the level and pick up the Starite before the remaining guerillas attack.

CRAZY SOLUTION

Let's get that Starite without having to worry about guerilla fighters and balloons and barrels and booms. Jot down a ramp and place it directly below the Starite. When you throw the blue switch, the Starite rolls to the right and comes to rest on the ledge above the balloon. Pick it up and end the level in starry triumph.

FRONTIER 8-8

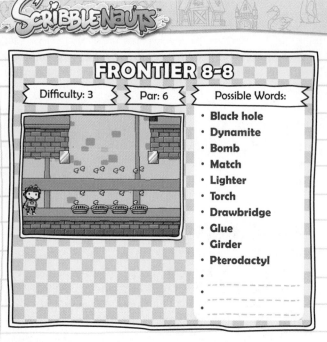

Difficulty: 3 > Par: 6 > Possible Words:

- **Black hole**
- **Dynamite**
- **Bomb**
- **Match**
- **Lighter**
- **Torch**
- **Drawbridge**
- **Glue**
- **Girder**
- **Pterodactyl**
- •
- •
- •

This level looks tough at the beginning. Four air vents are blasting air up at two spiked steel balls hanging from the ceiling. If Maxwell steps into the vents, he's pushed to certain doom. But he has to get across the vents somehow, because the red switch that opens the door to the Starite is over to the right. How can he neutralize the spiked balls or at least beat the air vents?

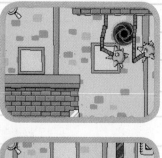

The black hole trick always works. Conjure up a black hole and use it to destroy the spiked balls during one solution. The spiked balls can also be destroyed with dynamite and bombs tossed into the air streams.

The pterodactyl can cross the air vents once without being pushed up, as long as you fly in a straight line and do not stop midway through the journey.

When you throw the red switch, the red door opens. Now, just float up and tap to the right so that when Maxwell flies past the opening, he scoots into the alcove and grabs the Starite.

There are more ways to beat this level. Write down three drawbridges and stretch them across the air vents. Layer them like this and then run under them as the air pushes you up. Do not stop. Once you have hit the red switch, push the drawbridges so they fly up into the spikes.

Two gobs of glue and two girders create enough of a block over the air vents so Maxwell can run to the switch.

CRAZY SOLUTION

Tape is not as strong as glue or adhesive, but it will hold objects in place. Tape two boards to the pieces of metal above the air vents. The air pushes the boards up, but the tape gamely hangs in there. Now, tape an air vent to the bottom of the left board so it pushes Maxwell down as he crosses the air vents. Once he gets past that open spot in the middle of the boards, he's golden.

FRONTIER 8-9

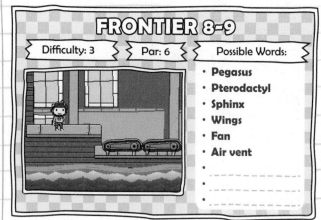

Difficulty: 3 > Par: 6 > Possible Words:

- **Pegasus**
- **Pterodactyl**
- **Sphinx**
- **Wings**
- **Fan**
- **Air vent**
- •
- •
- •

Conveyor belts, metal-teeth traps, and lava: What's not to love about this action level? Maxwell must somehow cross the room to reach the Starite. The bottom path is treacherous because of the teeth in the passage at the center of the level. The top route looks more amenable, but those two pieces of metal racing across the ceiling can put Maxwell in a pinch.

Fly up to the top ledge in the center of the level on the back of a pegasus or a pterodactyl or by using wings. The flying animal is too big to fit through the narrow opening, though. So, dismount and step through it with only Maxwell. Now, grab the animal and place it back on Maxwell. Fly to the Starite.

If you want to fly through the lower route, use a fan or an air vent and push the steel teeth into the lava to create a safe opening.

CRAZY SOLUTION

The metal pieces that slide left and right across the ceiling can be used to travel across the level. Give Maxwell a grappling hook. The hook doesn't have enough string to reach the ceiling, so place Maxwell on top of a crate. Shoot the metal piece. The hook grabs it and pulls Maxwell to the ceiling. Drop off the metal piece at the center of the level and then use the hook on the other piece of metal to continue the extreme journey to the Starite.

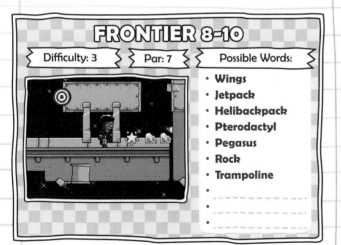

FRONTIER 8–10

Difficulty: 3	Par: 7	Possible Words:

Possible Words:
- **Wings**
- **Jetpack**
- **Helibackpack**
- **Pterodactyl**
- **Pegasus**
- **Rock**
- **Trampoline**
-
-
-

This action level is set up like a heist. There are security cameras everywhere that drop land mines on a robber who has managed to grab a diamond from the vault at the top of the level. When Maxwell arrives, it looks like a previous robbery has gone poorly. A diamond sits in the middle of the level—the robber likely a victim of a land mine.

The accomplice is at the top of the level, trapped in a room with a Starite. If Maxwell can bring the other diamond to the robber and raise the wall that traps him, the robber will hand over the Starite.

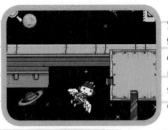

Start the level by opening the red door. Maxwell can either fly to it with wings (or a creature) or throw something at it, such as a rock.

When Maxwell has the diamond, the land mines start falling near the security cameras. You can shoot the cameras with a gun to obscure Maxwell's passage. Or, you can fly as close to the ceiling as possible to avoid the land mines on the floor. Just make sure that no matter what, you have the diamond in hand.

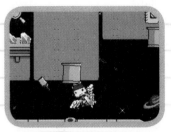

TIP

You can also bounce Maxwell up the tiers in this level with a trampoline.

Use the diamond to hit the target near the vault. Grab the diamond and give it to the robber as the wall lifts so he will not block passage to the Starite. Watch out for the security camera on the ceiling, though. If it spots Maxwell, it drops another land mine right on top of him. Stay off the floor!

CRAZY SOLUTION

There is a target on the left side of the level. If you shoot the target, it raises some stairs. Do not throw a diamond at these stairs. Instead, shoot the target to raise the stairs and keep Maxwell from accidentally dropping back down to the bottom of the level.

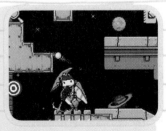

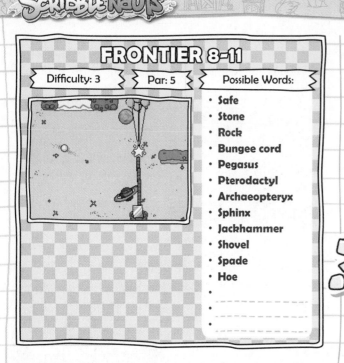

FRONTIER 8-11

Difficulty: 3	Par: 5	Possible Words:

- **Safe**
- **Stone**
- **Rock**
- **Bungee cord**
- **Pegasus**
- **Pterodactyl**
- **Archaeopteryx**
- **Sphinx**
- **Jackhammer**
- **Shovel**
- **Spade**
- **Hoe**
-
-
-

The Starite is this cosmic action level is floating above the great beyond by three balloons. The Starite does not float away, though, because it is tethered to a piece of metal by a rope. When Maxwell crosses a tripwire near his starting position, the rope snaps, and the balloons carry the Starite up. Maxwell must hurry to the Starite before it flies away.

Anchor the Starite to the ledge to the right of it. Place a safe or a stone on the ledge. Now, hook the Starite up to the safe with a lighter cord, such as a bungee cord. (The chain is too heavy. It will pull the safe off the ledge.) With the Starite tied to the safe, it cannot fly away when the rope is broken.

Just fly down and pick up the Starite!

There is an alternate way through the level that does not trigger the tripwire. Dig through the soil in the center of the level with a shovel or a jackhammer while on the back of a flying creature, such as a pegasus or a sphinx. You cannot do this with wings because you just drop when you break through the bottom. Once you finish burrowing, simply fly over to claim the Starite.

CRAZY SOLUTION

Psst. Wanna know a secret? Those balloons lifting the Starite are slower than a pegasus or a pterodactyl. You can just rush through the tripwire and catch up with the Starite long before it has any chance to escape the level. Wow—now you are four under par.

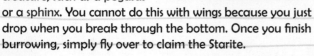

WORLD 9: DARK HOLLOW

PUZZLE LEVELS

DARK HOLLOW 9-1

Difficulty: 3	Par: 5	Possible Words:

- **Halo**
- **Pegasus**
- **Sphinx**
- **Vine**
- **Wings**
- **Handcuffs**
- **God**
- **Holy water**
-
-
-

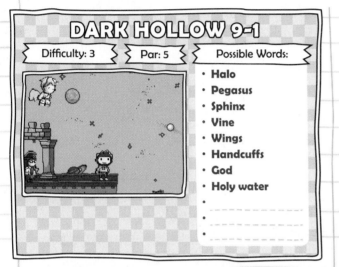

Judgment has been rendered, and the guilty are to be punished to an eternity of the inferno. However, forgiveness is the currency of the saints, and now Maxwell has the power to rescue these doomed souls just before they are cast out forever. How can you help Maxwell bring the three condemned souls into heaven?

The easiest thing to do is write down no fewer than three halos. Place a halo on each of the condemned, and they immediately soar to heaven.

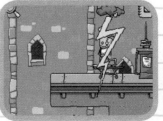

You can also go about things in the traditional way. Place Maxwell on the back of a flying steed, such as a pegasus or a pterodactyl, and lasso each condemned person with a rope or a chain. Attach the rope to the flying animal and carry them physically up to heaven. When the third body is at the Pearly Gates, the Starite appears.

CRAZY SOLUTION

Here's a hint: What's she buying? That's right. You can solve this problem by mimicking the title of everybody's favorite dorm-room jam.

DARK HOLLOW 9-2

Difficulty: 2	Par: 4	Possible Words:

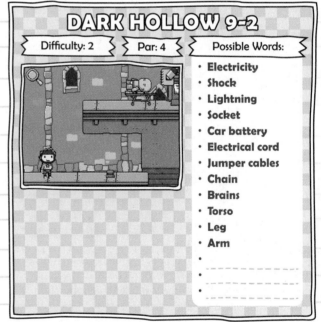

- **Electricity**
- **Shock**
- **Lightning**
- **Socket**
- **Car battery**
- **Electrical cord**
- **Jumper cables**
- **Chain**
- **Brains**
- **Torso**
- **Leg**
- **Arm**
-
-
-

Welcome to the laboratory. There is a body strapped to a table on the upstairs level of this level, hooked up to a bunch of wires and diodes. The good doctor is attempting to give life to dead tissue, and you are to be his Igor. To solve this level, you must devise the means for imbuing the literal spark of life to the cadaver, thus perverting the natural order of life and death. Good luck!

There are many ways to shock this body to life. Place a lightning cloud directly over the body. The crackling electricity jolts the corpse to life.

Once you have coaxed life back into the body, though, things go wrong. The monster is not friendly. It's quite violent, in fact. You must lure it into the cage to the left and then slam the door on it by throwing the blue switch. To lure the monster, trying leaving out body parts or brains. Keep moving the brains closer to the cage until the monster is inside of it. Then, while the monster chows down on some gray matter, throw the switch and close the door.

A car battery and set of jumper cables provides enough juice to shock the body to life.

 TIP

Just write down shock in the Notepad to receive a literal bolt of blue electricity. Drop it on the body to bring it to life.

CRAZY SOLUTION

Some monsters need a little more than just a brain or a femur. That'll just arouse the appetite without bedding it back down. Indulge your personal dark side and summon a baby. Apparently that monster will eat anything. Place the baby in the cage and then close the door. Whether you take the baby away from the monster before it starts snacking is entirely up to you. Sicko.

This level is set inside the famous fairy tale "Little Red Riding Hood." Maxwell catches up with Red at her grandma's house. The poor old woman is in bed. Everything looks peaceful, but you know the story here. The moment you near that bed, the grandma act comes off, and the wolf leaps into action. (In this level, though, the wolf is actually a werewolf.) How can you solve this situation for Red's safety?

Place a monster, such as a behemoth or a harpy, and drop it right next to the bed. The wolf jumps up for a fight but is just no match for your monster. Enjoy the Starite reward for thwarting the wolf's subterfuge. Just make sure you dispose of the monster before trying to collect the Starite.

CRAZY SOLUTION

There is a pretty powerful object you can drop into the mix to punish the mean ol' wolf: God. Complete with flowing robes, a shock of white hair, and a serious beard, this God looks like he just stepped off the ceiling of the Sistine Chapel to put an appearance in here.

DARK HOLLOW 9-4

Difficulty: 2	Par: 3	Possible Words:

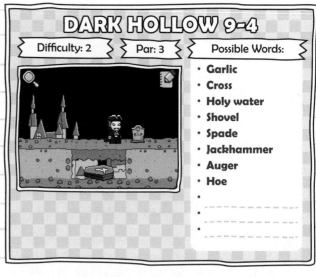

Possible Words:
- **Garlic**
- **Cross**
- **Holy water**
- **Shovel**
- **Spade**
- **Jackhammer**
- **Auger**
- **Hoe**

DARK HOLLOW 9-3

Difficulty: 2	Par: 3	Possible Words:

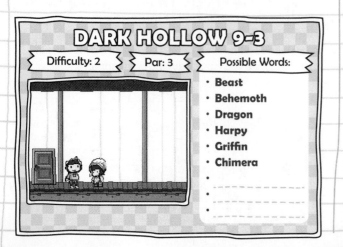

Possible Words:
- **Beast**
- **Behemoth**
- **Dragon**
- **Harpy**
- **Griffin**
- **Chimera**

The Starite in this level is tucked inside the coffin buried six feet under. Maxwell must dig up the coffin and open it to get the Starite. Sounds fine, right? Where's the shovel? Not so fast. There is a nasty vampire holding court in the graveyard that will attack if you attempt to dig up the coffin. You must keep the vampire at bay in order to safely dig up the coffin.

Call upon your vast knowledge of vampires to find a solution. What do vampires just loathe? Garlic. Crosses. Holy water. Write down any of these and drop them on the ground to make the vampire recoil in horror. Keep picking up the relic and moving it closer to the vampire until the ground above the coffin is clear. Leave the object in place, though.

With a shovel, a spade, or a jackhammer, dig down to the coffin and open it to fetch the Starite.

CRAZY SOLUTION

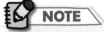

Up to now, you've been soft on the vampire. Just using garlic and whatnot keeps the vampire back, but what about a more permanent solution? Jot down the sun and hang it in the heavens. Daylight makes the vampire collapse and wither, leaving behind only a neat pile of ash.

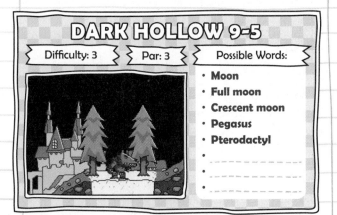

DARK HOLLOW 9-5
Difficulty: 3 Par: 3 Possible Words:
- **Moon**
- **Full moon**
- **Crescent moon**
- **Pegasus**
- **Pterodactyl**
- ____
- ____
- ____

Okay, so you were a little hard on the vampire in the previous level. You can make it up to his friend in this level by helping him get his mail. Maxwell and the mail carrier are stuck at the bottom of a hill, unable to get past the werewolf halfway up. You must neutralize (without killing) the werewolf so the carrier can deliver a letter to the vampire at the top of the hill.

Hang a moon in the sky. Any kind of moon will do: moon, crescent moon, gibbous moon, or full moon. The presence of the moon causes the werewolf to revert back to human form. Now you and the mail carrier can walk right by it on the way to the vampire's abode.

NOTE

Variations on an object are a good way to accomplish the same goal in multiple attempts at a single level. Moon and crescent moon may look the same, but the game counts them as different words for the sake of the level.

Fly over the werewolf with a pegasus. Instead of trying to drag the mail carrier, though, give him a pegasus. He will follow you through the night sky.

CRAZY SOLUTION

Werewolves have a few weakness, but none quite like silver. Drop some silver into Maxwell's hand. The werewolf runs from Maxwell and the mail carrier as you walk up the hill to the vampire house. The werewolf is so spooked by the silver that it will not bother the vampire.

DARK HOLLOW 9-6

Difficulty: 2	Par: 5	Possible Words:

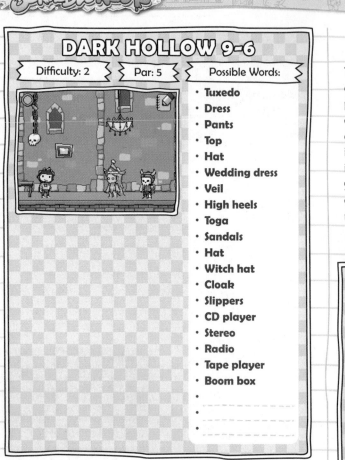

Possible Words:
- Tuxedo
- Dress
- Pants
- Top
- Hat
- Wedding dress
- Veil
- High heels
- Toga
- Sandals
- Hat
- Witch hat
- Cloak
- Slippers
- CD player
- Stereo
- Radio
- Tape player
- Boom box
- ⋯
- ⋯
- ⋯

Maxwell has been invited to a mashing of monsters. The party isn't quite hopping when Maxwell arrives, though. No graveyards are being smashed. Jenny Greenteeth here looks like she'd rather be anywhere else. The skeleton warrior is drying out by the second. Get this party started by creating a costume for Maxwell from three pieces of clothing and a source of music, such as a boom box or a CD player. Place the music object on the table behind Maxwell.

Have fun dressing up Maxwell for the party. Give him a fun steam-goth outfit with a top hat and a cape or dress him up like a bride, complete with a veil and a wedding dress. As soon as you place three fun costume pieces on Maxwell, the partygoers are impressed with his getup.

CRAZY SOLUTION

The costume contest is a chance to dig into the proverbial closet and pull out some goodies, such as an invisibility cloak that indeed renders Maxwell invisible. (But the cloak itself is still visible, which is why you haven't been using it to sneak past monsters and guards throughout the entire game.) Give Maxwell some more costume jewelry or gear, such as a monocle.

DARK HOLLOW 9-7

Difficulty: 4	Par: 5	Possible Words:

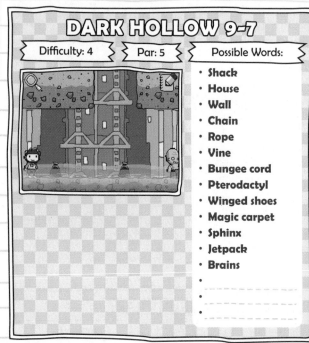

Possible Words:
- Shack
- House
- Wall
- Chain
- Rope
- Vine
- Bungee cord
- Pterodactyl
- Winged shoes
- Magic carpet
- Sphinx
- Jetpack
- Brains
- ⋯
- ⋯
- ⋯

If there is one thing monsters do not like, it's a messy neighborhood, They prefer to eat their brains in clear surroundings. So, Maxwell has been charged with collecting three bags of trash from the monster underworld and carrying them topside for the humans to deal with. When the third bag of trash is on the surface, the Starite appears.

The catch, of course, is that despite Maxwell trying to do the right thing here, monsters will be monsters. If Maxwell gets too close, the monsters lunge and attack. So, you must figure out a way to get these monsters to stay put. Place a shack near the monsters and chain them to it. Variations on this, such as a house and ropes, work, too.

NOTE

Trash bags are light enough that Maxwell can pick one up with his hands.

Give Maxwell the means of flight, such as some winged shoes or a pterodactyl, and cart the garbage bags to the streets above the monster paradise.

CRAZY SOLUTION

Though the trash bags are light enough, Maxwell can do this job the old-fashioned way if he is on a flying steed and cannot risk popping off to pick up the bag. (If a monster attacks a pegasus, for example, you cannot ride that pegasus again—you need to create a new one.) So, even though it is a bit slower—and slow equals crazy when monsters are afoot—use a cord to pick up the trash.

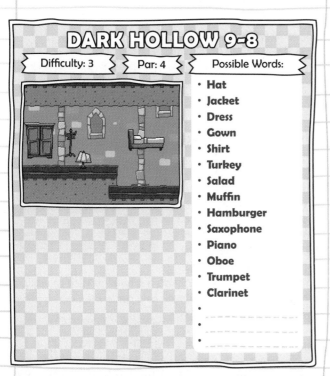

DARK HOLLOW 9-8

Difficulty: 3   Par: 4   Possible Words:

- **Hat**
- **Jacket**
- **Dress**
- **Gown**
- **Shirt**
- **Turkey**
- **Salad**
- **Muffin**
- **Hamburger**
- **Saxophone**
- **Piano**
- **Oboe**
- **Trumpet**
- **Clarinet**
-
-
-

Welcome to a real haunted house. This place is frequented by the spirits of Mr. Chef, Mr. Jazz, and Mr. Fashion. They shake, rattle, and roll objects in their respective rooms.

To soothe these restless spirits and earn the Starite, Maxwell must place a new object in each room that the ghost would have enjoyed in healthier times. Use the names of the ghosts as hints for what kind of object ought to be placed in which room.

Stay under par and use the ladders in this level to get around.

The bedroom is the domain of Mr. Fashion. To make the ghost happy, place an article of clothing on the bed in the room. Jot down something like a hat or a jacket and drop it on the bed. If the ghost likes it, you will see a smiley face pop out of nowhere. Now, move on to the dining room/kitchen area. Mr. Chef loves food, so whip up a dish and place it on the table. Try a turkey or a salad (or any food, really) and offer it to Mr. Chef. If he approves of the object, you see another smiley.

The essence of Mr. Jazz lingers in the upstairs lounge. Mr. Jazz loved music in his corporeal days, so think of a musical instrument and place it in the room. Think of all of the instruments associated with jazz for inspiration, such as the saxophone, the piano, or the clarinet.

As the ghosts are satisfied, they appear in this small side chamber along with the object they were haunting. Mr. Jazz was in the DVD, Mr. Chef was in the chair, and Mr. Fashion was shaking the bedroom lamp.

CRAZY SOLUTION

This is a good level for trying out objects you may not have used up to now and earning the New Object merit. Surely you have not tried a tiara. Write that down and throw it on the bed to please Mr. Fashion. How about a pistachio for Mr. Chef? Or an oboe for Mr. Jazz? Have fun and pick fresh objects to use.

DARK HOLLOW 9-9

| Difficulty: 3 | Par: 4 | Possible Words: |

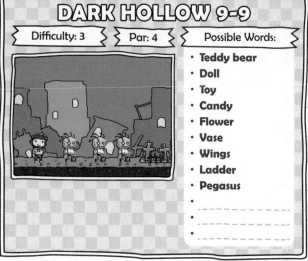

Possible Words:
- Teddy bear
- Doll
- Toy
- Candy
- Flower
- Vase
- Wings
- Ladder
- Pegasus

Three enemy soldiers have been cornered by a horde of zombies. Naturally, your allegiance falls with the undead crew advancing on the bad guys. If you help the zombies turn the three soldiers into gibbering sacks of undead flesh, you earn the Starite. So, how can you help the zombie crowd in this level?

Each of the soldiers is armed and will open fire on the zombies when they close in on the soldiers. Replace the soldiers' guns with other objects they cannot resist holding, such as teddy bears, flowers, and kittens. Once
the soldiers have been disarmed, they are pretty much done for. Watch the show.

When the last soldier has been turned, the Starite appears.

 **TIP**

Hurry up and grab the Starite. The zombies are still hungry, and with the soldiers gone, they turn to the next source of fresh flesh: you.

CRAZY SOLUTION

You can help the zombies out by removing the soldiers' weapons, but why not really make this a party and drop zombies right on the
three meatbags? The zombies turn the soldiers right away before the horde even reaches them, speeding you toward the next Starite.

DARK HOLLOW 9-10

| Difficulty: 3 | Par: 4 | Possible Words: |

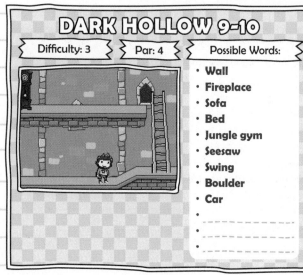

Possible Words:
- Wall
- Fireplace
- Sofa
- Bed
- Jungle gym
- Seesaw
- Swing
- Boulder
- Car

This level is tricky—fun, but tricky! There is a spectral grandfather clock in the level that seems always out of reach. If Maxwell rushes for it, the clock disappears and materializes in another corner of the room. The clock only appears in corners, though—that has to be a hint on how to stop it from moving around so much....

When you run at the clock and it disappears, place another object in its place. The grandfather clock cannot materialize on top of another object. Place a wall in each of the corners, for example. When you fill in three corners, the clock
has nowhere else to go. You do not have to stick to walls, though. Try other objects, such as a car, a fireplace, a jungle gym, or a swing set.

Once the clock can no longer move around the room, tackle it to earn the Starite.

CRAZY SOLUTION

Try themed collections of goods, such as Greek mythology. Conjure up Zeus, Hercules, and Cerberus. Place them in each corner to stop the roaming grandfather clock and earn some New Object merits.

The mobs move fast, so if you want to fly the giant out of reach, you must be just as quick about jotting down a rope and a flying creature, such as a pegasus. Tether the giant to the pegasus and fly straight up to pull the giant clear from attacks.

CRAZY SOLUTION

You must keep the mob from hurting your large friend. Turn the freeze ray on the giant. The giant is temporarily encased in a huge block of ice that keeps the mob from getting at him. Stand ready to hit the giant with the freeze ray again, just in case the ice melts or breaks before the Starite appears.

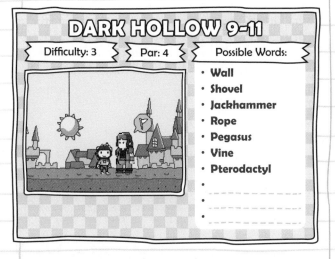

DARK HOLLOW 9-11

Difficulty: 3   Par: 4   Possible Words:

- Wall
- Shovel
- Jackhammer
- Rope
- Pegasus
- Vine
- Pterodactyl

In the past, you have tried to stop giants. You only misunderstood them. Now that you have seen the light, you must save the giant in this level from being attacked by a pitchfork mob and two ambitious knights. The villagers come from the left and the knight from the right. You cannot hurt any of these folks, though. You must figure out the means for just stopping them long enough to earn the Starite, which is about 10 seconds.

The knights can jump, so if you bring in large stationary objects, such as a wall or a tank, you need to stack them. The villagers are earthbound. They only need one wall to keep them back.

Try digging holes in the ground to keep the mob at bay. Use a shovel, a spade, or a jackhammer and get to work.

ACTION LEVELS

DARK HOLLOW 9-1

| Difficulty: 3 | Par: 4 | Possible Words: |

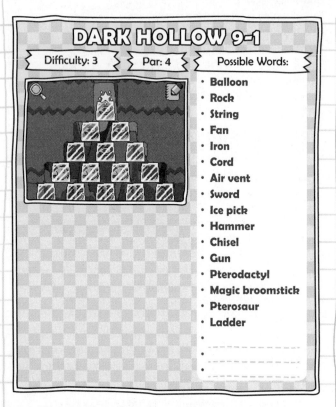

Possible Words:
- **Balloon**
- **Rock**
- **String**
- **Fan**
- **Iron**
- **Cord**
- **Air vent**
- **Sword**
- **Ice pick**
- **Hammer**
- **Chisel**
- **Gun**
- **Pterodactyl**
- **Magic broomstick**
- **Pterosaur**
- **Ladder**
- _____
- _____
- _____

The Starite in this action level is atop an icy pyramid, safe from the land mines and spiked balls just below it. Fortunately, those hazards are encased in ice, but this situation could change in the blink of an eye. A chain reaction or two, and the whole level goes up, taking the Starite with it. You need to somehow separate the Starite from the other ice blocks so you can safely and systematically work your way up to it. Along the way, you need to be ready to deal with the other frozen dangers, such as the bats and the land mines.

The first order of business is to get the Starite out of harm's way for when you chew up the ice pyramid. Tie the Starite to a rock or a safe with a string or a cord. Then, use a fan or an air vent to push the jerry-rigged contraption to the left. The shorter string or cord lifts the Starite away from the land mine.

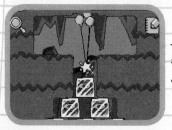

Three balloons attached to the Starite will also lift it away from the ice pyramid.

The reason it is so critical to move the Starite back despite it never touching the actual land mines is that if the ice block around the land mine is broken, the Starite will touch it before it falls to the floor. So, now

that the Starite is safe, you can fly up and dismantle the pyramid with a flying creature that can chew up ice and bats, such as the pterodactyl or the pterosaur, or on the back of a magic broomstick with a hammer or an ice pick. As long as Maxwell stays off the floor of the room, which is where the spiked steel balls land, he will be fine.

 **TIP**

While breaking the ice around the spiked balls or the land mines, stay to one side of the block. Do not fly directly below it, or you will fail when the dangerous object falls directly on you.

CRAZY SOLUTION

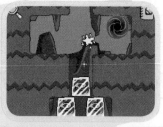

This takes a little guts—but you have that in spades, right? Use a black hole to lift the Starite away from the ice pyramid. Place the black hole in the corner of the upper chamber and then immediately "grab" it with the stylus as soon as the gravity pulls on the Starite. The Starite will drop down on the rock ledge. Now you can dispose of the black hole. Or, if you have chiseled some spiked balls out of the pyramid already, use the black hole to get rid of them.

DARK HOLLOW 9-2

| Difficulty: 2 | Par: 2 | Possible Words: |

Possible Words:
- **Fire**
- **Kid**
- **Brother**
- **Sister**
- **Vampire hunter**
- _____
- _____
- _____

This level is packed, man. The Starite is located at the bottom of the level, tucked into a small alcove. The way down to the Starite winds along three tiers. Each tier is lined with evenly spaced mothballs. There are cherries at each "corner" of the route. But this maze is hardly abandoned. Three ghosts also linger at the corners of the maze, locked behind doors but able to warp right through them when Maxwell gets close.

You can actually complete this level without using any objects, but you need to be fast to stay ahead of the ghosts. As soon as you drop into the maze, rush to the left. As Maxwell falls off the ledge, cut to the right to stay one step ahead of the ghosts. Avoid the cherries, as they will slow Maxwell down.

Just survive the maze to pick up the Starite.

If the mothballs and cherries seem to slow you down too much, burn them away with fire. Move a fire, campfire, or torch through the maze, burning up the objects so there is absolutely nothing between you and the Starite—save for the three ghosts, natch.

Place people in the maze who will get scared of the ghosts and keep them busy, if only for a second. Drop a kid, a sister, and a brother into the maze. Maxwell runs by them unhindered.

CRAZY SOLUTION

What's with all this undead-on-undead violence? Place a mummy in the first ghost's chamber. The mummy attacks the ghost, keeping it busy so Maxwell can skim by without any risk of injury.

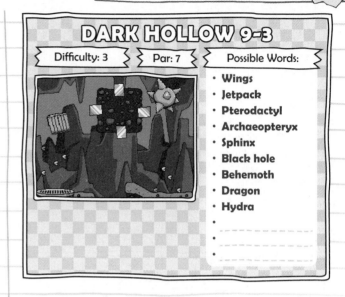

DARK HOLLOW 9-3

Difficulty: 3 · Par: 7 · Possible Words:

- **Wings**
- **Jetpack**
- **Pterodactyl**
- **Archaeopteryx**
- **Sphinx**
- **Black hole**
- **Behemoth**
- **Dragon**
- **Hydra**
-
-
-

The Starite this time around is at the very top of the level, guarded by two harpies. But those harpies are the least of your worries, because the center of the level is dominated by a vortex of death. A system of large air vents sends a giant spiked steel ball and steel crate swirling around the central chamber. If caught against a wall by the spiked ball, Maxwell is done for. You must find a way to survive the vortex as well as defeat the harpies in order to recover the Starite.

To enter the vortex chamber, you need to throw the red switch on the ground floor. The door only stays open for a moment, so you need to scoot through. But do not rush it. Wait until the time is just right before flying up into the vortex with wings or a pterodactyl. As soon as the spiked ball flies past, that's when you should enter the vortex and fly to the very top, armed with an axe to break through the loose rock that stands between you and the harpies.

A black hole inside the vortex will eliminate the spiked ball and crate—but that only works for one try at the level.

The harpies at the top of the screen should be dealt with as soon as possible. A giant creature, such as a hydra or a dragon, makes short work of the harpies so Maxwell can just fly straight for the Starite after surviving the vortex.

CRAZY SOLUTION

The speeding spiked ball will chew through most stuff you place in the vortex. However, you can stop it with another large metal object. First, place

some glue on the bottom piece of metal in the vortex. Then, conjure up a ramp. Release the ramp so it falls and bounces into a vertical position. Grab it and then attach it to the glue. The spiked ball slams into it and stops.

Inside the ice block, the frost giant cannot do much harm. To attack the frost giant with a monster, you must first break it out of the ice block. Place a fire source, such as a campfire or a lighter, near the ice until you see it sweat. Then the frost giant pops out, ready for a fight.

The frost giant is actually afraid of fire. If you leave the fire source next to him in that contained space, he cowers.

DARK HOLLOW 9-4

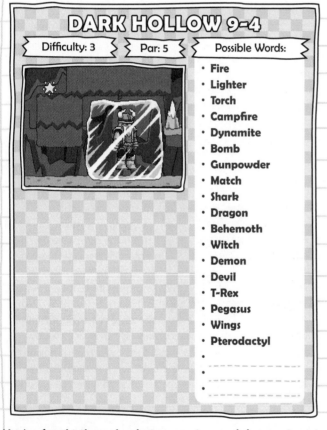

Difficulty: 3	Par: 5	Possible Words:

Possible Words:
- **Fire**
- **Lighter**
- **Torch**
- **Campfire**
- **Dynamite**
- **Bomb**
- **Gunpowder**
- **Match**
- **Shark**
- **Dragon**
- **Behemoth**
- **Witch**
- **Demon**
- **Devil**
- **T-Rex**
- **Pegasus**
- **Wings**
- **Pterodactyl**

The frost giant can also be eliminated with explosives while it is within the ice. Plant some dynamite or a bomb near the ice and then drop a match on it. The explosion not only shatters the ice block, but it also destroys the frost giant.

The sea witch must be ruined before you fly toward the Starite. Before suiting up Maxwell with some wings or placing him on a pegasus, drop a monster near the sea witch, such as a dragon. A regular

witch works, too, as it will cast a spell on the sea witch and turn it into a frog. Now you can fly right over the water and zero in on the Starite.

You've fought through robots, vampires, and dragons to get here—now what? Frost giants, friend. In this action level, a frost giant is trapped inside a giant ice block that plugs up the route to the Starite. You must not only figure out a way to get through the frost giant, but also eliminate an eel in the waters below the level and a sea witch that guards the entrance into the center of the level. The two monsters on land must be dealt with right away, but if you stay out of the water, the eel is not a factor.

CRAZY SOLUTION

The frost giant can be laid low with a magic wand placed in Maxwell's hands. Shoot the frost giant with it to turn it into a harmless frog. Now you can just waltz by it and fly up to the Starite.

DARK HOLLOW 9-5

| Difficulty: 4 | Par: 6 | Possible Words: |

- **Giant enemy crab**
- **Beast**
- **Behemoth**
- **Hammer**
- **Pickaxe**
- **Sword**
- **Spade**
- **Shovel**
- **Gun**
- **Rifle**
- **Shotgun**
- **Bazooka**
- **Snowball**
- **Ice ball**
- **Ice block**
- **Rain**
- **Fan**
- **Pterodactyl**
- **Pegasus**
- **Sphinx**
- **Archaeopteryx**
- **Wings**
- ....
- ....
- ....

The Starite is this level is guarded by a necromancer and his platoon of skeleton warriors. These foes will not give up the treasure without a fight, so that is what you must give them. (Or at least give them a push. An air vent to the left of the necromancer and skeleton warriors pushes them right off the ledge and into the lava below.) Do not even try to fly over the lava and head for the Starite without first taking care of the bleached bone army.

Before flying to the Starite, you also need to take care of the large fire vent. Drop a snowball or an ice ball on it to snuff out the flames.

The skeleton warriors are tough, but not even they can withstand an attack from a ferocious beast or behemoth. These monsters are just small enough to fit in the confined space

leading to the Starite, but they are certainly large enough to cause real carnage.

The route to the edge of the upper tunnel where Maxwell starts the level is blocked by a stalactite and a stalagmite. Get rid of them with a pick or a hammer.

There is another hazard along the top of the level that must also be dealt with before flying off to the Starite on the back of a pegasus or a pterodactyl: spiked balls. These are held up by some loose rocks and will fall as soon as you step off the edge of the platform. No matter how quickly you move, they will fall on you. So, before taking flight, use a projectile (such as a gun or a rifle) to shoot out the loose rocks below the spiked balls so they fall into the lava and pester you no more.

CRAZY SOLUTION

Go on. Be a monster. Lure the necromancer and the skeleton warriors off the edge of this platform with a little toddler. They simply cannot resist.

The baby is a good way to put some space between the skeleton warriors and the Starite, too, so you can get in there and install an air vent or a fan to push them into the lava.

DARK HOLLOW 9-6

Difficulty: 3 · Par: 5 · Possible Words:

Possible Words:
- Fire
- Campfire
- Lighter
- Torch
- Flamethrower
- Shovel
- Spade
- Pickaxe
- Dynamite
- Bomb
- Gunpowder
- Gun
- Rifle
- Machine gun
- Black hole
- Devil
- Demon
-
-
-

This level has a serious mummy problem. The whole area is infected with bandaged-up dead dudes. For Maxwell to collect the Starite, he must fight his way through the mummies and then burrow into the catacombs below the surface—where he must challenge even more mummies. And that's not the entire crew, either. There is a tomb down there that releases a cyclops if Maxwell gets close to it. So, before even docking Maxwell's pirate ship and jumping onto land, take some steps to clear the area of trouble.

Due to those dry rags hanging off them, mummies are extremely flammable. Drop a fire source right on top of each mummy. Use a fire, a campfire, a torch, or a lighter. Any of these will send the mummy up in flames. Then it takes just a few seconds for the mummy to be reduced to harmless ashes.

After burning through the mummies, it is time to dig down to the catacombs. Jot down a shovel, a pickaxe, or a spade and hand it to Maxwell. The sand and stones give way to the digging utensil easily enough.

The cyclops erupts from the tomb as soon as you touch down in the catacombs. If you still have the fire, place it next to the tomb to contain it. Otherwise, you need to fight back against the cyclops with a gun or a rifle. A laser pistol is particularly effective against this mythological monster.

The Starite is in a small chamber that is too small for you to access. You must bring the Starite to you. A rope, a chain or a bungee cord works. You can also tie the Starite to a small animal, such as a cat, and then tease the animal with its favorite food. The animal runs for the food and brings the Starite with it.

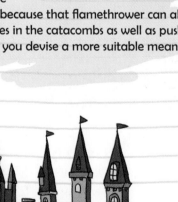

The cyclops can be preemptively destroyed by placing the fire source you used to torch the mummies next to the tomb. Then, drop a bomb or some dynamite right on top of it.

CRAZY SOLUTION

Death from above! Hand Maxwell a flamethrower and soar over the mummies above the catacombs and lace them with hot blasts from the weapon. Hold onto it, because that flamethrower can also incinerate the mummies in the catacombs as well as push the cyclops back while you devise a more suitable means of dealing with it.

DARK HOLLOW 9-7

Difficulty: 3 **Par: 6** **Possible Words:**

- Scuba
- Flippers
- Wetsuit
- Respiration
- Dive helmet
- Dragon
- Behemoth
- Beast
- T-Rex
- Witch
- Black hole
- ....
- ....

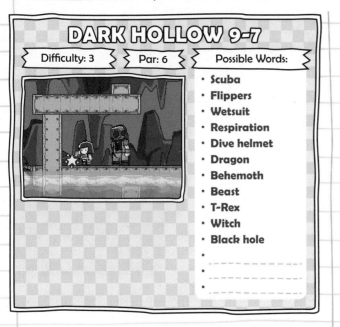

This underwater city was supposed to be paradise. A place where great men and women could leave the world behind and focus on great works of science and art... Where government would treat the working man the same as it would the king... But then something went wrong. Horribly wrong. And now all that is left of the dream are monsters in diving helmets and small sisters that guard the precious Starites. Maxwell must dive into this failed Utopia and retrieve the Starite without hurting the small girl.

The Loch Ness monster patrols the waters below the small girl. Before slipping into the waves, be sure to eliminate the monster with one of your own. A dragon shreds Nessie.

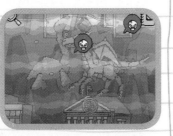

That same dragon can be used to eliminate the little girl's guardian. If you try to attack it directly, the size of the guardian will overwhelm you. So keep your distance and deal with it from afar via a dragon, a hydra, or a T-Rex. Any mid- to large-sized monster will rip the guardian apart. Just make sure to junk the monster before it threatens the little girl.

As soon as the guardian and the Loch Ness monster have been neutralized, don some scuba gear or flippers and swim to the hole in the floor that leads up to the little girl and the Starite.

CRAZY SOLUTION

Attack the guardian from afar with powerful blasts of fire and electricity. Create some fireballs and shocks and drop them right on the guardian's head, imagining that these powers were somehow coming right out of your own hand and arcing across the screen. Yeah, imagine that....

DARK HOLLOW 9-8

Difficulty: 2 **Par: 3** **Possible Words:**

- Dragon
- Behemoth
- Beast
- Hydra
- Cthulhu
- ....
- ....
- ....

Below the surface, the elder gods slumber. While they sleep in their kingdoms, they dream. They dream of the war with the shoggoths that helped build these eldritch palaces before turning on their masters. Most of the shoggoths were killed in the war, but some survived. And now one is loose in this level, guarding a precious Starite. To get the Starite, you must raise the shoggoth to the surface and be ready for its attack.

Use the red switch on the wall next to all of the doppelgangers to start raising the shoggoth.

As the shoggoth rises, prep a monster, such as a dragon or a hydra, in the Notepad. Place the monster aside so it cannot attack Maxwell. But as soon as the shoggoth is on the surface, move the monster into the level and

watch the battle commence. You can also summon a black hole and send the shoggoth to another dimension as it rises to the surface.

CRAZY SOLUTION

Let's do this level up right. If you need to take down a shoggoth, then you'd better conjure up Cthulhu for one of the solutions. Cthulhu rages against the shoggoth, slamming it back to oblivion with its giant fists. Just make sure you banish Cthulhu to the trash before heading out to pick up the Starite.

Make sure you throw the red and green switches so the lava pit at the bottom of the level is covered.

CRAZY SOLUTION

The origins of the Flatwoods Monster stretch back to 1952. Folks in the town of Flatwoods, West Virginia, claimed a UFO dropped off at least

one alien creature, described as having burning red eyes and a huge cowl-like headdress. It has not been seen since, but it is a popular part of local folklore. Why not help these aliens get back to their homes with a portal? Oh, the portal only releases monsters? Well, then the ahool that pops out will help here, too.

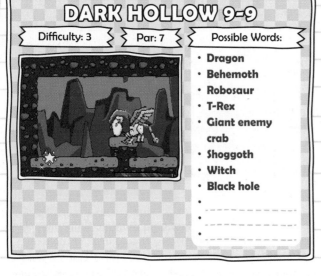

DARK HOLLOW 9-9

Difficulty: 3	Par: 7	Possible Words:

- **Dragon**
- **Behemoth**
- **Robosaur**
- **T-Rex**
- **Giant enemy crab**
- **Shoggoth**
- **Witch**
- **Black hole**
-
-
-

This level is a rogue's gallery of urban legend monsters. The Jersey Devil is joined by Flatwoods Monsters, living stone gargoyles, and a chimera. Before even setting foot in the tunnels that lead to the Starite at the bottom, you must destroy these monsters. Only when the path is clear can you move toward the Starite, throwing the red and green switches as you move to erect a bridge over the lava pit at the very bottom of the level.

Start with the chimera and work your way up. The chimera is the toughest monster in this level and is likely to do the most damage to your monster. Once you have beaten the chimera, then move on to the Jersey Devil.

Large monsters might be too big to eliminate the two Flatwoods Monsters in the middle of the level, so try a medium-sized beast or behemoth.

DARK HOLLOW 9-10

Difficulty: 4	Par: 5	Possible Words:

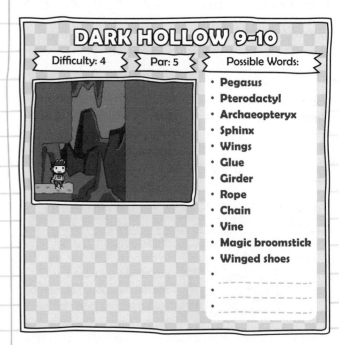

- **Pegasus**
- **Pterodactyl**
- **Archaeopteryx**
- **Sphinx**
- **Wings**
- **Glue**
- **Girder**
- **Rope**
- **Chain**
- **Vine**
- **Magic broomstick**
- **Winged shoes**
-
-
-

This is a deceptively easy level to complete. The Starite is in a small alcove on the opposite side of the level from Maxwell. There are two slender shafts that extend up and down the right and left sides of the level. With very little to grab hold of and use to pull Maxwell up to the top of the level, you must instead use flying creatures, such as a pegasus or a pterodactyl, to do all the heavy lifting.

There are a couple of metal pieces sticking out of the walls in the shafts. These can be used to make makeshift platforms. Glue a girder to the metal and then dangle a rope down for Maxwell to grab onto. Fly up to the rope with wings, winged shoes, or a magic broomstick. (Be mindful of distance, though. These objects only last for a few moments before they stop and must be refreshed.) Then fly over the girder and release the rope. From here, you can reach the top of the level.

Flutter down the right side of the level to pick up the Starite.

CRAZY SOLUTION

This is such an easy level to over-think, but that is part of the trick. You really only need to use a flying animal, such as a pegasus, a sphinx, a pterodactyl, or

an archaeopteryx to reach the Starite. Because par is five, you come in way under, which helps you earn the World Under Par merit for Dark Hollow.

DARK HOLLOW 9-11

| Difficulty: 4 | Par: 8 | Possible Words: |

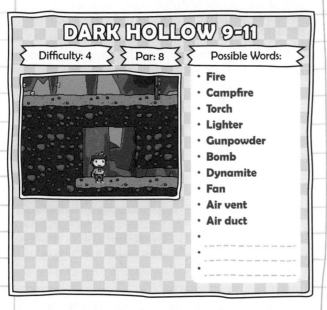

Possible Words:
- **Fire**
- **Campfire**
- **Torch**
- **Lighter**
- **Gunpowder**
- **Bomb**
- **Dynamite**
- **Fan**
- **Air vent**
- **Air duct**
- _____
- _____
- _____

In the final Dark Hollow level, Maxwell is trapped. He must make the Starite come to him. The level is set up for this,

but you just need to help things along to make it actually work. This level requires a lot of fire, so expect to be using matches, fires, campfires, torches, fireballs, and lava spouts for all your pyrotechnic needs.

First, you need to burn through the rickety wood wall.

Next, ignite the gunpowder to blow through the dirt below the Starite. Now light the rope holding up the Starite ablaze.

 TIP

If you accidentally set the Starite itself on fire, drizzle it with water to put out the little flames.

Once the Starite falls, you must push it along the ledge so it drops down next to Maxwell. A fan and an air vent are the two obvious solutions. However, for the third and fourth attempts, you need to employ the hungry animal trick. Attach the Starite to a critter and then tease the animal with some food to make it run and drag the Starite along behind it.

Push the Starite through the narrow opening at the bottom of the level. A magnet and a piece of metal glued to the Starite will also pull it along.

CRAZY SOLUTION

Tie the Starite to a mouse with a guitar string. You'll hear sweet music as you lure the mouse into Maxwell's cave with some cheese.

WORLD 10: MISH MASH

PUZZLE LEVELS

MISH MASH 10-1

| Difficulty: 2 | Par: 2 | Possible Words: |

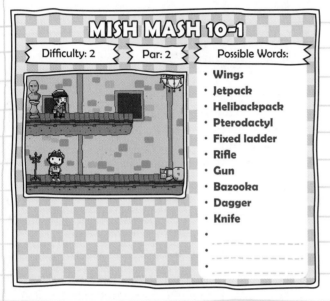

Possible Words:
- Wings
- Jetpack
- Helibackpack
- Pterodactyl
- Fixed ladder
- Rifle
- Gun
- Bazooka
- Dagger
- Knife
-
-
-

Maxwell has been called to the scene of the crime, a grand mansion on a grim night, to determine who is the killer. A body lies in the center of the level. Guests and hired help surround it. The goal here is simple. Maxwell must figure out...whodunnit.

The solution to this mystery is simple: It was the maid. (You were expecting the butler?) To earn the Starite, though, you must effectively finger the maid as the killer. You must reach the ledge she is on, so try using some wings, a pegasus, or a fixed ladder. Once you close in on the maid, give Maxwell a weapon so she knows you mean business. At the sight of a gun or a knife, the maid flees. Mystery solved.

CRAZY SOLUTION

The maid is so jittery about what she's done that she will give herself away at the sight of any weapon. Even a slingshot in Maxwell's hand elicits a confession.

MISH MASH 10-2

| Difficulty: 1 | Par: 3 | Possible Words: |

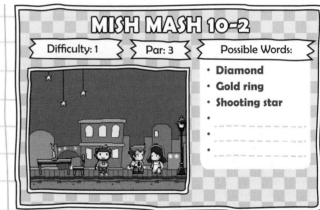

Possible Words:
- Diamond
- Gold ring
- Shooting star
-
-
-

'Tis a night for romance. A lovely young couple stands on the shores of a river in an aging city. A candlelit table is set for a wonderful meal. Love is in the air. All this night needs is a spark to turn into a *l'amour* inferno. And that's where Maxwell comes in. He needs to make this level super-romantic by adding at least one object to it that perfects the mood.

Could it be time for a proposal? Give a diamond or a gold ring to the woman. The couple squeals with delight when the jewelry appears, causing a Starite to appear. But sometimes romance needs not the material to flow. All it needs is the perfect scenery. Try hanging a shooting star in the sky to enchant the couple.

CRAZY SOLUTION

Stretch your imagination when giving a gift to the woman in this level. Jot some selenite down in your Notepad. The mystical-looking gypsum appears and puts a smile on everybody's face. Try other minerals and crystals in this level to keep getting New Object merits.

MISH MASH 10-3

Difficulty: 2   Par: 3   Possible Words:

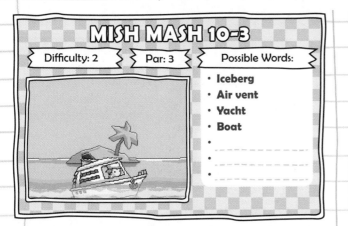

- Iceberg
- Air vent
- Yacht
- Boat
-
-
-

In Greek legend, the song of the sirens was so beautiful that when it filled the ears of sailors, they had no choice but to steer their ships toward it. Captains would crash their ships into rocks and sink, all under the spell of the sirens' voices. In this level, the sirens have returned from myth and are filling the air with their dulcet tones. A sailor on a ship in the middle of the lake is caught between the song and safety. Maxwell must help him to either fate in order to earn the Starite.

There are many ways to push or pull the sailor. Dropping an iceberg in the water right next to the ship creates waves that push the ship toward either shore.

Push the ship toward the siren with your own boat or yacht. Just make sure you write down a bigger vessel so you have the power to move the sailor's boat.

CRAZY SOLUTION

The siren should inspire you to consider other threats to sailors from the great poem "The Odyssey." Conjure up Scylla, the sea monster, and drop it in the water right next to the sailor. The sight of Scylla freaks him out, prompting him to flee. Depending on which side of the ship you place Scylla, that could end in delight or disaster.

MISH MASH 10-4

Difficulty: 3   Par: 3   Possible Words:

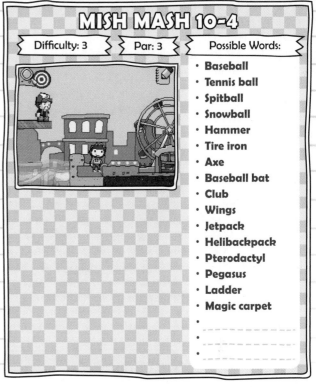

- Baseball
- Tennis ball
- Spitball
- Snowball
- Hammer
- Tire iron
- Axe
- Baseball bat
- Club
- Wings
- Jetpack
- Helibackpack
- Pterodactyl
- Pegasus
- Ladder
- Magic carpet
-
-
-

Welcome to an afternoon at the fair. The Ferris wheel cycles lazily against the afternoon sun. The midway is full of smiling folks, emptying their pockets for a chance to win the big stuffed elephant. Maxwell is more than happy to be here, ready to play some games and win the best prize of all: a Starite.

There are three events you must play in this level to win: dunk tank, whack-a-mole, and hammer swing. You do not have to do them in any particular order. When the third event is finished, the Starite appears.

The dunk tank on the left side of the level is easy to complete. Just create a ball for Maxwell (shooting the target will not work) and throw it at the target. Use a small ball that Maxwell can throw high, such as a baseball or a tennis ball. Maxwell struggles to throw a heavier ball from the ground. Now, if you have wings or a jetpack to fly closer to the target, you can use something heavier, such as a rugby ball. You can use these flying objects or a ladder to scale the whack-a-mole station.

Three moles pop in and out of their burrows near the clown. You must smack each mole. A bat or a sword works here, but you need the means to fly to get the top mole.

Test your strength at the hammer swing. Come down hard on the button in front of the bell to ring it. Dropping on it from a great height works well, as does smashing the button with a tool, such as a baseball bat or a tire iron.

CRAZY SOLUTION

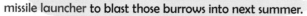

Why bother playing whack-a-mole when you can play blast-a-mole? Eliminate the three moles with extreme prejudice by using a bazooka or a missile launcher to blast those burrows into next summer.

Give a projectile weapon to your gunslinger, such as a rifle or a shotgun. Then drag the object onto Maxwell. The moment you see him turn blue, release the weapon into his possession.

CRAZY SOLUTION

Who wants to play cowboys and aliens? Give the gunslinger a weapon of the sci-fi future for this match: a laser pistol. The laser pistol blasts the evil gunslinger and takes him down with a single shot.

MISH MASH 10-5

Difficulty: 3	Par: 3	Possible Words:

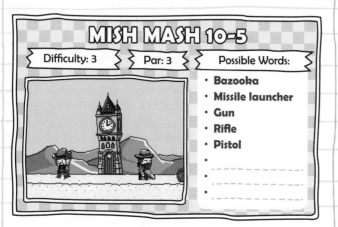

Possible Words:
- **Bazooka**
- **Missile launcher**
- **Gun**
- **Rifle**
- **Pistol**
- _____
- _____
- _____

Two gunslingers agree to meet in the street to settle their differences the old-fashioned way—crippling violence. Unfortunately, one of the gunslingers is only a slinger today—he forgot his gun. Maxwell must help this fella participate—and win—the gunfight to earn the Starite. The only solution here is to give the gunslinger a weapon. Maxwell cannot shoot the other gunslinger on the fellow's behalf.

TIP

Act quickly! As soon as the level begins, you have maybe three seconds to give the gunslinger a weapon before the other shooter opens fire and guns the slinger down in the shade of the clock tower.

MISH MASH 10-6

Difficulty: 2	Par: 4	Possible Words:

Possible Words:
- **TV**
- **Radio**
- **DVD player**
- **Computer**
- **Brother**
- **Mother**
- **Sister**
- **Aunt**
- **Doctor**
- **Surgeon**
- **Pathologist**
- _____
- _____
- _____

Maxwell pays a visit to the hospital in this level. He's charged with bringing a little joy to the ward. How can Maxwell turn these frowns upside down? By giving the three patients in the level something they want. The patient requests today are medical attention, entertainment, and family. So, you must think of objects to satisfy these needs in order to win the Starite.

The patient in the lower-right corner of the level needs some medical attention. She's feeling really awful. Give her a doctor. Try different types of doctors to satisfy her needs, such as a surgeon or a general practitioner. When the doctor is dropped next to her bed, she smiles. That's one down.

The patient directly above the one who needed a doctor would love some entertainment to pass the time. Provide a TV or a DVD player to put a smile on her face.

The patient in the upper-left corner of the level just wants a visit from her family. Write down a family member, such as a mother, a brother, or a sister and place that person next to the patient's bed. At the sight of the family member, she smiles. The Starite appears as soon as that third smile brightens the ward.

CRAZY SOLUTION

What's more entertaining than video games? Give a video game to the patient who needs a little distraction. Place the handheld system in her hands to coax a smile to her face. As for the patient below her...she asked for medical attention, but she did not exactly specify what kind of doctor she wanted to see. Would the sight of a proctologist make her smile?

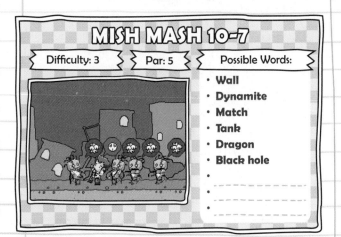

MISH MASH 10-7

Difficulty: 3	Par: 5	Possible Words:

- **Wall**
- **Dynamite**
- **Match**
- **Tank**
- **Dragon**
- **Black hole**

The zombies are on the march again. The slavering horde stumbles toward a family. The father is overcome at the start of the level. He is turned into a zombie before his wife and child. They will have time to mourn him later. Right now, they need Maxwell's help to survive this horror. Destroy the zombie army and save what's left of the family to earn the Starite. It is a bittersweet victory indeed.

Slow the advancing horde by placing a wall in their path. The zombies walk into the wall and pile up. With the zombies gathered close, drop some dynamite or a bomb in their midst. Ignite the fuse with a match or a torch and turn those zombies into ash.

 **TIP**

If there are any straggler zombies, giving them some brains will lure them to the rest of the pack. Just pick up the brains and keep moving them closer and closer to the rest of the zombies until they are all together. As the zombies feed, you can plan their destruction.

You can also send a dragon or a behemoth to confront the zombie horde. These huge beasts cannot be turned into zombies by their touch.

CRAZY SOLUTION

Up to now, Maxwell's solutions have not required him to get his hands dirty. Place Maxwell in a tank and drive through the level, shelling the zombies. You have to keep moving to eliminate the horde before they reach the family, but a single shell from the tank is enough to bring down one or two zombies.

MISH MASH 10-8

| Difficulty: 3 | Par: 6 | Possible Words: |

Possible Words:
- **Wings**
- **Jetpack**
- **Sphinx**
- **Missile launcher**
- **Knife**
- **Dagger**
- **Gun**
- **Rope**
- **Handcuffs**
- **Steak**
- **Hamburger**
- _____
- _____
- _____

Jailbreak! There has been an escape at the prison, and the guards need Maxwell's help to rein in the fleeing prisoners. These are dangerous men, so Maxwell has his choice of dead or alive when hunting the convicts. There are three prisoners in this level. Two of them are to the right. One has a hostage that must not be hurt, or else the level ends. The other is protected by a vicious dog. Try not to hurt the dog, if you can avoid it. The third prisoner has changed into civilian clothes and is mingling with two fans at the stadium to the left. You must avoid hurting the two fans and just collar the crook.

It is easiest to shoot the criminal with the hostage in the cave. Wait for the crook to be apart from the girl and then open fire with a pistol or a rifle.

CAUTION

Only use a precision weapon for this level. If you try something with too much boom, you will hurt innocents.

The prisoner above the hostage situation is protected by the snarling dog. If the dog sees you, it will attack. You can feed the dog three times (steak, hamburger, and meat all work) to make it sleepy and then fly to grab the crook or eliminate him. If you want to bring him in alive, use a rope or handcuffs to tether the

convict to Maxwell and then drag him to the prison. When any of the crooks is brought to the jail, they slump their shoulders and accept their fate. They do not put up a fuss past this point.

The convict who blended into the crowd at the stadium is tough to spot at first. He's the one without any facial hair and with the ball cap. Strike the convict with a weapon to drop him or grab him and drag him back to the prison.

CRAZY SOLUTION

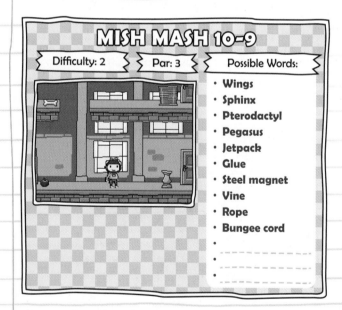

Not every convict is willing to go back to jail with pretty please. Conjure up a bulldozer and push the prisoner at the stadium back to jail kicking and screaming. The other two fans are pretty jazzed about the appearance of the bulldozer, actually. You may even see one climb up on the roof for a free ride.

MISH MASH 10-9

| Difficulty: 2 | Par: 3 | Possible Words: |

Possible Words:
- **Wings**
- **Sphinx**
- **Pterodactyl**
- **Pegasus**
- **Jetpack**
- **Glue**
- **Steel magnet**
- **Vine**
- **Rope**
- **Bungee cord**
- _____
- _____
- _____

Maxwell plays the part of a delivery man in this one. There are six doors in this level. A delivery sits in front of each door, but it's the wrong item for the person or object inside. Maxwell must correct the misplaced orders to earn the Starite. This level requires flight, so create some wings or a jetpack for Maxwell. He cannot carry some of these objects up the ladder—they are too heavy.

You must make the matches to complete the level. When you bring the correct object to the proper door, Maxwell smiles. Match similar objects to make progress and earn the Starite. For example, take the apple to the door with the orange. The pedestal goes to the door with the lamp. The bone belongs at the door with the dog.

The dog tags go to the door with the soldier.

You need to use a rope, a chain, or a cord to fly the heavier objects, such as the pedestal and the window dressing, around the level. The shades go up to the door with the window in the upper-left corner of the building.

CRAZY SOLUTION

The heavier objects can be moved by the power of magnets. Glue a piece of metal to the objects and then hand Maxwell a magnet. The magnet pulls the metal toward Maxwell and takes the object with it.

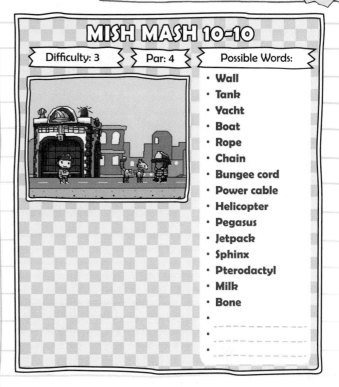

MISH MASH 10-10

Difficulty: 3	Par: 4	Possible Words:

- **Wall**
- **Tank**
- **Yacht**
- **Boat**
- **Rope**
- **Chain**
- **Bungee cord**
- **Power cable**
- **Helicopter**
- **Pegasus**
- **Jetpack**
- **Sphinx**
- **Pterodactyl**
- **Milk**
- **Bone**
-
-
-

When Maxwell arrives in this level, he stands in front of a firehouse. There is a firefighter in front of it, next to a cat. Wait a second—don't firehouses normally have dalmatians? What's this guy doing with a cat? Well, it turns out the dalmatian is across the pond in the center of the level. The dog is standing next to an older lady. Maxwell must get these pets back to their rightful owners to earn the Starite. But since cats and dogs tend to scrap, he must keep them apart. If the dog attacks the cat, the level ends.

Wall off the cat from the firefighter by luring it into the corner with some milk. Once the cat has been separated, you can safely retrieve the dog from the old lady without causing a big scene.

Neither the dog nor the cat particularly wants to be dragged through the water, so give Maxwell some wings or a flying creature, such as a pterodactyl.

Once the dog has been placed in front of the firehouse, you can take the cat to the old lady. Tether the cat to Max with a rope or a chain and fly it through the air. When you drop the cat off in front of the lady, she smiles. The Starite appears, and the level has been solved.

CRAZY SOLUTION

Why move the pets when you can move the people? After all, the pet owners will not put up a fight if they are in the same area together. Fly the old lady over the cat and then take the firefighter over to the dalmatian. As long as the match is made, the Starite is awarded.

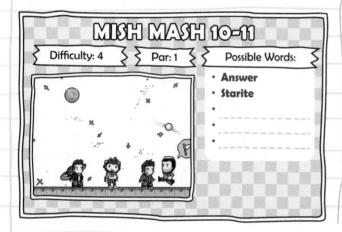

MISH MASH 10-11
Difficulty: 4 | Par: 1 | Possible Words:
- Answer
- Starite

This level is a neat trick. Maxwell arrives in a rather cosmic-looking room with some of the 5TH Cell developers at his side. There is no sign of the Starite. All the hint says is to "Write the answer." What is the answer? The answer to what? Life's deepest questions? 42? How can you solve this level with little more than an obscure clue?

Wait a second. The hint *is* the answer. Jot "answer" down in your Notepad. The Starite appears. Actually, a lot of Starites appear. Collect one to end the level.

CRAZY SOLUTION

Well, you cannot just write "answer" four times to complete the level. What else can you write in there to finish the level? Just write Starite in the Notepad. That's an equally suitable answer.

ACTION LEVELS

MISH MASH 10-1
Difficulty: 4 | Par: 4 | Possible Words:
- Balloon
- Glue
- Tape
- Adhesive
- Girder
- Board
- Air vent
- Fan

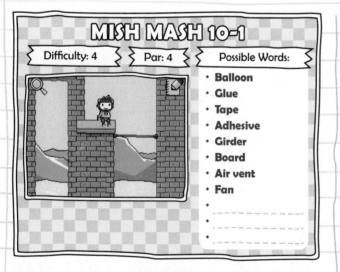

The Starite in this action level is located in a tall chamber, held up by a door that is moved as soon as Maxwell triggers the tripwire next to his feet. The bottom of the level is lined with spiked balls. If the door opens and there is nothing to catch the Starite, it will drop directly into the spikes and be ruined. You must come up with the means to slow or stop

the Starite's descent so Maxwell can fly down the level and pick it up before it reaches the spikes.

Tie three balloons to the Starite. Once the third balloon is attached, the Starite actually starts to rise in its side chamber. Now Maxwell can fly down to the Starite and chase it on a pegasus, a sphinx, or a pterodactyl. Because the room is so tall, any flight object other than a flying mount will not effectively work.

There is a piece of metal sticking out of the side of the level below the Starite. You can build something here to catch the Starite. Glue a girder to the metal. Then, place an air vent on the girder to "catch" the Starite when it falls. Make sure to place the air vent close to the edge of the girder so the Starite does not bounce away.

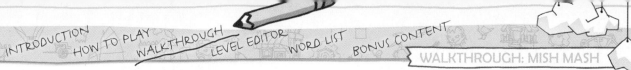
Now, fly down and fetch the Starite from its airy cradle. You can also build this set up with tape, a board, and a fan.

CRAZY SOLUTION

Jot down a guitar string and tie the Starite to a bird, such as an eagle. The Starite is heavy, but the eagle does its best to stay aloft. This setup slows the Starite's fall toward the spikes, so as soon as the door is removed by triggering the tripwire, fly straight for the Starite.

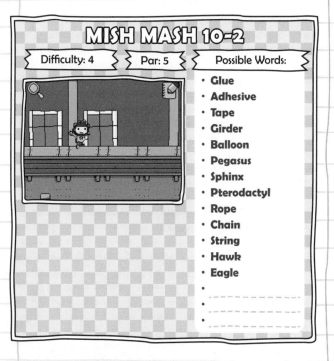

MISH MASH 10-2

Difficulty: 4	Par: 5	Possible Words:

- Glue
- Adhesive
- Tape
- Girder
- Balloon
- Pegasus
- Sphinx
- Pterodactyl
- Rope
- Chain
- String
- Hawk
- Eagle
- _____
- _____
- _____

This level is a machine. The Starite is located on a track directly below Maxwell's feet. As he walks to the right, a wall pushes the Starite along with him. However, the Starite track is shorter than Maxwell's. Before Maxwell can reach the end of his track and then fly down to grab the Starite, it has already fallen into an abyss. So, as in the previous level, you must think up a contraption to slow or stop the Starite's fall until Maxwell can reach it on the back of a pegasus or a pterodactyl.

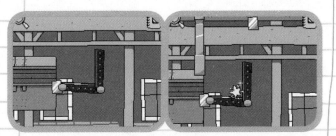

You have one more object in this level than in the previous one, so glue together a "bucket" make of two girders and

attach it to the piece of metal just below the Starite's track. The wall just pushes the Starite into your bucket. You can create this bucket with other materials, too, such as adhesive and boards.

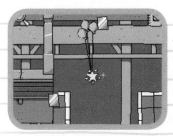

Three balloons tied to the Starite keep it from falling into the void when pushed out of its track.

CRAZY SOLUTION

Because you can use multiples of the same object in a single solution, use two pterodactyls to finish the level. Place Maxwell on a pterodactyl

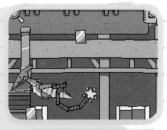

so he can fly down and pick up the Starite. But then use the second pterodactyl to keep the Starite aloft. Tie the Starite to the pterodactyl. The pterodactyl will not fall right off the screen. It flaps its wings to stay up. But you need to hurry to reach the Starite before it slowly sinks.

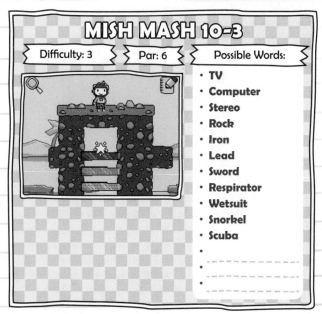

MISH MASH 10-3

Difficulty: 3	Par: 6	Possible Words:

- TV
- Computer
- Stereo
- Rock
- Iron
- Lead
- Sword
- Respirator
- Wetsuit
- Snorkel
- Scuba
- _____
- _____
- _____

The Starite in this level is held above a pool of water by three doors. Each door is controlled by a button or switch in the level. The red and green doors are controlled by buttons in the lake. The blue door is activated by a switch in a small pool to the right. You must activate these doors in order to drop the Starite into the water and pick it up. However, there are a few complications, as you might expect.

For example, there are a werewolf and a devil in the water just below the Starite. Each is wearing a snorkel so they can swim underwater and attack if Maxwell makes a run for the prize.

The first thing you need to do is activate the blue switch. There is a vampire guarding it. However, because the vampire is in the water, it can be shocked with an electronic object. Drop a TV in the water to give the vamp a jolt. The buzz not only eliminates the vampire, but it also throws the switch. Now the blue door is open.

Next: Take out the monsters in the water. Drop another TV in the water to zap them out of the picture.

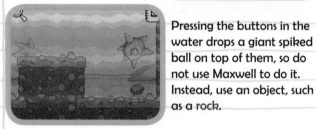

Pressing the buttons in the water drops a giant spiked ball on top of them, so do not use Maxwell to do it. Instead, use an object, such as a rock.

Once the Starite has been dropped into the water, jot down some scuba gear or flippers and dive after it. Now, you could dive to press the buttons earlier if you used a black hole to get rid of the spiked balls. But if you are not quick enough to move the black hole around the level, you are better off sticking with objects to press the buttons.

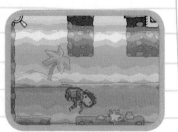

CRAZY SOLUTION

You can kill the vampire and revert the werewolf back to a harmless man by hanging a sun in the skies over the level.

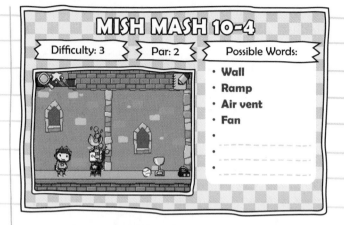

MISH MASH 10-4

Difficulty: 3   Par: 2   Possible Words:

- **Wall**
- **Ramp**
- **Air vent**
- **Fan**
-
-
-

The puzzle in this level is behind a door in the ceiling. There is no switch that removes the door, so you need to instead figure out which object on the floor must be picked up to activate the door. There are two Scribblenauts patrolling the room with flamberges, so you need to keep them at bay while pursuing the object, but they cannot be injured. If either is killed, the level ends.

Push the two Scribblenauts aside with a fan or an air vent. You can also contain them with a wall.

To unlock the Starite, pick up the x-ray goggles. When Maxwell puts the goggles on his face, you see things just like an x-ray. The Starite falls from the ceiling and can be easily scooped up to end the level.

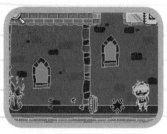

If you are using a wall to block the Scribblenauts, try placing a ramp on top of it so the Starite just rolls right to you.

CRAZY SOLUTION

Push the Scribblenauts aside by blasting them with the freeze ray. When one is encased in ice, you can just push him into his friend and block him off in the left corner of the room. Now go grab the goggles to release the Starite.

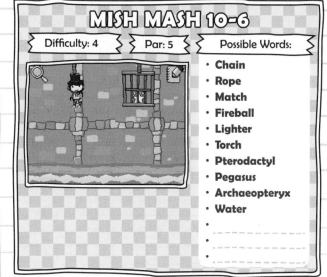

MISH MASH 10-6

Difficulty: 4	Par: 5	Possible Words:

Possible Words:
- **Chain**
- **Rope**
- **Match**
- **Fireball**
- **Lighter**
- **Torch**
- **Pterodactyl**
- **Pegasus**
- **Archaeopteryx**
- **Water**
- ⋯
- ⋯
- ⋯

MISH MASH 10-5

Difficulty: 3	Par: 2	Possible Words:

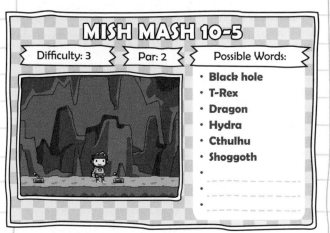

Possible Words:
- **Black hole**
- **T-Rex**
- **Dragon**
- **Hydra**
- **Cthulhu**
- **Shoggoth**
- ⋯
- ⋯
- ⋯

At the beginning of this level, Maxwell is presented with a series of switches. Each switch controls a door on the ceiling. The Starite is behind the last door.

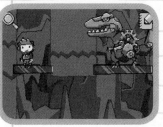

But the other doors are all that's holding back a doppelganger, a robosaur, and a grim reaper. If Maxwell hits the wrong switch, he'll have a real headache on his hands.

The switch that drops the Starite is on the left side of the level. Throw the switch and then collect your prize without any hassle from the monsters in the ceiling.

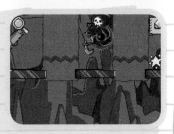

CRAZY SOLUTION

However...if you would feel better about exterminating the threats in the ceiling, summon a black hole and drag it into each alcove to remove the threat. End with the grim reaper, because Death does not go easily.

The Starite is not in immediate danger in this level, but it could be with one false move. Maxwell hangs from the ceiling next to a caged Starite. Both are just inches from falling into a pit of lava. Maxwell must somehow disconnect from his tether without falling and free the Starite from its cage without it rolling right into the molten earth.

The easiest thing to do is place Maxwell on a flying creature, such as a pterodactyl, and then separate him from the ceiling by burning through the rope. A match or a lighter works, but you have to wait for the fire to burn through the rope. Dropping a fireball on the rope immediately severs it.

When Maxwell is free, he can fly to the cage and interact with it to release the Starite. Do not fly into the cage and get it swinging. If you release the Starite while the cage is perfectly still, you can fly up and grab it before it rolls into the lava. If the cage sways, the Starite usually just bounces right into the fire.

CRAZY SOLUTION

Attach Maxwell to the piece of metal holding up the cage with a chain. Then, sever Maxwell from his own rope. When Maxwell swings into the cage, do nothing. Wait. When Maxwell and the cage settle into place, then you can safely free the Starite and end the level.

MISH MASH 10-7

Difficulty: 3	Par: 5	Possible Words:

- Shovel
- Spade
- Pickaxe
- Jackhammer
- Wings
- Pegasus
- Helibackpack
- Pterodactyl
- Archaeopteryx
- Fighter Jet

Ever heard of a nuckelavee? It's a monster from Pictish legend, and it looks like it was designed to scare children into minding their parents. The nuckelavee is a centaur-like creature with no skin and yellow veins. It is all muscle and all evil. In this level, it is luckily locked away in a dirt chamber. But the Starite is located on the top of that dirt, so Maxwell must figure out something to do with this monster or at least minimize its threat before going for the Starite.

There are three large boulders that plug a secondary shaft up to the Starite. These boulders are released if you press a red button on the wall near Maxwell's starting point. You can dig into the dirt on the right (near the nuckelavee) to create some space for the boulders. Use a shovel or a spade to dig into the dirt. Dig out a holding area so the boulders have a place to settle when you drop them.

You can also use these boulders to contain the nuckalavee. Dig through to the monster, but then retreat and drop the boulders. Use a fan or an air vent to push the boulders into the monster.

Once you have removed the boulders, you can fly up with wings or a pterodactyl and pick up the Starite.

If you write down a pegasus or a sphinx, you can actually fly up the shaft below the boulders and then dig around the nuckalavee's chamber and come up under the Starite.

CRAZY SOLUTION

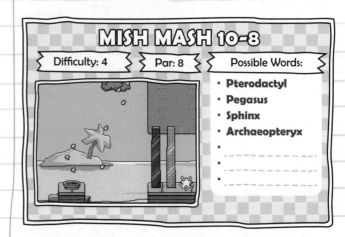

Board a fighter jet and blast your way through this level. Target the nuckelavee and Maxwell shoots through the dirt. Fly through the hole, but then pick up the jet and drop it on the button to release the boulders. Now, give the jet back to Maxwell. Target the boulders to shoot your way out of the sand and then fly up to the Starite to complete this level with just a single object. That puts you four under par!

MISH MASH 10-8

Difficulty: 4	Par: 8	Possible Words:

- Pterodactyl
- Pegasus
- Sphinx
- Archaeopteryx

The Starite in this level is located behind two colorful doors. There are two buttons in the level that open up the doors, but they are on the sides of the pillars adorned with air vents. These vents blast air up and down through the level, which can make flying with wings or a jetpack difficult. Plus, there is a rain cloud near the Starite that will short out any electrical flight object, such as a helibackpack.

Use a flying creature, such as a pegasus or a pterodactyl, to beat the wind and just fly into the buttons.

CRAZY SOLUTION

A UFO has the maneuverability to squeeze between the pillars and slam into the buttons. However, the cosmic craft is too big to fit into the Starite's alcove. Wedge it in there as well as you can and then tap the Starite to have Maxwell hop out and pick it up.

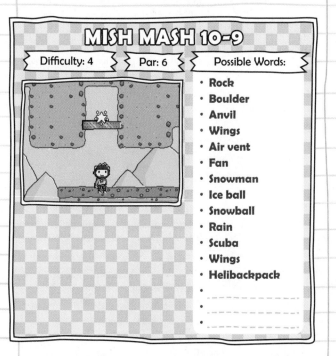

MISH MASH 10-9

Difficulty: 4	Par: 6	Possible Words:

- **Rock**
- **Boulder**
- **Anvil**
- **Wings**
- **Air vent**
- **Fan**
- **Snowman**
- **Ice ball**
- **Snowball**
- **Rain**
- **Scuba**
- **Wings**
- **Helibackpack**
- ....
- ....
- ....

The Starite in this level is locked behind a green door. This door will not open unless Maxwell presses three green buttons around the level simultaneously. All three must be held down at the same time, or else nothing happens. One of the buttons is on the ceiling to the right of Maxwell. The one on the left is in the middle of a fire vent. The third is in the water below, which is patrolled by piranha.

The button in the fire vent is easy enough to work with. Put out the fire with rain and then place an object on it. Or, snuff out the fire with a snowball or an ice ball and then leave it there to hold the button down.

The button in the water can be pressed without getting Maxwell's toes wet. Just drop a rock or an anvil on it.

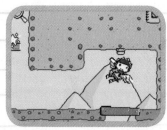

Once the other two buttons have been pressed, Maxwell can just fly up into the button on the ceiling to free the Starite. Give Maxwell some wings or a jetpack. As soon as he touches the button, the Starite falls to the floor. Just pick it up to end the level in success.

CRAZY SOLUTION

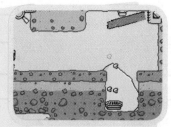

You can actually solve this level without moving an inch. Putting out the fire and pressing the button in the water are easy. But what about the button on the ceiling? Place an air vent in the hole below the pit. This blows the board that spans the pit into the button on the ceiling. The Starite drops right into Maxwell's hands!

MISH MASH 10-10

Difficulty: 4 〉 Par: 4 〉 Possible Words:

- **Balloon**
- **Winged shoes**
- **Helibackpack**
- **Jetpack**
- **Pegasus**
- **Magic carpet**
- **Glue**
- **Magnet**
- **Adhesive**
- **Girder**
- **Air vent**
- ....
- ....
- ....

Trophies are wonderful prizes, but they do not sparkle quite like a Starite. The Starite in this level is located on a teetering stack of trophies. There is an air vent next to the Starite that will blow it into spikes if Maxwell throws the blue switch that also unlocks the door to the trophy room. So, what can you do to save the Starite from being smashed against the spikes? You must build something to catch the Starite.

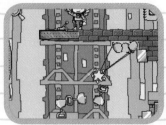

Three balloons tied to the Starite float it against the ceiling. When the wind rushes through, the Starite is just blown to the side of the trophy room. However, do not linger. Get in there with some winged shoes or a jetpack and grab the Starite before the wind blows the balloons so hard against the wall that it pushes them down, bringing the Starite close to the spikes.

Glue a magnet to the metal piece on the wall pictured here. As soon as the magnet is in place, it grabs the trophies. The Starite then falls on the pedestal below. When you open the door to enter the chamber, the air from the vent does not affect the Starite.

Try to catch the Starite with your own air vent. Attach a girder to the metal piece seen here with some adhesive. Place the air vent on the end of the girder so when you open the door, the Starite is blown right into your contraption. Your air vent keeps the Starite from rolling into the spikes. Now just fly into the chamber and retrieve it.

CRAZY SOLUTION

Those trophies look a lot like hockey trophies. How about placing a skating rink in the chamber next to the Starite? When the fan blows, the Starite is caught on the roof of the rink.

The buttons are between giant spikes and guarded by a behemoth.

The switches are also tucked between spikes and watched over by the grim reaper.

You cannot destroy the spikes. You can eliminate the monsters with other creatures or a black hole, but those spikes? Nothing will remove them. Not a black hole. Not an explosive. Not a magnet. Nothing. So how do you raise those doors if you cannot access the buttons and switches?

MISH MASH 10-11

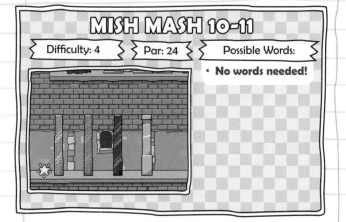

Difficulty: 4   Par: 24   Possible Words:

• **No words needed!**

CRAZY SOLUTION

Oh, now that is just *mean*. This whole level is a trick. You do not need to do anything with the spikes, buttons, or switches. As soon as Maxwell walks toward the doors, they start rising on their own. The final Starite is yours for the taking.

Wow. When you start this level, the Starite is behind a series of doors. These colored doors match switches and buttons placed throughout the level. But it will not be easy to access them and raise those doors to claim the Starite. Really, check this out....

LEVEL EDITOR

So, you've conquered all 220 levels in the game, collecting every single Starite? Is it time to pull the game from your Nintendo DS? Hardly. *Scribblenauts* includes a Level Editor that lets you create custom levels that you can either play yourself or share with friends over the Nintendo Wi-Fi Connection. Now the game will last until the day you can no longer use your imagination—a day we all hope never comes.

The Level Editor lets you essentially customize levels you have already completed. All objects are stripped away, leaving a relatively blank slate for you to play with. The landscape is all that remains, so if the original level was built on the side of a lake with beach and water, the beach and water exist in the Level Editor. Any creatures in the water or a boathouse on the shore are gone. With this clean level as your canvas, you can dig in and try to come up with puzzles and action levels that outsmart even the amazing levels created by the folks at 5TH Cell!

HOW-TO

Let's get through the basic steps of creating your own level in the Level Editor before we move on and show you eight sample levels we made with the provided tools. The building blocks of a level are the level itself, the objects you place within the level, the directions to assign to objects (such as humans and creatures), and the parameters for the level, such as par.

Select a Level

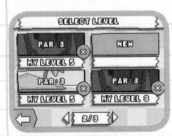

When you decide to create a level with the Editor, you must choose a new slot. There are a total of 12 save slots for storing levels you create. If you want to edit a level you have already started and saved, just tap it with the stylus. If you need to delete a level in order to create a new one, tap the yellow X next to the level's save slot.

Once you have selected a slot to save your work, you need to then select a level to use as a template. First, you select the world. You can only select worlds you have unlocked with your hard-earned Ollars. Then, you can only select a level that you have opened while playing in Challenge Mode. You can see all of the levels in both Puzzle Mode and Action Mode, but levels you have not completed have a

lock on them. So, if you want more templates to use in the Level Editor, you better get back into Challenge Mode and collect some more Starites and Ollars.

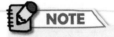
NOTE

To switch between puzzle and action levels, simply tap the symbol in the lower-left corner of the screen, just as if you were playing in Challenge Mode.

Once you select a level, you enter the Level Editor tool for adding objects to the level. Notice how all of the objects have been removed? The world is now your oyster. It's entirely up to you to fill the level with objects and create an exciting challenge for yourself or your friends.

Here's a level in Challenge Mode...

...and here's what it looks like in the Level Editor.

Arrange Objects

Now that you've picked a level that suits an idea you have rattling around in your head, it's time to populate it with objects. You can write any object into your level, as you can when attempting to solve a level in Challenge Mode. Using objects works exactly the same in the Level Editor. Just tap the Notepad in the upper-right corner of the screen and spell out words to create objects. The more objects you create, the more the Object Meter fills. When the Object Meter finally is full, you can no longer create objects.

All objects you create count against the meter, including objects you build ostensibly for decoration, such as hanging the moon in the sky or erecting a house in the backdrop. So, you may want to save as much of the meter as possible for objects that the player will interact with, such as monsters.

Drop creatures in the level that will attack Maxwell or at least run interference for the Starite.

TIP

Use the levels you have completed as inspiration. Think of your favorites and then build on those ideas.

Since you are working with template-like empty levels, you have the run of the place. You can build things by gluing objects together, place obstacles along paths, and piece together puzzle-like gauntlets.

Because there is no penalty for trying something that may not exactly work, such as placing a rain cloud over a fire vent that keeps a monster at bay, have fun experimenting with the Editor.

Every level needs a Starite. You cannot save a level without it, even if it is just a work in progress. Create a Starite using your Notepad and place it somewhere in the level as a goal for Maxwell.

What's My Motivation?

When you drop animate objects into a level, they revert to their traditional actions. A dragon will attack. A dog will chase a cat. A cow will just stand there and chew its cud. That's fine, but perhaps your level requires a little more direction. Once you have added an object that moves and acts on its own to a level, you can assign specific directions to that object.

To assign an action, just tap the object once it has been placed in the level. Tapping the object creates a thought balloon over the object. This is the object's action. There are several actions from which to choose. Tap the left and right arrows next to the balloon to scroll through the potential choices, such as guard or consume.

Here are all of the actions and what they do:

Protects: This action directs the object to protect another object. If you choose a bear and then select it to protect Maxwell, the bear will then fight anything that threatens Maxwell in the level.

Attacks: This action orders an object to specifically attack another object—or Maxwell. This will not necessarily override instinct. If you place a bear directly next to a dragon and order both attack Maxwell, they will likely fight each other right away, and then the victor will attack Maxwell.

Scared Of: Assigning this action to an object makes it cower from another specified object in the level. Use this to tweak conventions, such as making a dog scared of a cat. It is also a good way to set up a level with multiple objects for Maxwell to choose from. If Maxwell picks up the correct object, the Starite guardian will fear him, no matter what.

Consumes: This action directs an object to feast on an assigned object. If you have a food-themed level in mind, this is a good way to direct objects to zero in on particular food objects.

Follows: Want to give Maxwell a shadow? Assign this action to an object and then direct it to follow Maxwell. The object will now trail Maxwell through the level. You can have an object follow any other object. You do not need to limit yourself to animate objects. If you have a dog follow a particular sword, and Maxwell picks up that sword, the dog will then follow Maxwell. That could be a fun way to start a level.

 Guards: This action directs an object to guard another object. The easiest use for this is assigning a monster to guard the Starite from Maxwell's greedy little fingers. But you can also assign creatures to guard Maxwell or to guard a ladder that is central to your level.

 Uses: Many of the action levels have buttons or switches that control doors. This action will direct objects to interact with those buttons and switches or to grab an object you have placed inside a level.

 Mounts: Use this action to task an object with riding or driving another object. If you create a horse and a knight, for example, you can then tell the knight to run for and ride the horse. If you ordered the knight to attack Maxwell, the knight would then rush Maxwell while on the horse. This works for cars, planes, tanks, UFOs, sphinxes, and all sorts of moving vehicle-like objects.

 **Steals:** This action directs an object to attempt to steal another object. If you have created a level that relies on Maxwell grabbing a specific object, then tasking another object with stealing that makes Maxwell's life a little more complicated.

After settling on an action, you can then direct that action toward another object. For example, if you created a monster that you want to actually guard Maxwell, you then tap Maxwell after changing the action in the thought balloon to guards. See the white line of arrows that appears? That indicates which object is now the focus of the assigned action. You can change these up as many times as you like while creating a level, but you can only select one action per object and then only one focus of that action. You cannot assign a knight to both guard a cake and mount a horse.

 NOTE

Assigning actions does not affect the Object Meter at all.

Use actions to have fun with conventional assumptions about items. Why not have a vampire scared of a little girl instead of the other way around? By changing how objects interact with each other, you add interesting twists to your levels that may throw off your friends. They'll see a dragon and immediately assume they need to attack it. But what if that dragon was set to guard Maxwell while he pushed through a line of zombies?

Set the Parameters

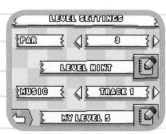

After assembling the level by placing objects and adding actions, you can then adjust the settings for your level. Tap on the arrow in the upper-left corner of the screen to pull out a small menu. Tap the gear in that menu to access the settings. In this menu, you can name the level, select the par for that level, create a hint that appears when the player first starts the level, and assign a music track to the level.

NOTE

Want more music tracks? Buy them in the Ollar Store so you can use them in the Level Editor.

Pay close attention to the par for your level. This is another way you can mess with your friends. If you really limit the number of objects they can think up, you can run them through the wringer. However, do not be so miserly that you effectively cut them off from making any solution. Give them a fighting chance. The default is three, but you can even go as low as zero. If you choose zero, you'd better make sure there are objects already placed within the level that your friends can use to solve the level. Otherwise, the level just will not work.

Test, Save, and Share

While creating a level, you may want to try out something you made before saving and sharing it. Open the menu in the upper-left corner of the screen and tap the green arrow to test the level. The green arrow turns into a big red square. While testing the level, you can play and interact with everything. This is a good way to see whether your assigned actions work or whether you gave the player a high enough par to work with.

When you are happy with the level (or you just need to go do something else), you can save it by tapping the small disk icon. Then, select an available save slot or save over an existing level. If you choose to save over an existing level, you must confirm the decision to overwrite the file before the level is saved.

When you want to share your levels with friends or try out one of theirs, you must go back to the Main Menu of the game and tap the Wi-Fi icon to open up the Nintendo Wi-Fi Connection menu. From here, you can connect to friends over a local wireless connection or the Nintendo Wi-Fi Connection to swap levels.

NOTE

For more information on getting online with your Nintendo DS, please see the manual that came with your DS.

SAMPLE LEVELS

We've gone over the basics of level creation. Now let's actually put together some levels with the Level Editor and see how it works in practice.

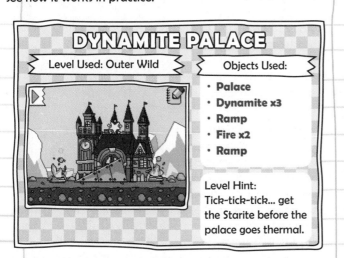

DYNAMITE PALACE

Level Used: Outer Wild

Objects Used:
- **Palace**
- **Dynamite x3**
- **Ramp**
- **Fire x2**
- **Ramp**

Level Hint:
Tick-tick-tick... get the Starite before the palace goes thermal.

This level is all about rushing to save the Starite. The palace here will go up in flames soon, and when it does, the Starite will fall on the ramp and roll into the flames. But to complicate matters even more, the palace has been packed with three sticks of dynamite. So, not only will the palace burn, but the dynamite might fly into the fire and explode, potentially destroying the Starite. This setup forces the player to hurry and get to the top of the palace before disaster strikes.

Here's how we put together this level:

1. Jot down a palace and place it in a flat section of the level so there is plenty of room on each side.

2. Place the dynamite inside the palace. You can switch out dynamite for bombs or fireworks, too.

3. Now place fires on each side of the palace. Make sure one is actually touching the palace so when the level begins, the timer is set. Within several seconds, the fire will burn the palace.

4. Next, set the Starite on the palace balcony so the player has a chance to actually grab it before the whole thing explodes.

5. The ramp in front of the palace will roll the Starite into a fire in the event that the explosion does not ruin the Starite. So, even if the player is lucky and the dynamite doesn't blow up the Starite, the player still needs to hurry so the Starite doesn't burn.

So, here's what happens if the player is a slowpoke. The fire burns through the side of the palace, which causes the object to pop. The pop sends the three sticks of dynamite flying. If the dynamite falls into the fire, it, too, explodes. Should the Starite be too close, the blast takes out the Starite, ending the level in failure for the player.

The solution then is to summon some wings or a jetpack and fly to the top of the palace as soon as the level begins. By picking a large level and placing Maxwell on the opposite side of the it, you increase the tension. Not only does Maxwell have to fly up to the balcony to grab the Starite, but he must also close the gap between his starting position and the palace.

MONSTER CAVE

Level Used: Frontier	Objects Used:

Objects Used:
- **Werewolf**
- **T-Rex**
- **Air vent**
- **Lava spot**
- **Starite**

Level Hint: The roar of the T Rex isn't only Maxwell's problem...

During Challenge Mode, you saw how useful monsters are for clearing out troublesome creatures. However, in this level, the monsters are strictly Maxwell's problem. He starts the level right next to a werewolf and a T-Rex that will eat him within seconds if he does not move. This adds some immediacy to the level, forcing the player to move as soon as the action begins. Here, we've squeezed Maxwell between a monster and a lava pit, so he has to pick the lesser of two evils. Let's go through the creation of this level:

1. Place the two monsters on the platform along with Maxwell. The platform is too small for two giant monsters, so we're sticking with just one big monster and a smaller beast, such as the werewolf.

2. Let's give these monsters some motivation. The T-Rex is assigned to actually attack the werewolf. This gives Maxwell a couple seconds to escape the monsters, because they will immediately tussle with each other before the victor (always the T-Rex in this match-up) turns its attention to Maxwell.

Prima Official Game Guide

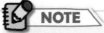

NOTE

By design, monsters always attack whatever is closest to them. You can use this natural behavior to set up lots of big fights and then drop Maxwell in the middle of them. At first, players will be freaked by the level, but when they realize the heat isn't on them, they have a chance to figure out a way out of the skirmish.

3. Now we need to set up the Starite. Leaving it on a ledge is too easy. Place an air vent next to the Starite.

4. Attach a lava spout to the ceiling above the air vent, creating a fire trap that must be either quickly passed through or snuffed out with something like an ice ball.

When the level begins, the fight starts. Due to their proximity to Maxwell, it looks like both monsters are going to attack him. But when the T-Rex gets close to the werewolf, it turns those teeth on the werewolf. While the monsters fight, Maxwell can escape.

The fire trap in front of the Starite is a bit tricky because Maxwell will bounce back from fire when he touches it. Touch fire too many times, and Maxwell perishes. So, instead of threading the needle with wings or a jetpack, a ladder actually works very well here. Maxwell can hop over the air vent and slide up to the Starite.

DIGGING UP TROUBLE

Level Used: Metro

Objects Used:

- **Land mine x5**
- **Boulder x4**
- **Wall**
- **Starite**

Level Hint: Buried not-so-treasure threatens the Starite... and Maxwell!

A loaded trap, ready to spring, is a great way to greet the player. In this level, the Starite is buried in the desert. Just dig down to it, right? Nope. Not if you fill the other air pockets in the desert with land mines. Now the player must figure out a way through the land mines to grab the Starite without setting off a chain reaction that threatens to blow up the Starite. How can we take this level, though, and make it even more dangerous?

1. Place the Starite in the air pocket at the very bottom of the desert.

2. Fill the other air pockets with land mines. Each land mine helps fill the Object Meter, but you need to use as many as will fit in those pockets to make this level tough.

3. Digging around the land mines would be too easy. Add a little potential trouble by placing boulders above the sand. That way, the player must be mindful of not letting the boulders fall into the sand while digging, lest they set off a land mine.

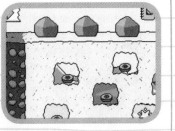

4. Place a wall near the side of the desert so the player cannot just push all of the boulders out of the way. You need to make the player deal with the problem at hand, not find a simple workaround.

Now, by placing the boulders within the confines of a wall and an incline, you force Maxwell to deal with them. He can push them from side to side a little, but he cannot completely push them out of the way.

However, if players write down a tough digging instrument, they can break down the boulders a little. If you want to keep players from even trying that solution, replace the boulders with spiked steel balls.

See how the boulders can slip into the sand and potentially set off a land mine?

While digging for the Starite, the player must be mindful of the land mines. Touching one sets it off, which causes a chain reaction. Sticking to one side of the desert works well for reaching the Starite and ending the level.

ZOMBIE ARMY

Level Used: Frontier

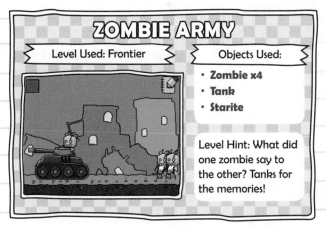

Objects Used:

- **Zombie x4**
- **Tank**
- **Starite**

Level Hint: What did one zombie say to the other? Tanks for the memories!

What could be more fearsome than a zombie horde? How about a zombie horde with control over a tank? This level sets Maxwell against an army of zombies that stand between him and the Starite. By weaponizing at least one of the zombies, Maxwell must deal with the threat of attack. The player cannot just sit back and destroy all of the zombies from afar. Here's how we set up this level:

1. Write down a tank and place it near Maxwell. Not right on top of him, but close enough to make him nervous. Now, either place a zombie next to the tank and assign it the mount action or just place the zombie directly in the tank.

2. Next, place the remaining zombies around the Starite.

Be mindful of how actions affect enemy behavior. Setting a zombie to guard the Starite sounds like a good idea. However, this action then takes precedence over all other instincts. The guarding zombie will attack the other zombies if they come too close to the Starite. This makes the level way too easy if the zombies all kill each other.

Once the level begins, Maxwell must deal with the tank-driving zombie. Another tank is a good solution. Exchange shells with the zombie tank. If Maxwell goes first, he will win the fight.

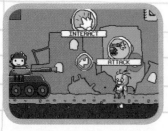

Then the player can just use the tank to get rid of the rest of the zombies.

SWIMMING FOR STARITES

Level Used: Shoreline	Objects Used:

Objects Used:
- **Shark**
- **Piranha x2**
- **Air vent x2**
- **Spiked steel ball x2**
- **Starite**

Level Hint: Does Maxwell have to sleep with the fishes to save the Starite?

Maxwell has no problem swimming with the right equipment, so let's make this underwater journey a little tougher for the hero. By adding several dangers around the Starite, the player must think in advance of how to circumvent problems before slipping into the water. We have placed three dangers in this level: shark, piranha, and spiked steel balls. Let's set up this level and show how the placement of dangers in relation to each other can increase the difficulty of a level.

1. Place the Starite at the bottom of the lake. Then add two air vents next to it.

2. Place spiked steel balls over the air vents. The air vents will push these spiked steel balls up but also create a current that could potentially push into them Maxwell or any creature he creates to fight off the shark.

3. Let's add some attack creatures. Place a shark near the beach so Maxwell has an immediate danger to deal with before even thinking of going for the Starite.

4. Next, place two piranha near the Starite. These will naturally attack Maxwell if he gets too close.

The placement of the piranha next to the Starite limits the use of the electronic-object-in-water trick. A TV will buzz up and kill the shark just fine. But because the piranha are so close to the Starite, the shock will destroy the Starite, too. Instead, Maxwell must come up with a different solution for the toothy fish.

Another sea creature to use against the piranha is a better solution, but be mindful of the air vents. The current pushes the creature up toward the spiked steel balls, which will injure any creature, no matter how strong.

See how placing a hammerhead next to the shark forces it back into the spiked steel balls? That's more likely to eliminate the shark than the hammerhead's attack is.

Once the shark and piranha have been dealt with, now Maxwell can strap on his scuba gear and swim for the Starite. As long as players move past the air vent without stopping, they can beat the current and solve the level.

FIERCE CREATURES

Level Used: Frontier	Objects Used:
	• **Hydra** • **Dragon** • **Behemoth** • **Wall** • **Starite**
	Level Hint: Monsters are like drill sergeants. They respect strength.

This level sets up a gauntlet of monsters for Maxwell to fight through in order to reach the Starite. However, you

know that monsters too close to each other will end up just fighting among themselves and making things easy for Maxwell. So, let's set up this level in a way that will prevent the monsters from battling each other and keep their fire strictly on Maxwell.

1. First, place the Starite on the far side of the level and then drop in a hydra right next to it.

2. There is enough room on the platform for a behemoth, too. Place a wall between the two monsters, though, so they do not attack each other.

3. Next, place a dragon and a werewolf closer to Maxwell. This means he must fight through four monsters. Don't be too strict with par in this level so the player has a chance to create the necessary weapons or attack creatures to work through the gauntlet.

4. Place a wall at the start of the gauntlet so Maxwell must fly into the face of trouble.

5. Set the actions of each monster so they are ordered to attack Maxwell.

Oops—the dragon and werewolf are too close together. Instead of placing another wall in the level that would give

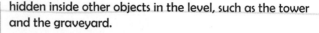

Maxwell a safe place to land while flying over the monsters, just separate them a little more so they are not in each other's sight lines.

Now it's time to test this level. The black hole trick works well on the first few monsters because they are far enough from the Starite that the black hole will not threaten it. By placing the hydra so close to the Starite later in the level, you neutralize the effectiveness of the black hole attack. The player might also try to use an attack creature to eliminate the monsters, but because you placed such large ones in the level, the player needs to use big ones, too. Depending on how close you pack the monsters, you may limit the room players have to deploy a large attack creature. That's good—it makes them think.

So, instead of attacking the behemoth and the hydra with a big creature, such as a shoggoth, players instead need to think of using weapons, such as a missile launcher.

FRIGHTFUL NIGHTFALL

Level Used: Dark Hollow

Objects Used:
- **Graveyard**
- **Tower**
- **Vampire**
- **Werewolf**
- **Silver**
- **Holy water**
- **Starite**

Level Hint: A vampire, werewolf, and zero par? Could Maxwell dig himself out of this trouble?

This level is about finding the solutions to trouble within the environment itself. We're setting the par for this level at zero to force the player to think about how to attack both a werewolf and a vampire without being able to write down a single object. This forces players to think of alternative ways levels might be set up. Hopefully, it will not take them too long to realize the solutions have been

hidden inside other objects in the level, such as the tower and the graveyard.

Here's how we put together this level:

1. Place the Starite in the shallow grave and then drop a vampire next to it.

2. Write down a werewolf and place it on the other side of the grave. Next, place a tower or a house behind the werewolf. The placement of the tower here is important because we are going to hide in the tower the shovel needed to dig. If the werewolf is in front of the tower, the player must then figure out a way to move the werewolf.

3. Place a graveyard next to Maxwell's starting position. You can use anything that holds multiple objects, such as another tower, but the graveyard goes with the theme here.

4. Place silver and holy water inside the graveyard by holding the objects over the graves and releasing them.

5. Now hide a shovel inside the tower.

At the start of the level, players see they have zero par. They must figure this thing out without conjuring up any help. The first thing they need to do is empty the graveyard to release the silver and the holy water.

By holding the silver, the player can force the werewolf back from the tower. Once the werewolf has been backed up past the Starite, the player can throw the silver at the werewolf. The silver bounces off the werewolf but lands on the ground in front of it. The werewolf can now no longer approach Maxwell.

The vampire can, though. So the player needs to grab the holy water and throw it at the vampire. The holy water kills the vampire. (Well, it re-kills the vampire, since vampires are technically already dead.)

To solve the level, the player just needs to empty the tower to fetch the hidden shovel and dig up the Starite. The werewolf is stuck behind the silver and must watch helplessly as Maxwell digs down to the Starite.

COFFIN PIÑATAS

Level Used: Metro	Objects Used:
	• Air vent x3
	• Coffin x3
	• Zombie
	• Starite
	Level Hint: Can Maxwell resurrect the Starite?

The level is something of a piñata party, except the piñatas have been replaced with coffins, and not every coffin contains a treat. In fact, one of these coffins contains a downright nasty surprise: a zombie. The player needs to pick the right coffin to solve the level. It's a simple level, but it's fun nonetheless.

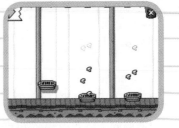

1. Place three air vents on the ground. These will prop up the coffins.

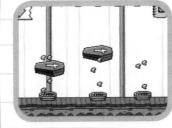

2. Create three coffins and place them over each of the air vents. You are starting to run out of objects now, so you can only fill two of the coffins.

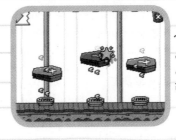

3. Place the Starite in one of the coffins. It's your choice, but the middle one is a good bet.

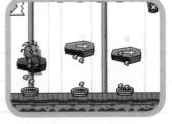

4. Finally, add the zombie surprise to one of the other coffins. One of the coffins will remain empty, but because opening a coffin releases a ghost no matter what, the player is still in for a fright.

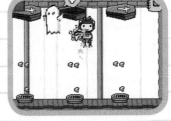

Now, players just need to decide which coffin they want to open, They have no idea which coffin contains the Starite, nor that any of the other coffins holds a zombie. They can just use the air vents to ride up to the coffins. But if players release the zombie, this also means they have a floating zombie to deal with while seeking out the Starite.

ADVICE FROM THE TEAM

The team at 5TH Cell has a handful of tips and tricks for budding level editors creating their first *Scribblenauts* levels. One of the first things you should consider is moving the focus of the level from the Starite to Maxwell. If you fill a level with monsters, the player can just use their own attack creatures to eliminate the monsters before stepping away from the starting position and going for the Starite. Alternately, just placing the Starite on a high ledge or across a gap makes for an easy level, too, because the player can always use wings or a pterodactyl the reach it.

Instead, create levels where Maxwell must do the heavy lifting. Create situations that put the Starite in immediate danger, like fire or falling into an abyss. If Maxwell becomes the main actor in a level as opposed to the player just relying on a big dragon to clear the area, the level becomes much more challenging.

When creating levels, try not to rely on the same ideas over and over. If you are giving your friends a few levels, don't make them all levels that concentrate on flying or throwing switches. Keep things fresh by changing things up. Make one level about figuring out how release a humanoid that has been directed to use a switch. Make the next about getting the Starite away from a bunch of monsters. Continuing changing the focus of your levels and your friends will be asking for more.

Finally, have fun with the hints you can offer at the beginning of the level. Don't give it all away up-front, but don't be purposefully obtuse. Use humor like puns or little jokes to nudge the player in the right direction.

10 LEVEL EDITOR TIPS

1. Fire burns through an object in about five seconds. Tuck the Starite inside another object and place a fire source next to it to create a "timed" level.

2. Mess with player assumptions by changing the motivations and actions of hostile creatures. A chef might look completely innocent and certainly acts that way during Challenge Mode, but by directing it to attack Maxwell, the player will be in for quite a surprise when they walk up to the chef.

3. If you have a level that requires the player to fly, use rain clouds to limit them from relying on jetpacks and the helibackpack.

4. Place a hostile creature close to the Starite in an underwater level. This will force the player to not rely on the TV-in-the-water trick since the shock would destroy the Starite as well as the monster.

5. Remember that unless you direct them otherwise, monsters and hostile creatures will attack Maxwell and other hostile creatures by default. If you place too many hostile creatures too close together, they will just fight each other and make things too easy for the player.

6. Use some of your favorite levels in Challenge Mode as inspiration for your own levels. Think how those levels were solved and then tweak with that idea for your own level. So, instead of starting a level with Maxwell on land and the Starite in the water, reverse it so Maxwell is in the water and the Starite is on land.

7. Give the player a fighting chance at the beginning of every level. You can put them in danger, but not immediate danger so they perish within two seconds. Placing Maxwell on a tiny ledge with a behemoth is not fair. Placing Maxwell near a behemoth on a medium-sized ledge with a little room between them gives the player a chance to react and come up with a solution.

8. Hide useful objects in your levels inside other objects, like what we did with our "Frightful Nightfall" level. The holy water and silver that lets Maxwell fight back against the werewolf and vampire are ready—the player just needs to look for them. If a player must take down a robber or villain, hide a gun inside a house and set the par low enough that the player must consider whether or not you hid something useful in the level.

9. Place fire around levels where you think the player might try to use a flying creature or monster to solve it. Many creatures are afraid of fire, so this will limit movement or object options unless the player does something to put out the fires first.

10. Be strict with par on your levels, but do not be mean. Make sure the player has enough par to solve them without pulling their hair out. As you create a level, think of as many solutions as possible and then use the average when you assign a par to your level.

WORD LIST

POWERFUL LANGUAGE

The world of *Scribblenauts* is a world of language. The more creative you are with words, the more things you can conjure into the game. There are tens of thousands of recognized words in *Scribblenauts* that result in objects or beings. Animal, vegetable, and mineral are only the start of it. Monsters, weapons, and machines are also ready to materialize in the levels in hopes of getting Maxwell closer to his Starite goals.

This word list does not contain all of the words in *Scribblenauts*. In fact, it's only a fraction of the words you can use. However, this list of terms use in the level solutions should get you well on your way to coming up with incredible, creative (and sometimes outright bizarre) means for capturing Starites.

Adhesives

Need to stick two or more objects together to make a contraption, such as making a Starite catcher or attaching a weapon to a vehicle? You need adhesives. These objects bind objects together.

- Adhesive
- Glue
- Tape

Your Words:

Attack Creatures

Many of the creatures you create via the Notepad are friendly, but there is a menagerie of animals and monsters that are most definitely not. These creatures default to aggressive behavior and will attack other nearby creatures and humanoids.

- Alligator
- Asp
- Barracuda 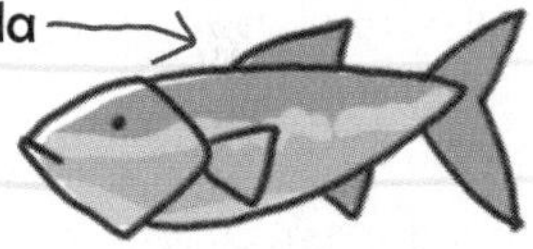
- Bat
- Bear
- Behemoth
- Cerberus
- Chimera
- Cobra
- Crocodile
- Cyclops

- Death
- Devil
- Dragon
- Electric eel
- Gargoyle
- Ghost
- Ghoul
- Griffin
- Great white
- Hammerhead
- Harpy
- Hydra
- Killer bee
- Kraken
- Lion
- Loch Ness monster
- Medusa
- Minotaur
- Mongoose
- Monster

- Mothman
- Mummy
- Ninja
- Orca
- Piranha
- Pterodactyl
- Rattlesnake
- Robosaur
- Samurai
- Scylla
- Sea monster
- Sea witch
- Shark
- Shoggoth
- Snake
- Sphinx
- Swordfish
- Tiger
- T-Rex
- Vampire
- Velociraptor

- Werewolf

- Witch

- Yeti

- Zombie

Your Words:

Your Words:

Peaceful Creatures

- -

These creatures are the antithesis to the previous list of objects. These animals are docile by design and will not attack without provocation. However, many can be excited by offering them their favorite food or placing their natural prey nearby.

- Archaeopteryx
- Beaver
- Beluga
- Bird
- Calf
- Cat
- Charonosaurus 
- Chicken 
- Cow
- Crab
- Dalmatian
- Dinosaur 
- Dodo
- Dog 
- Dolphin
- Donkey
- Dove

- Eagle
- Fish
- Frog
- Giraffe
- Goose 
- Hawk
- Horse
- Kangaroo
- Kitten
- Lamb

Your Words:

- Mole
- Monkey
- Mouse
- Octopus
- Owl
- Ox
- Pegasus
- Pig
- Piglet
- Puppy

- Sheep
- Skunk
- Starfish
- Termite
- Unicorn
- Vulture
- Walrus
- Whale
- Zebra

Your Words:

Your Words:

Big Monsters

These are the biggest monsters you can place in a level. They require a lot of space, so they will not work in tight quarters. If you need a creature that is not only aggressive but dominant, jot down one of these monsters in the Notepad.

- Behemoth
- Charybdis
- Cthulhu
- Dragon
- Giant enemy crab
- Hydra
- Kraken
- Leviathan
- Minotaur
- Monster
- Mothman

- Scylla
- Sea monster
- Shoggoth
- T-Rex
- Yeti

Your Words:

Dinosaurs

There are many dinosaurs in the game, including the sampling below. Dinosaurs have a variety of functions, from pure attack power to friendly mount.

- Archeopteryx

- Charonosaur

- Dinosaur

- Pterodactyl

- Pterosaur

- T-Rex

- Velociraptor

Your Words:

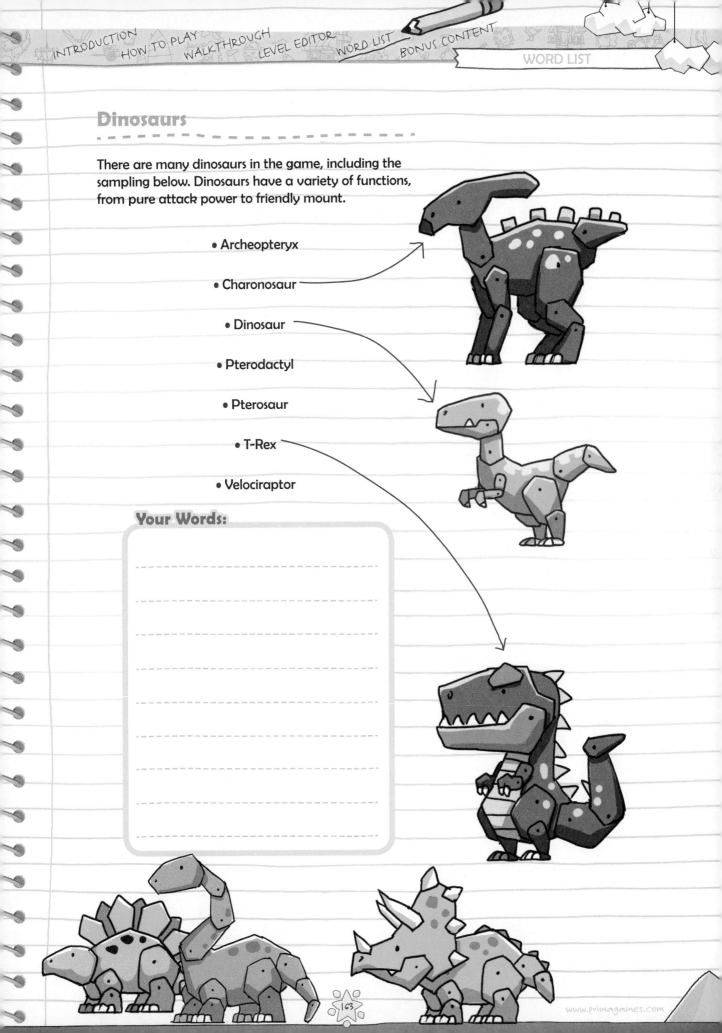

www.primagames.com

Boats

Boats help Maxwell cross the waters. There are many boats you can try out, from a basic dinghy to a mighty Viking ship.

- Anchor
- Boat ⟶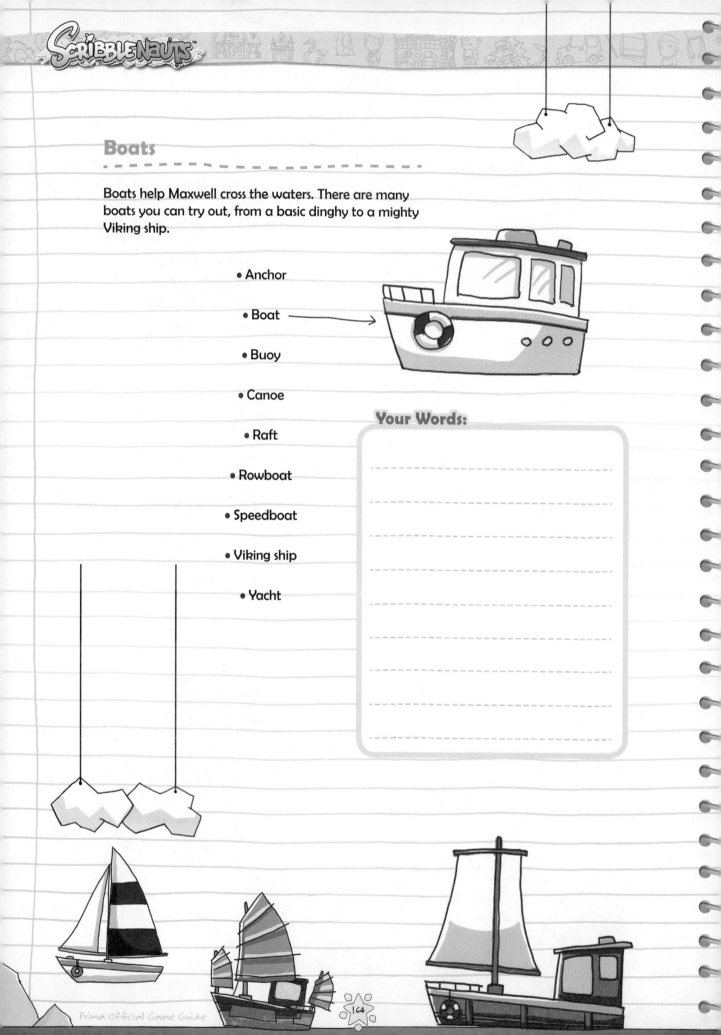
- Buoy
- Canoe
- Raft
- Rowboat
- Speedboat
- Viking ship
- Yacht

Your Words:

Swimming Objects

Without a special swimming object, Maxwell can only move across the tops of the waves. If you need him to dive underwater, you must give him a swimming object such as those in this list.

- Dive helmet
- Diving bell
- Diving helmet
- Dolphin
- Flippers
- Respirator
- Scuba gear
- Snorkel
- Wetsuit

Your Words:

Digging & Breaking Utensils

Maxwell can burrow through soft or loose soil with a digging utensil, such as a shovel or jackhammer. Many digging utensils can also be used to break objects and ice, just like tire irons and ice picks.

- Auger
- Bucket excavator
- Bulldozer
- Chisel
- Hoe
- Ice pick
- Jackhammer
- Knife
- Pickaxe
- Saw
- Shovel
- Spade
- Tire Iron

Your Words:

Flying Vehicles

Sometimes Maxwell need to take flight. Give him a flying object so he can successfully leave terra firma. These objects vary as wildly as wings you strap on to Maxwell to a hot air balloon.

- Balloon
- Fighter jet
- Glider
- Hang glider
- Helibackpack
- Helicopter
- Hot air balloon 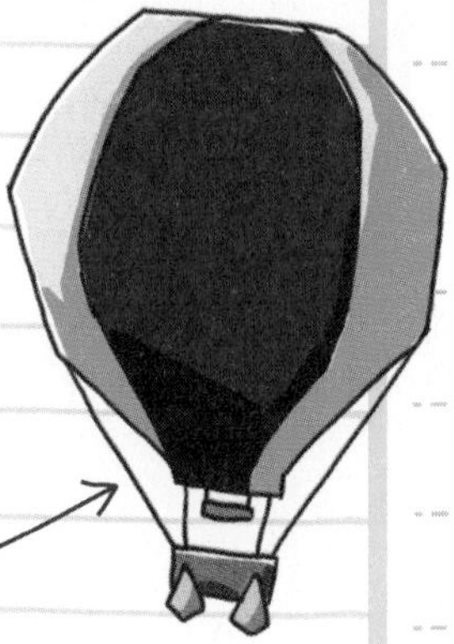
- Jet
- Jetpack
- Magic broomstick
- Magic carpet
- Parachute
- Seaplane
- Spaceship 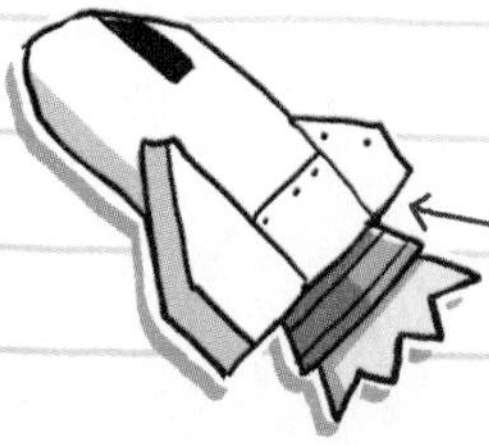
- UFO
- Winged shoes
- Wings

Your Words:

Land-based Vehicles

When Maxwell needs to get from point A to point B as fast as he can, write a land-based vehicle in the Notepad and then place the little hero behind the wheel.

- Bicycle
- Bike
- Bucket excavator
- Bulldozer
- Bus

- Car

- Crane

- Dump truck

- Forklift

- Ice cream truck

- Limo

- Mech

- Motorbike

- Pogo stick

- Race car

- Roller skate

- RV

- Scooter

- Skateboard

- Steamroller

- Stock car

- Tank

- Unicycle

Your Words:

Flying Creatures

There are special flying creatures that Maxwell can ride to great heights. These creatures do not need to stop and refresh like a jetpack or wings. Some flying creatures can even attack targets, such as other creatures.

- Archeopteryx

- Pegasus

- Pterodactyl

- Pterosaur

- Sphinx

Your Words:

Buildings

Buildings often rest in the backdrop, but can be interacted with. Taller buildings often have balconies that can prop up objects and most buildings can double as containers for other objects.

- Barn
- Drawbridge
- Fence
- Fixed ladder
- House
- Jungle gym
- Ladder
- Shack
- Skating rink
- Ziggurat

Your Words:

www.primagames.com

Ropes & Tethers

These objects let you tie two objects together or pick up an object (such as a crate) and drag it behind Maxwell.

- Bungee cord
- Cable
- Chain
- Electrical cord
- Extension cord
- Handcuffs
- Hose
- Jumper cables
- Leash
- Net
- Rope
- String
- Vine
- Wire

Your Words:

Containers

These objects hold other objects. The bigger the object, the more it can hold.

- Bag
- Basket
- Bucket
- Cage
- Can

- Coffin

- Crate

- Fish tank

- Lunch box

- Sarcophagus

- Trunk

Your Words:

Building Features

Building features include things you might find at a construction site or within a building, such as an elevator or pool.

- Bridge

- Elevator

- Haystack

- Pool

- Ramp

- Scaffold

- Stairs

- Wall

Your Words:

Water & Ice

Water and ice have a number of functions in this game, such as putting out fire or being thrown, like a snowball.

- Ice
- Ice ball
- Ice block
- Iceberg
- Puddle
- Snow
- Snowball
- Snowman
- Water

Your Words:

Minerals

There are many gems and minerals in the game you can create and give to other humanoids as presents or valuables, or just use as a regular object to weigh down a button.

- Diamond
- Emerald
- Gold
- Gold ring
- Iron
- Metal
- Moonstone
- Onyx
- Rock
- Ruby
- Selenite
- Silver
- Topaz

Your Words:

Fire

Fire objects set other objects ablaze. Fire can also be used to scare other creatures or keep them at bay.

- Bunsen burner
- Campfire
- Candle
- Fire
- Fireball
- Flamberge
- Flamethrower
- Lava spout
- Lighter
- Match
- Torch

Your Words:

Melee Weapons

These handheld objects can be used to attack other objects, such as aggressive creatures. Many can also be used to break objects, such as boxes and rocks.

- Axe
- Bat
- Bear trap
- Billy club
- Chainsaw
- Dagger
- Flamberge
- Flyswatter
- Hammer
- Handsaw
- Hoe
- Ice pick
- Knife
- Nunchucks
- Pickaxe
- Saw
- Scimitar

- Scythe

- Shovel

- Sickle

- Spade

- Sword

- Tire iron

- Whip

- Wooden sword

Your Words:

Projectile Weapons

Projectile weapons let Maxwell attack other objects and creatures from a safe distance. Many have limited ammunition and will disappear after just one or two uses.

- Bazooka

- Bow and arrow

- Cupid's arrow

- Flamethrower

- Freeze ray

- Grappling hook

- Gun

- Holy water

- Howitzer

- Laser pistol

- Machine gun

- Magic wand

- Missile launcher

- Mortar

- Rifle

- Shotgun

- Shrink ray

- Slingshot

- Spitball

- Stun gun

Special Weapons

These special weapons have exciting properties, such as the shrink ray that miniaturizes a target or Cupid's arrow, which soothes an aggressive creature and makes them follow Maxwell.

- Blue magic

- Cupid's arrow

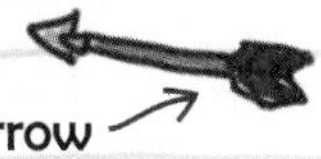

- Freeze ray

- Magic wand

- Shrink ray

Your Words:

Your Words:

Heavenly Bodies

Hang one of these objects in the skies to sometimes impress other humanoids or create special effects, such as reverting a werewolf back to a humanoid with a moon.

- Aurora borealis
- Black hole
- Comet
- Crescent moon
- Full moon
- Gibbous moon
- Jupiter
- Mars
- Meteor
- Moon
- Pluto
- Saturn
- Shooting star
- Sun

Your Words:

Food

Got the munchies? Does another creature in the level need a quick bite? Add some food to the level and feed them. Some foods will help you manipulate the behavior of other creatures.

- Apple
- Baklava
- Banana
- Cake
- Candy
- Carrot
- Casserole
- Cheese
- Cherries
- Chicken
- Cola
- Cookie
- Doughnut
- Egg
- Eggplant
- Garlic
- Hamburger
- Honey

- Ice cream cone

- Iced tea

- Lasagna

- Lettuce

- Lime

- Meat

- Milk

- Milkshake

- Muffin

- Omelette

- Orange

- Pancakes

- Pie

- Pills

- Pistachio

- Pizza

- Pork chop

- Pot roast

- Salad

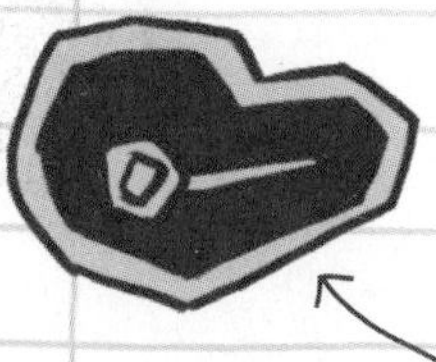

- Steak

- Tea

- Turkey

- Venison

- Wedding cake

- Yogurt

Your Words:

Urban Legends

These monsters are creatures pulled from myth, such as the lumbering Bigfoot of the Pacific Northwest.

- Bigfoot

- Jenny Greenteeth

- Mothman

Your Words:

Humanoids

Humanoids are objects that you can place into a level to do things or serve the needs of other humanoids.

- Abraham Lincoln

- Aunt

- Baby

- Bomb disposal expert

- Brother

- Cyclops

- Death

- Doctor

- Elf

- Fairy godmother

- Friend

- General practitioner

- George Washington

- God

- Hercules

- Kid

- Mother

- Mrs. Claus

- Ninja

- Pathologist

- Pirate

- Proctologist

- Ra

- Robot

- Samurai

- Sister

- Student

- Surgeon

- Toddler

- Vampire hunter

- Werewolf

- Wizard

- Zeus

Body Parts

These objects are parts of a humanoid body that will satisfy any hungry creature or zombie.

- Arm

- Brain

- Leg

- Torso

Your Words:

Your Words:

www.primagames.com

Environmental

These objects have an effect on the environment in a level.

- Electricity 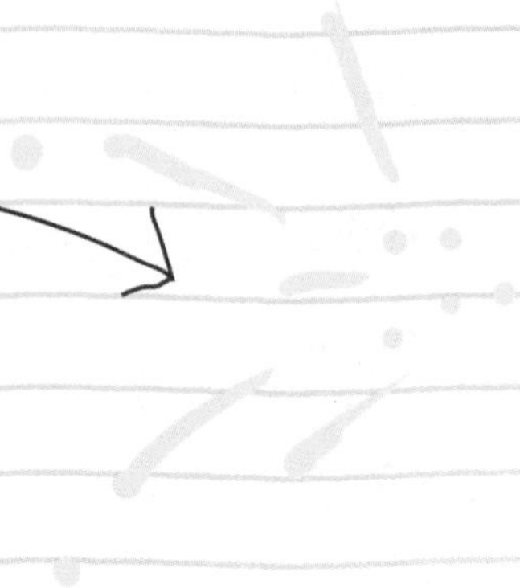
- Fire 
- Fireball
- Ice
- Iceberg
- Lava
- Rain 
- Shock
- Volcano
- Water

Your Words:

Weather

These objects effect the weather in a level, such as making it rain or casting bolts of lightning from the sky.

- Lightning
- Rain
- Rainbow
- Snow
- Sun

Your Words:

Wardrobe

Dress Maxwell or other humanoids up in clothes for fun—or to satisfy level objectives to earn Starites.

- Blouse
- Cape
- Chasuble
- Cloak
- Contact lenses
- Dress
- Glasses
- Gown
- Hat
- High heels
- Invisibility cloak
- Jacket
- Jewelry
- Mask
- Monocle
- Pants
- Periwig
- Robe
- Sandals
- Shirt

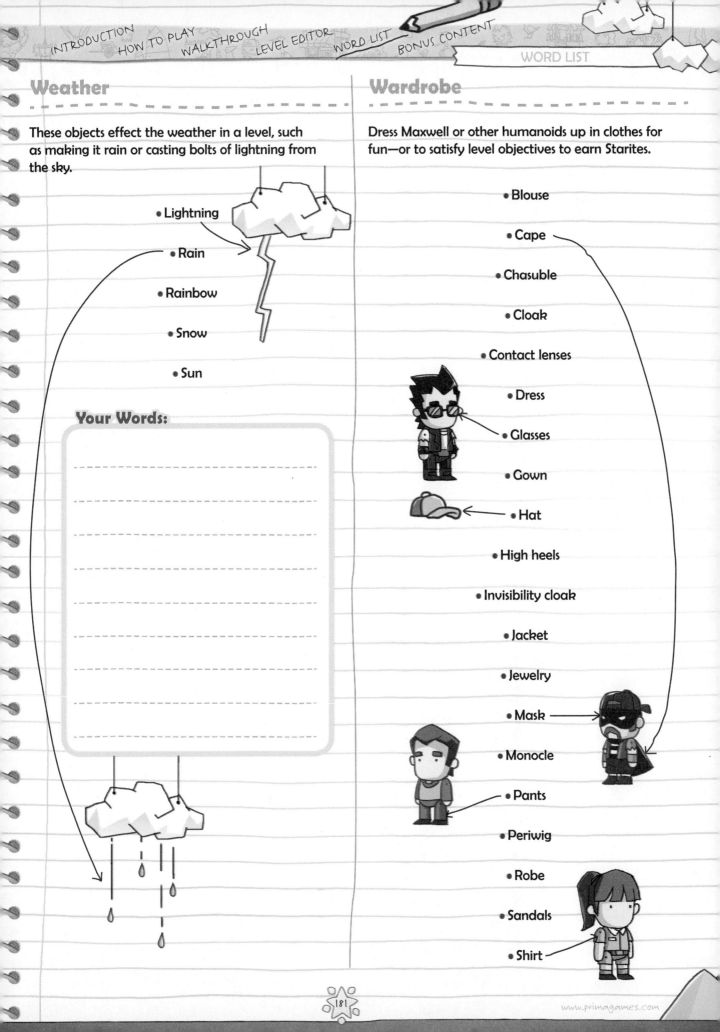

Your Words:

- Shoe
- Slippers
- Tiara
- Toga
- Top Hat
- Tuxedo
- Veil
- Wedding dress
- Witch hat
- Wizard hat

Explosives

These objects cause damage when set next to other objects. Typically, they need to be set off with a fire source, but they can also be detonated by forcefully slamming into another object.

- Bomb

- Claymore

- Dynamite

- Exploding barrel

- Explosive

- Fireworks

- Gunpowder

- Land mine

- Missile

- Nuke

Your Words:

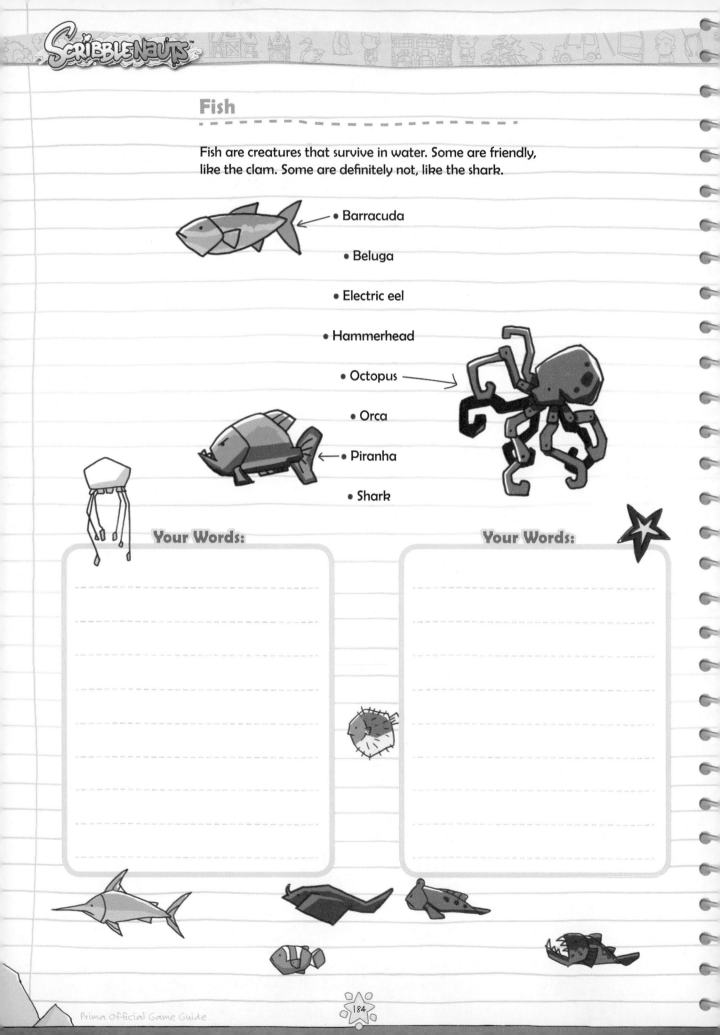

Fish

Fish are creatures that survive in water. Some are friendly, like the clam. Some are definitely not, like the shark.

- • Barracuda
- • Beluga
- • Electric eel
- • Hammerhead
- • Octopus
- • Orca
- • Piranha
- • Shark

Your Words:

Your Words:

Instruments

Musical instruments create sounds when used.

- Bass

- Cello

- Clarinet

- Congo

- Didgeridoo

- Djembe

- Drums

- Flute

- Gong

- Guitar

- Mic

- Oboe

- Piano

- Saxophone

- Triangle

- Trombone

- Trumpet

- Tuba

- Violin

Your Words:

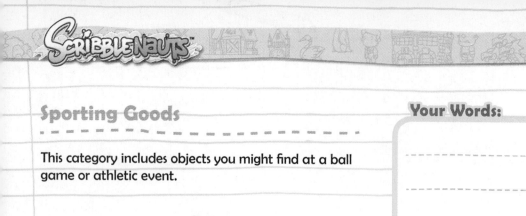

Sporting Goods

This category includes objects you might find at a ball game or athletic event.

- Ball

- Baseball

- Bat

- Compass

- Dodgeball

- Dumbbell

- Football

- Hockey puck

- Kickball

- Medicine ball

- Rugby ball

- Soccer ball

- Tennis ball

- Wiffle ball

Your Words:

Plants

Plants can be used to decorate a level or feed to an herbivore, such as a cow.

- Bamboo
- Bush
- Clover
- Flower
- Grass
- Hay
- Leaf
- Manure
- Mistletoe

Your Words:

Electronics

Electronics are objects powered by electricity, Some are used for entertainment purposes, such as the TV or DVD player. However, when dropped in water, electronics can cause quite a shock and injure nearby creatures.

- Blow dryer
- Boom box
- Car battery
- CD player
- Computer
- DVD player
- Electrical cord
- Electricity
- EMP
- Extension cord
- Fan
- Jumper cables
- Lamp
- Microwave
- Outlet
- Oven
- Radio

Your Words:

- Robosaur
- Shock
- Socket
- Socks
- Stereo
- Tape player
- Telephone
- Toaster
- Tractor beam
- TV
- VCR
- Video games
- Wire

Furniture

Furniture has many uses in the world, such as decorating a level or creating makeshift ledges for Maxwell to jump on.

- Baby bed
- Bed
- Couch
- Lamp
- Mirror
- Oven
- Sofa
- Stove
- Waterbed

Your Words:

Art Supplies

These objects can be used together to create art and solve levels.

- Canvas
- Chalk
- Easel
- Paint
- Paper
- Pen
- Pencil
- Spray paint

Your Words:

General Purpose

General purpose objects are things you might use often, such as rocks or fans, in your pursuit to solve levels and collect Starites.

- Air vent
- Anchor
- Anvil
- Axe
- Binoculars
- Black hole
- Board
- Book
- Boulder
- Buoy

- Confetti
- Cross
- Diamond
- Disco ball
- Doll
- Flashlight
- Fork
- Gift
- Girder
- Glowstick
- Hammer
- Handsaw
- Hay

Your Words:

Your Words:

- Haystack
- Highway
- Iron
- Ladder
- Lane
- Lantern
- Log
- Magnet
- Magnifying glass
- Manure
- Map
- Mattress
- Metal

- Mop
- Oil rag
- Oven
- Pan
- Plates
- Portal
- Present
- Road
- Rock
- Safe
- Schoolbook
- Seesaw
- Skull

Your Words:

Your Words:

- Sleeping bag
- Spatula
- Spoon
- Stairs
- Statue
- Stethoscope
- Stick
- Stone
- String
- Swing
- Tarp

- Teddy bear
- Telephone
- Tent
- Towel
- Toy
- Trampoline
- Vase
- Wall
- Waterbed
- Yardstick

Your Words:

Your Words:

BONUS CONTENT

INTERVIEW WITH 5TH CELL

Jeremiah Slaczka
Co-Founder and Creative Director,
5TH Cell

With a game as crazy as *Scribblenauts*, we knew there had to be some crazy stories behind it. Since Maxwell is kind of the strong, silent type, we instead chatted with 5TH Cell Co-Founder and Creative Director Jeremiah Slaczka about the development of the game, how objects were selected, and some of the zaniest contraptions he ever saw people create within the game.

Prima: How did the idea of *Scribblenauts* come about?

Jeremiah Slaczka, 5TH Cell: The concept originally came from an idea called Once Upon a Time, the premise there was you could write sentences and paragraphs on the bottom screen to create stories on the top screen. So people could write "the brown dog ran through the forest" and you'd see a brown dog appear that would run through the forest. The problem was that there wasn't any point to the game, and people don't want to write sentences or care about grammar and structure - they just want keywords. Later on a I had a dream about being in an Aztec temple which had these white rooms with no doors. In order to get an exit to appear I had to solve a puzzle in the room. Like a painting was crooked so if I aligned it correctly the exit would appear. I woke up and scribbled the idea down as I thought it'd be a fun idea. The problem was it had no replay value. So I merged the two ideas together into a game where you write anything to solve puzzle levels and out came *Scribblenauts*!

Prima: What were the challenges of putting together a game where the player could essentially create anything?

Slaczka: The biggest challenge was making sure we covered all our bases with how the items would interact with each other. When you can create anything people expect what they write to work a certain way, like writing "pogo stick" should allow Maxwell to hop up and down on it.

Prima: Do you have any personal advice to players just starting out in the game?

Slaczka: Play the way you want to play! If that's beating levels as simply and as fast as possible, go for it! If it's experimenting on the title screen, that's great too!

Prima: Maxwell's rooster helmet—who came up with that?

Slaczka: The rooster helmet's name was coined by Destructoid.com and we just kind of ran with it. But why is Maxwell wearing it? If you could write anything, what kind of hat what would you wear? I think he made a wise choice.

Prima: There are a lot of Internet memes in *Scribblenauts*, like "keyboard cat" and "all your base are belong to us." Did you have one person dedicated to scouring the Internet for popular trends, like the lolcats?

Slaczka: That was me actually. I guess I'm a big internet nerd because I was like, "We gotta go through and put all these random internet memes in!" A lot of people rolled their eyes at me.

Prima: So, who at the office is the Lovecraft fan that insisted shoggoth and Cthulhu make it in the game?

Slaczka: It wasn't really any one person for the most part. We just wanted to make sure we included everything we possibly could. Shoggoth was a late entry though, that thing looks awesome in the game too.

Prima: What were discussions like when the team debated which objects to put into the game?

Slaczka: We hired a bunch of people to research all the objects in the game.

Prima: What are your favorite uses for George Washington and Abraham Lincoln? And why no love for James Garfield?

Slaczka: I love giving Abraham a mini-gun, it just feels right. George loves his axe though. Poor James never got to do much in office though. We just wanted to stick with the few public figures everyone knew.

Prima: What are some of the craziest contraptions or objects that you've seen people try out in the game?

Slaczka: Shooting a swordfish with a tranquilizer gun to make it fall asleep then use it as a sword was pretty inventive, as was using shrink ray on an animal then scooping it up in purse. It was crazy watching someone cut off Medusa's head the first time and use it to turn other people into stone!

Prima: Any words or objects you wish had made the final cut but did not?

Slaczka: I wish we could have put in celebrities and copyrighted stuff. There's just so many cool things out there that are copyrighted and so many celebrities you'd want to see react to situations in the game.

Prima: Are there any elements of the game that you wanted to put in but couldn't for one reason or another?

Slaczka: Plenty, with game development it's always about time and budget. We had a specific timeframe we wanted to release the game in - Fall of 2009. So we had to scale back some of the secondary features like the level editor and online portion.

Prima: What was the most challenging element about creating a game like this.

Slaczka: Everything! [laughs] It was just such a different development experience than every other game I've worked on. It was very challenging, but we all really enjoyed it. The people here are great.

Prima: Has there been a dramatic evolution of the game since its initial creation, or has the game been on track with its initial concept?

Slaczka: Surprisingly little has changed between the initial idea of *Scribblenauts* and the final design. A major change was the implementation of our interactive title screen, which all our games share. Another big change was to make sure we had two different level modes - Action and Puzzle - in the game.

Prima: How did the team go about finding all of the words to put into the game?

Slaczka: We had 5 people spend 6 months just going through dictionaries, encyclopedias, Wikipedia and even just looking around them in everyday life to find every object they could.

Prima: Do you plan to release a sequel?

Slaczka: Like most games, that really depends how well the original game does.

Prima: What was the concept behind the unique artistic style used throughout the game?

Slaczka: Edison Yan, our art director, and I went through about twenty different art styles before we settled on the one in the game. We wanted something that appealed to everyone, just like the concept itself does. We also needed to make sure the art was simple enough we could create it all within the schedule.

THE SCRIBBLENAUTS TEAM

Pictured from left to right: Christina Welk, Nikolay "Aleks" Aleksiev, Jeff Luke, Robert Hunt, Marius Fahlbusch, Cole Phillips, Jeremiah "Miah" Slaczka, Cody Haskell, Matt Cox, Justin Chambers, Brittany Aubert, Matt Gross, Chuck Skoda, Caleb Arseneaux, Joseph Tringali.

Not pictured: Liz England, Brett Caird, Edison Yan, Joshua Billeaudeau, Jonathan Armoza, Nick Deakins, Nathan Hernandez.

ART GALLERY

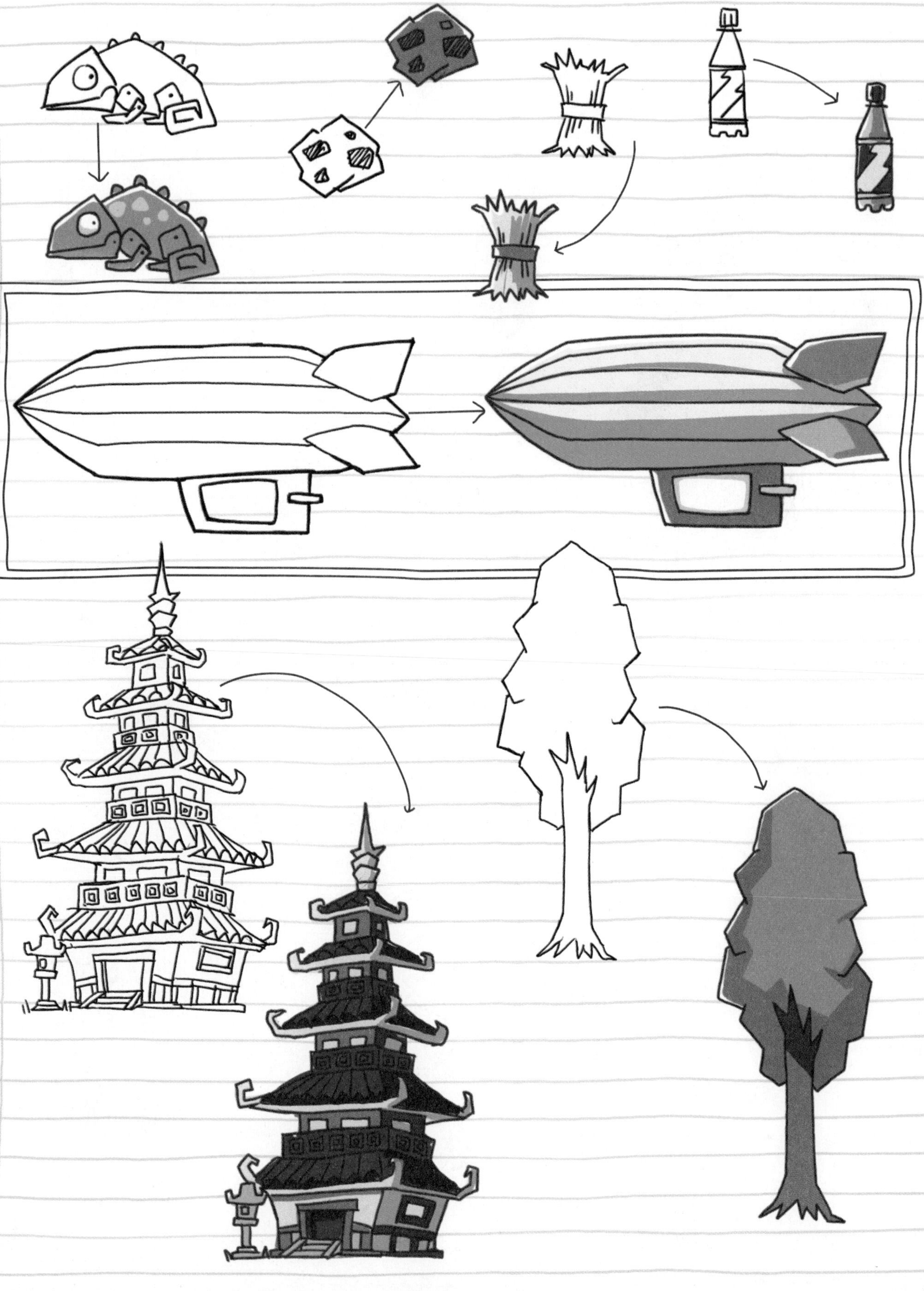

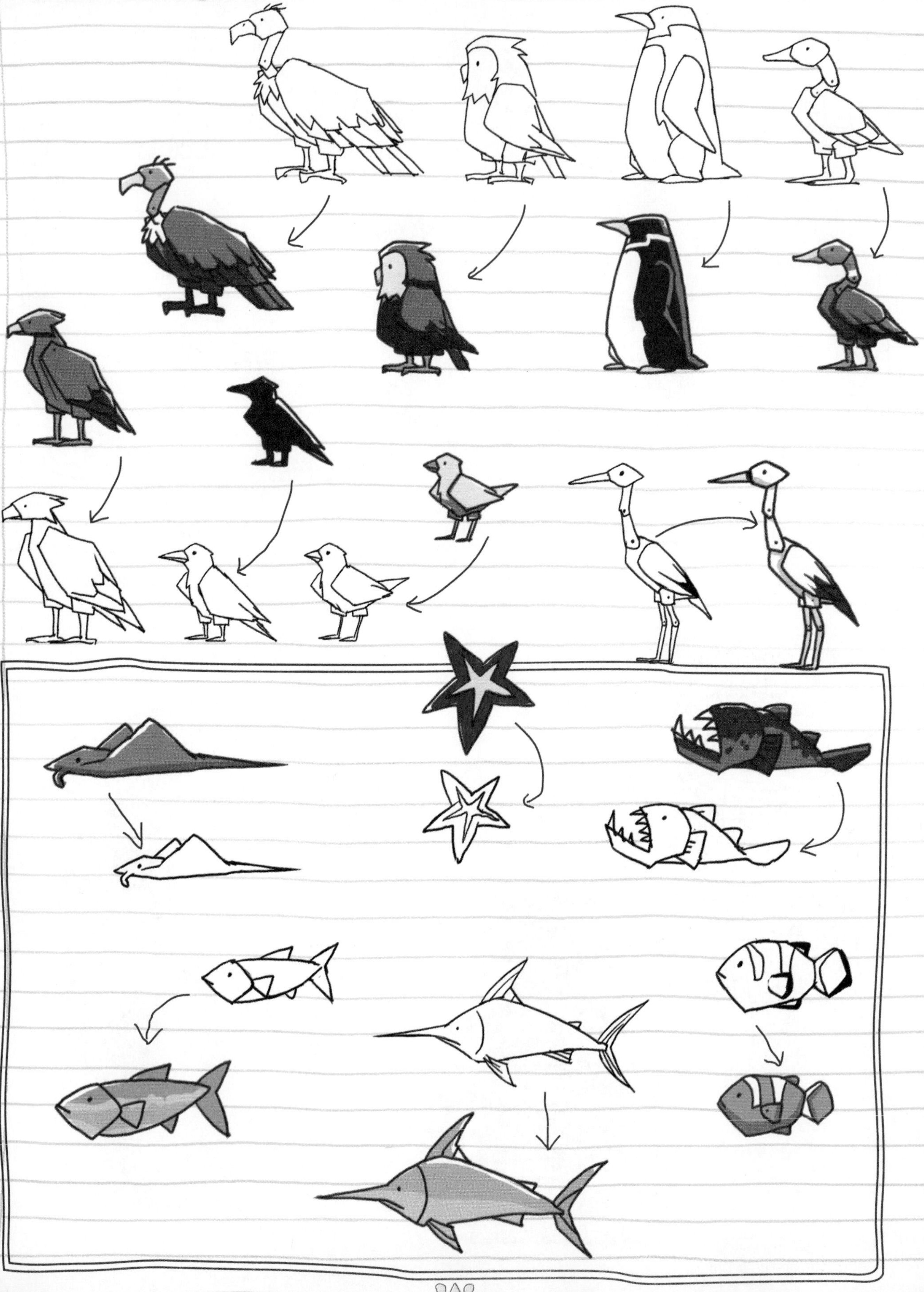

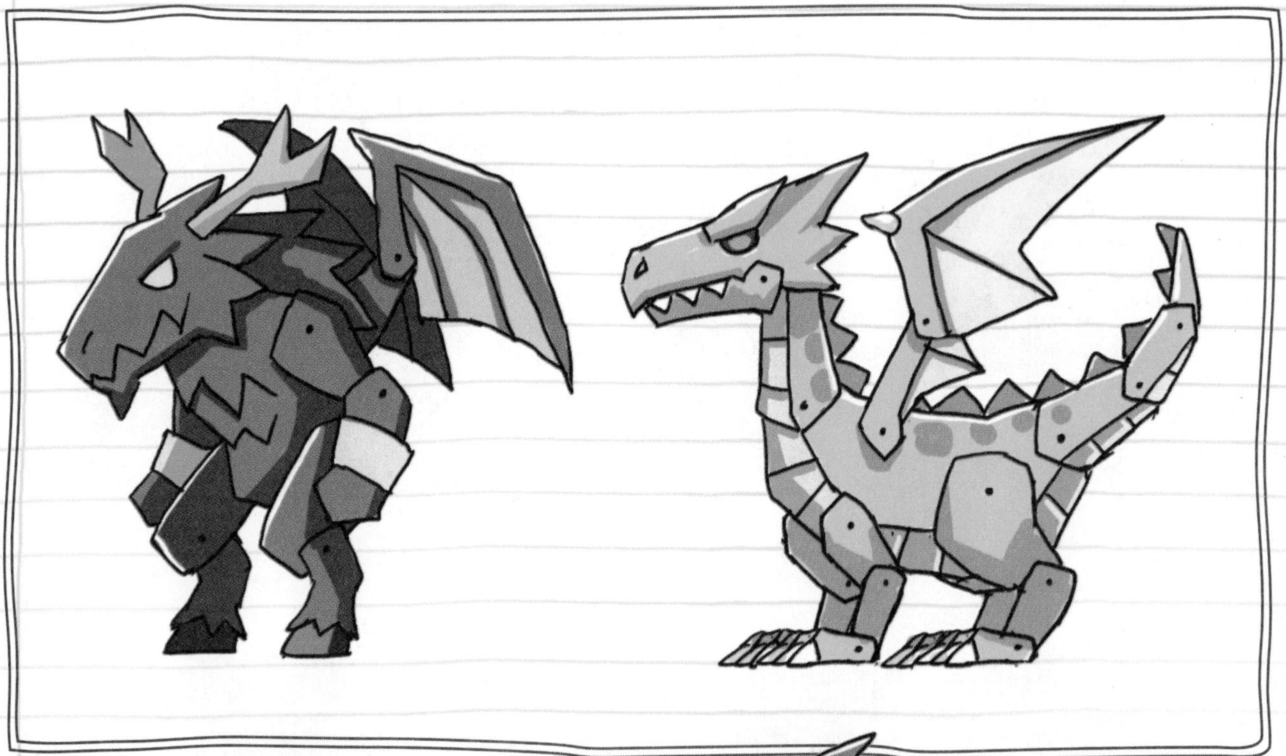

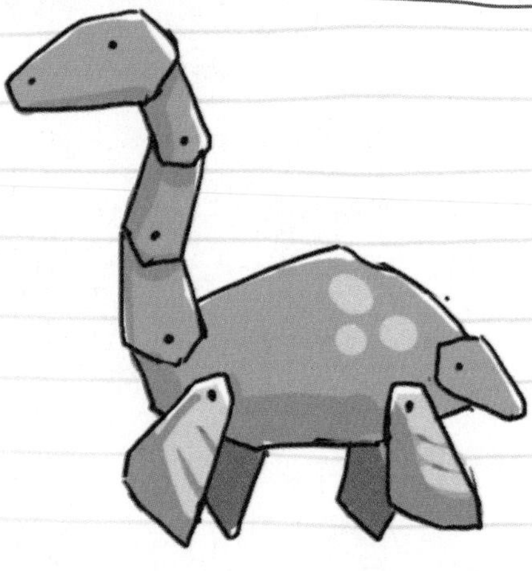

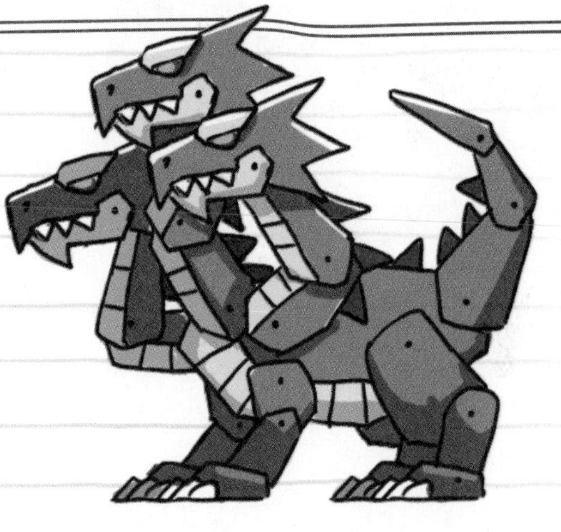

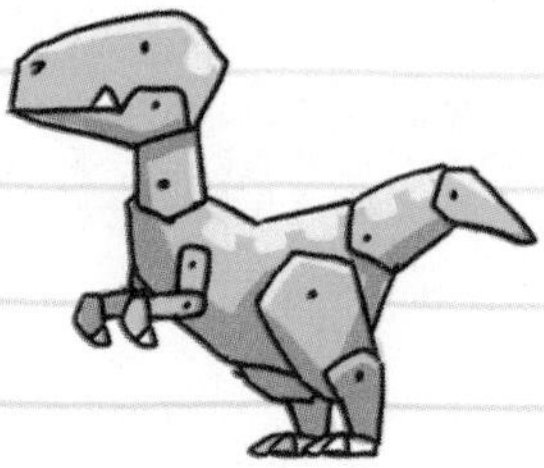

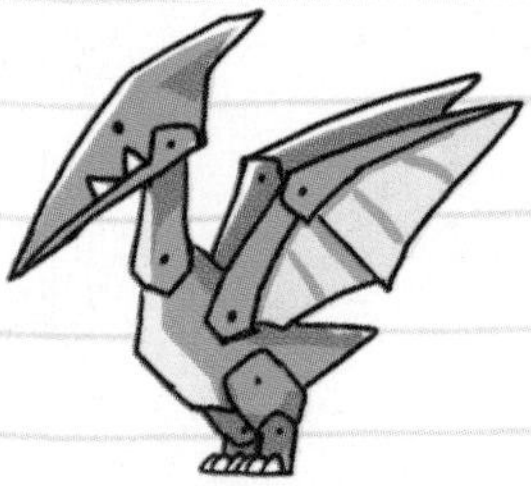

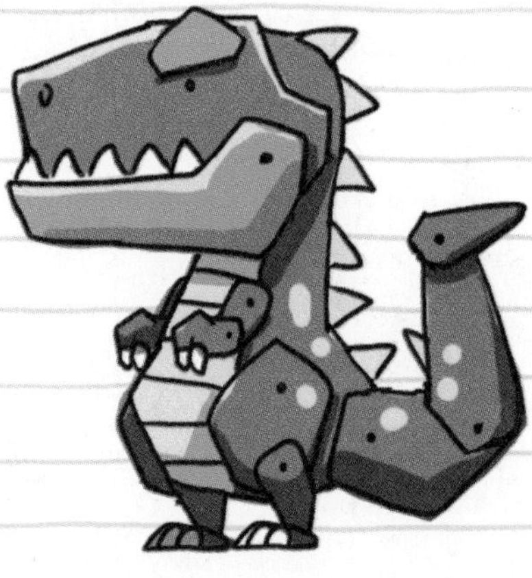

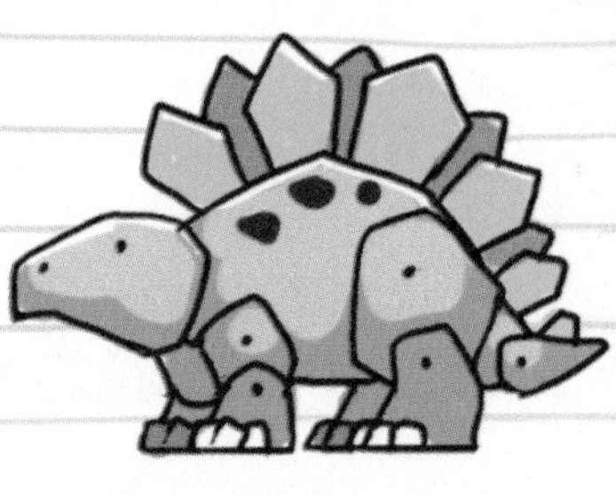

NOTES

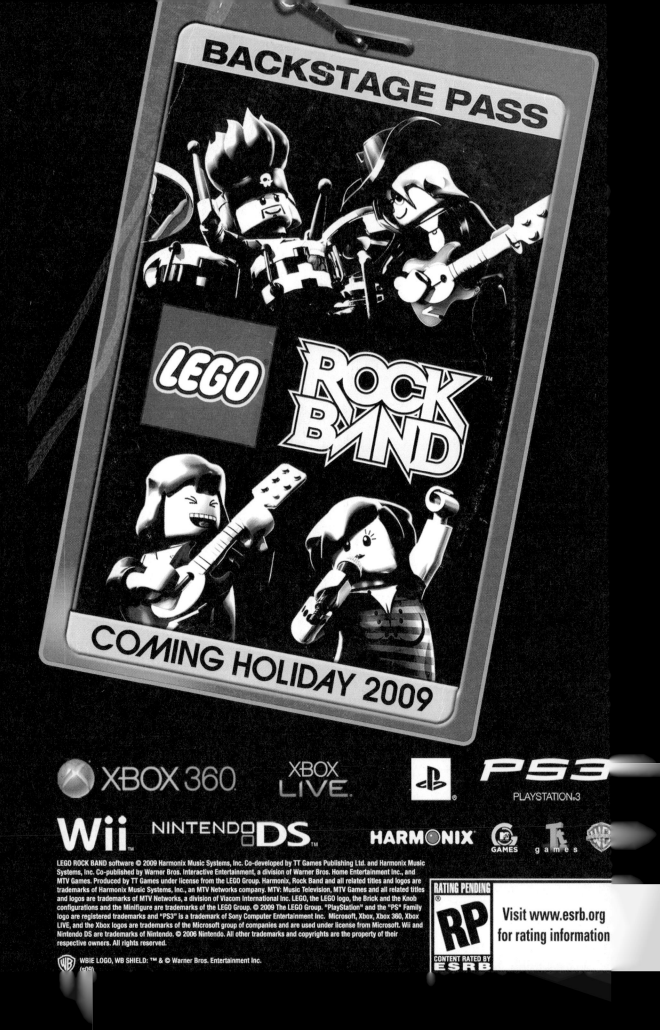